Early Writings

Albert Hirschman's Legacy
Works and Discussions

Luca Meldolesi
Series Editor

Vol. 6

Albert O. Hirschman

Early Writings

Edited by Luca Meldolesi

PETER LANG

New York - Berlin - Bruxelles - Chennai - Lausanne - Oxford

Library of Congress Cataloging-in-Publication Control Number: 2024016219

Bibliographic information published by the Deutsche Nationalbibliothek.
The German National Library lists this publication in the German
National Bibliography; detailed bibliographic data is available
on the Internet at http://dnb.d-nb.de.

Cover design by Peter Lang Group AG

ISSN 2576-9723 (print)
ISBN 9781636675398 (hardback)
ISBN 9781636675886 (ebook)
ISBN 9781636675893 (epub)
DOI 10.3726/b21105

Published by Peter Lang Publishing Inc., New York, USA
info@peterlang.com - www.peterlang.com

This publication has been peer reviewed.

CONTENTS

EARLY WRITINGS: TABLES, FIGURES, & GRAPHS

Chapter 1

Chapter 2

Chapter 3

Chapter 4

Chapter 6

Chapter 7

Chapter 8

INTRODUCTION

> "Asked in a questionnaire of which achievement in his life he was most proud, Hirschman listed his work with the Italian anti-Fascists and with Varian Fry first, before his academic work on development in Latin America, and his books and articles."
>
> —Lewis Coser (1984, p. 163).

> "In 1944 I heard about Eugenio's death. I was then in Algiers and learned the news from a group of Italian antifascists I had met. For me it was a terrible blow. I realized that he was the person who had counted most in my life."
>
> —Albert O. Hirschman (1998, p. 76).

The essays collected here were given to me personally by their author at the end of the 1980s.[1] Together they constitute the first phase of Albert Hirschman's[2] intellectual development—in 1937–1939.

1 These are texts that have only now become "available" internationally.

2 As is well known, he was then called Otto Albert Hirschmann. He only later acquired his definitive name (which, however, for simplicity's sake, we will hereafter also use retrospectively), through two changes: the first (reversing his two proper names) when he landed

As we shall see, young Albert was effectively able to make a virtue of necessity during his unstable and diverse experience as a university student. For the 1932–1933 academic year he had enrolled in the law school at the University of Berlin with the intention of becoming an economist.[3] But soon, after his father's death in April 1933, perhaps due in part to the influence of Eugenio Colorni,[4] he took refuge in France, where he spent two years at the École des Hautes Études Commerciales (HEC). Then, thanks to a scholarship, he spent the 1935–1936 academic year at the London School of Economics (LSE). Finally, after a brief involvement in the Spanish Civil War,[5] he moved to Trieste in the fall of 1936. There he resumed his studies and graduated on June 27, 1938.[6]

in the United States in late 1940; the second (losing the final n of his surname) when he enlisted in 1943 in the U.S. Army.

3 A decision that was certainly political, influenced by the economic and social consequences of the great economic crisis of 1929 (which ended up even affecting his family's savings: see Adelman, 2013, pp. 47–48). "At that time," Hirschman recalled (1998, p. 54), "I was still looking: I studied something between law and economics"—but only for a semester at the School of Law and Political Science at the University of Berlin's Institute for Political Science and Statistics. His papers on the subject were entitled, "The Critique of Smith's Doctrine of Money and Capital through Marx" and "The Limits and Scope of Ricardo's Labor Theory of Value" (Adelman, 2013, p. 76). (The choice of law school for the study of economics was long in vogue in our countries, even—as I can testify personally—thirty years later).

4 Hirschman had met Colorni in Berlin through his (elder) sister Ursula, who had met him at the Staatsbibliotheke where he was studying the myriad texts of Leibniz. "Ursula and Otto Albert plucked up the courage to ask Colorni to keep a printing machine in his room in a hostel in Charlottenbourg. There they could compose their broadsheet; since he was a foreigner the Nazi would not suspect his involvement. Thus began," Adelman wrote (2013, p. 80), "a formative influence." Current opinion in Berlin's polite society was that Hitler's rise to power would not last long. In contrast, Colorni, fresh from Italy's well-established Fascist experience, was of a different opinion. And indeed, Albert, as a militant social democrat and the first-born son of a family of Jewish descent, was even then in grave danger. As so often happened later, his "sixth sense," helped him personally make the difficult decision to emigrate to Paris.

5 During which, probably at the battle of Monte Pelado in late August 1936, he was slightly wounded (Adelman, 2013, pp. 133–134).

6 At that time, political economy was taught very differently in different European countries, from the German historical school in Berlin and the applied-statistical approach in Paris, to London's economics. Concerning the debate over the last of these, Hirschman told me personally that he found himself isolated yet again in Trieste. The point, however, is that when viewed from a different angle, this unevenness (which undoubtedly made life difficult for a young student exile), contributed quite by accident to an unusual process of education,

At the same time, his social-political education had also been progressing. We see this in his first commitments as a young social-democrat in Berlin, linked to the Neu Beginnen group,[7] and in his work with the (mainly Triestine) Italian anti-fascists[8] and with Varian Fry in Marseilles in 1940 which, as Lewis Coser informs us in this introduction's first epigraph, he was particularly proud of.

In the summer of 1935, Albert had vacationed at Forte dei Marmi as Eugenio Colorni's guest, and then also returned to Italy on the occasion of Colorni's marriage to his sister Ursula. Thus in 1936, after the interlude of the Spanish war, he planned to settle in Trieste. And it was here, in almost daily contact with Ursula and (above all) with her brother-in-law Eugenio, that his extraordinary creativity first blossomed.

Beyond his antifascist, federalist and socialist political activity, Albert above all admired Colorni's ability to be "a constant critic, questioner, stimulator."[9] "By 1937, at age twenty-two," Hirschman later recalled, "I had myself lost some of my earlier certainties, but, with my German upbringing, I still

the intellectual harbinger of interesting, unpredictable (and thus indeed ... unforeseen!) developments—both from the point of view of the multiplicity of environments and themes encountered along the way (perhaps at the expense of systematicity), and mainly (as we shall see below) in terms of the subject's central role, which was inevitably elicited by the unfolding of events and which he soon learned to turn gradually to his own advantage (fending for himself, getting by and adapting to reality while remaining vigilant and active) in terms of his own goals, pursued with extraordinary constancy and ingenuity.

7 Adelman (2013, Ch. 3), Fleck (2020), Hirschman (1998, Ch. 3).

8 This development of course deserves particular attention for our purposes. After the entrenchment of Hitler and the "black humor" that came to prevail in German émigré circles in Paris, Ursula and Albert were struck by a welcome Mediterranean libertarian breeze via Renzo Giua (not Guia, as Adelman, 2013, pp. 107–108ff., unfortunately called him) who became their Italian teacher in Paris, and then via Eugenio Colorni. It was Ursula who took the initiative. Thus it happened that later on "Colorni visited Paris and introduced Ursula and Albert to his exiled friends. Otto Albert was swept away by Eugenio's warmth, liveliness, and the fresh air he brought to what was becoming an increasing stultified milieu. [. . .] Colorni quickly became the colligative force in the Hirschmann's lives—Ursula's, Otto Albert's and even the young's Eva. Attractive, full of joy, a dispenser of uplifting and positive advice, [. . .] he was *the* person to whom they turned, as Eva put it" (Adelman, 2013, pp. 108–109).

9 As he later wrote in a letter to Ursula in the early 1970s (cit. in Adelman, 2013, p. 114). Colorni thus became Albert Hirschman's second mentor (The first, Heinrich Ehrmann, had initiated him at the tender age of fourteen into reading Karl Marx and then Austro-Marxism, Lenin, etc. Fortunately, our author never became a doctrinaire Marxist: cf. Hirschman, 1998, p. 48 and pp. 67–68).

sensed it as a real defect not to have a full-fledged Weltanschauung. Colorni, who was six years older than I, seemed on the contrary to cultivate and relish an intellectual style that took nothing for granted except his doubts. At the same time, he and his friends held fast to one certainty: they were firmly committed to opposing the Fascist regime. What was fascinating to me was that there was an intimate connection between the intellectual posture emphasizing the lack of firm ideological commitment and the commitment to perilous political action."[10]

There was, therefore, a close relationship between great freedom of thought and risky political action experienced as the "almost joyful counterpart" of such intellectual openness, without boundaries.[11] Under the Fascist regime this meant learning to discipline one's own life, rigorously separating its official and clandestine aspects.[12] That this was no simple matter is shown, among other things, by Albert's first paper, "Fertility of Italian Women by Age and Number of Children Born" (mimeo, March 1937), which implicitly

10 Hirschman (1995, pp. 118–119). The passage continues: "It was precisely the questioning and exploratory style with which Colorni and his friends were approaching philosophical, psychological and social issues that impelled them to action in situations where freedom of thought was suppressed, or where they felt that injustice was obvious and stupidity intolerable." Undoubtedly, outgoing as he was, Eugenio spoke with Albert about his studies in philosophy, psychology, physics, mathematics, etc. And in all likelihood he also explained how in the seventeenth-century Leibniz, by focusing on a specific topic each time (small perceptions included), had managed to achieve amazing cultural discoveries. It was probably this philosophical "rib" that gave rise to what Hirschman later wrote in the famous dedication to Colorni that opens *Exit, Voice, and Loyalty*: "To Eugenio Colorni (1909–1944), who taught me about small ideas and how they may grow" (Colorni, 2023; Hirschman, 1970; Meldolesi, 2023).

11 Address on the occasion of his *Laurea honoris causa* in political science conferred by the University of Torino on November 12, 1987. "This sort of combination of participation in public affairs with intellectual openness," Albert concluded insightfully (1995, p. 119) "seems to me the ideal micro-foundation of a democratic politics." At the time, however, access to Eugenio's world of rebellious thought and action proved to be anything but easy for the young Hirschman—to the point that, as he later confessed, he felt a certain amount of envy toward those closer to Colorni than himself (Adelman, 2013, p. 148). It was in any case a period of vast theoretical and practical learning for Albert, which only later began to emerge copiously in his work.

12 Paradoxically, it is this aspect of the issue that Norberto Bobbio (1975, p. xxxix), referring to Eugenio Colorni, did not in my view sufficiently take into account.

criticized the policy of the regime[13] and was for this reason *not* published by the *Giornale degli Economisti.*

Hirschman learned quickly.[14] Even so, we must not lose sight of the fact that the Trieste papers were written while Albert was doing "his work with the Italian anti-Fascists." He had not taken a position favoring any particular antifascist current. He had simply "made himself available" as a friend of the movement against the regime. He was accordingly entrusted with the delicate (and risky) task of serving as liaison[15] with certain Italian antifascist exiles in Paris, which included importing to Trieste some of the underground antifascist literature. This was then channeled into working-class circles according to a novel logic, elucidated simply and persuasively by Eugenio Colorni in a now-famous essay.[16] For Hirschman it amounted to a continuous back-and-forth[17]

13 Cf. below; Hirschman (1998, p. 66); and Finzi (2004, p. 129). The first photocopied page of the article, delivered to me personally by Albert, contains an annotation in the margin advising greater caution (perhaps written by Pierpaolo Luzzatto-Fegiz, director of the Institute of Statistics of the University of Trieste, or by Giorgio Mortara, editor of the *Giornale degli Economisti*) referring to A *Mathematical Theory of Population*, 1917, by George H. Knibbs. It reads: "Knibbs knew his subject well; which means he saw some difficulties that you do not see!" In any case, following this, in the summer of 1937, Mortara did warn Albert (Hirschman, 1998, p. 68) that the situation in Italy was bound to get much worse: "much time will be needed before this obsession, this cholera, will be spent." "Mortara recommended that Hirschman not publish any more essays that questioned fascist data and policies so long as he remained in Italy—and indeed urged him to consider returning to Paris and offered to put him in contact with several of his colleagues there" (Adelman, 2013, p. 150).

14 Indeed, in January 1938 Hirschman published a "Note on Two Recent Tables of Marriage Rates in the Italian Population" in the *Giornale degli Economisti* (cf. Hirschman, 1995, pp. 116–117; and Ch. 2 below) which came to the more modest (and not at all dangerous) conclusion that "*two different tables of marriage and mortality rates for bachelors should be constructed and consulted according to the type of investigation to be undertaken.*"

15 Mainly serving as a shuttle between Eugenio Colorni and Angelo Tasca (Hirschman 1998, p. 64). Indirectly, one can get an idea of this from Eugenio Colorni's 1937 correspondence with Joseph (Giuseppe Faravelli), cf. Colorni 2019a.

16 Colorni (1937; English tr. 2019). It is a surprising and innovative article, contrary, at the time, to the prevailing doctrines inside the workers movement.

17 Enabled by his ability to blend in (an attribute difficult to classify), along with his cool head, his premonition for what was about to happen, and his having quickly become something of a polyglot (with his native German, his perfect French, his English, and now his Italian); and also—it must be added—by the timidity (sense of inferiority, refuge in bureaucracy, etc.) with which Fascist officials of the time treated good-looking Germans. . .

that made use of his pristine German passport.[18] In addition, instead of double-bottomed suitcases, which Italian inspectors sometimes checked, he made use—as he told me personally—of double lids that had been specially crafted for the purpose. It was the first instance of the ingenuity in clandestine activity that would become proverbial in Marseille.[19]

In enrolling at the University of Trieste, Hirschman had of course presented ample documentation of his previous studies: attendance at a number of courses at the University of Berlin, his diploma from the École des Hautes Études Commerciales (HEC), and the courses he had taken at the London School of Economics (LSE).[20] He was thus permitted to enroll in the fourth year in the department of business and economics, but with the stipulation that in order to graduate he had to take five law exams[21] (as well as a "recommended" complementary exam—corporate law, of course).[22]

At the same time, Hirschman was thinking of his future profession.[23] In Paris he had attended, among others, the Institute de Statistique of the

18 "The strange thing was—Hirschman explained later (1998, p. 63)—that I had a German passport in good order, issued two years before, without any stamp indicting that I had entered Spain or that I had left it!"

19 His main tasks within the Committee, a rescue organization directed by Varian Fry, were "obtaining passports, identity cards and other emigration documents for the refugees, devising escape routes they could use to get out of the country, and founding mechanisms for transferring money from the United States to support the Committee's activities," Franco Ferraresi, "Laudatio," cit., November 13, 1987; in Albert O. Hirschman, *Tre Continenti*, cit. (1990; English tr. 2002, p. 23).

20 Cf. Finzi 2004, pp. 124–125. Courses in Elements of German Private and Public Law, History of Roman Law, General Political Economy, and Economic Policy at the University of Berlin; courses in Principles of Currency, International Trade and Foreign Exchanges, Banking, Banking in the United States and Financing of Industry at the London School of Economics.

21 Ibid., p. 126. These were: Public Law Institutions, Business Law II and III, International Law, Financial Law and Finance Science.

22 For Albert, this "intensive treatment" in law turned out to be more or less indigestible. Despite this, by June 1937 he had passed four of the six exams that stood between him and graduation. But on October 25, 1937, he failed (with a ten even written on the booklet) the Commercial Law II /III exam. In addition, his request to be allowed to retake the exam in the second round of the fall session was not granted. ("It was as if they had flunked me all over again"—he told me). Thus Hirschman had to re-sit this exam on June 12, 1938, still scoring a meager 24/30 (ibid., pp. 127–128), which—inter alia—prevented him, as we shall see, from obtaining honors in the following graduation session.

23 Or rather—we shall see this better later—a kind of multiple interrelated professions—a kind of reasoning (also, in a sense, of Leibnizian-Colornian inspiration) which he later

Université de Paris, which had issued him a "Certificat d'Aptitude." With this background, he was introduced in Trieste by Colorni to Pierpaolo Luzzatto-Fegiz, director of the Institute of Statistics at the local university, and began to do some volunteer work of a sort[24] at that Institute as an internal student.

This experience—as already mentioned—soon gave rise to a genuine contribution in statistics concerning Italian demography; and with it Hirschman glimpsed a first, possible, professional horizon. "My work at the time," he later maintained, "was mostly centered on demography, one of my real passions." And he added: "because the Fascist regime, to promote the natalist policy, helped to publish many statistical data and studies in this field which have never been published before: for example, on the fecundity of the Italian woman according to the number of children that have been conceived or have survived and so on. This was quite interesting data. I based an article on it in which I demonstrated that the official policy could have counterproductive results: for example, when you had six children there would be four survivors, but when you had seven children there might only be three survivors. Therefore, I asserted in the article that even from the point of view of a natalist policy it was absurd to give prizes to women who give birth to all these children! I thought it was a good argument and still think it is, but I did not succeed in getting it published. *Perhaps I shall publish it posthumously*."[25] This is, indeed, a significant aspect of our "Hirschman's Legacy"—in fact, publisher Peter Lang and I are finally able to publish the essay—more than eight decades after it was written![26]

called "how one thing leads (or does not lead) to another" (Hirschman, 1958, Meldolesi, 1995, Ch. 3); and which he eventually placed alongside his theses on "trespassing" and "crossing boundaries" (Hirschman, 1981, 1998).

24 Hirschman (1998, p. 132). The fact that Albert later considered this to be an assistant's position (1998, p. 63 and 66) is, in my opinion, one of the first of his famous "half-truths" (which I will mention later: see n. 58).

25 Hirschman (1998, pp. 66–67); emphasis added. Of course, this inspiration (admittedly amplified by memory) requires reading between the lines—readers can detect this for themselves by comparing this reasoning with the original text: see below, Ch. 1.

26 Note how the essay arose from the observation of some demographic statistics that potentially contradicted the conventional thinking on the subject that had led to their publication. So that already in this first youthful work there is a small idea that is made to grow (cf. above n. 10). As well known, Albert's first book—*National Power and the Structure of Foreign Trade* (1945)—took off from some statistics (concerning Germany's foreign trade with some small and poor Balkan countries) that were at first glance of little importance, but instead held decisive significance (and went against the grain!).

This brings us to a second horizon. "More important," Hirschman maintained retrospectively,[27] "I acquired a nicely limited area of competence: the Italian economy. I had come to Italy from France and had been asked by a Paris publication to send in, on a trial basis, some reports on the Italian economic situation. At the time, the Mussolini regime began increasingly to restrict the publication of official economic statistics, so that it took some attentive reading of what did get published and of the daily financial press (*Il Sole*, *Ventiquattro Ore*) to figure out what was going on [. . .]. I enjoyed the detective work involved, and whatever success I could claim in outwitting the Fascist authorities."[28]

Albert came out of all this—I observed—by means of "an accurate reconstruction of public finance (the budget, deficit financing, capital taxation of corporations), monetary policy, consumption, production and foreign trade. The overall picture that emerged [to be read in France of course, not in Italy] was of an economy well managed technically, but strangled by policy of economic autarky which, in conjunction with policies of war mobilization, resulted in a bloated public sector, an impoverished population, and suffocated productive and financial sectors."[29]

The essay, "Les finances et l'économie italienne. Situation actuelle et perspectives," published anonymously in Paris on 1 June 1938 in the *Supplément au bulletin quotidien* of the Société d'études et d'informations économiques,[30] demonstrates without a shadow of a doubt that the "trial period" under which Hirschman had been commissioned by the Société had been passed brilliantly. It was the (hoped-for) start of a possible profession as an economic journalist specializing in the Italian economy—a prospect that was instead

27 Hirschman (1995, p. 118).

28 Is it possible, Roberto Finzi wondered (2004, pp. 118–122), that Hirschman was given this assignment even before he had gained any expertise, however limited, in the Italian economy? Finzi looked for some clues in this regard (which, incidentally, did not concur) in various documents of the regime (which obviously were not to be taken retrospectively as gospel). I would answer his misgivings with the observation that in order to be able to claim that the commission (received "on probation" from Paris) must have materialized "toward the end of his stay in Trieste," my friend Roberto must not have had in his hands the essay in question—the one that Albert Hirschman gave me personally; and on whose photocopied facsimile he wrote in his own hand "Écrit en Italie et envoyé à Paris. Fin de mars 1938."

29 Meldolesi (1995, p. 8).

30 Cf. below, Ch. 3.

brutally interrupted by the enactment of the Fascist racial laws and then by the outbreak of the war.

Moreover, "Les finances et l'économie italienne" is a quite different kind of paper, much more lively and instructive than what might ex ante have been expected—not only for its intelligent and careful reconstruction of such a "Situation actuelle et perspectives," but also because it clearly shows the extraordinary continuity of the author's multidisciplinary inspiration (first and foremost psychological and social, as well as statistical, economic and financial)—in its developmental process.[31] It is as if, by focusing each time on a different aspect of his work, Hirschman was implicitly drawing together (or perhaps allowing to emerge in his mind spontaneously) the many acquisitions (at first glance disparate, but in reality highly relevant to his specific purpose), which he had "stored up," perhaps even unconsciously, during the course of his intellectual and political wanderings through some of the major European countries.

In this essay, in fact, Hirschman lists in rapid succession the three essential factors that had permeated Italian economic life in recent years (the war in Abyssinia, rearmament, and repeated strivings for autarky), along with their economic and financial consequences (which increased government spending from one-third to one-half of national income), and the main types of measures that were used to cover the deficit in the state budget (long-term loans, short-term loans, inflation, and miscellaneous means)—to then address in detail the tax on the capital of Joint Stock Companies.[32]

This last element in particular shows (unexpectedly) a distinctive technical virtuosity that leads Hirschman to the following conclusion: "L'opération, il faut bien le dire, est magistrale. L'actionnaire en réalité paie l'impôt pour la société, mais non seulement il ne s'en aperçoit presque pas puisqu'il reçoit une action en échange, mais il croit même réaliser un bénéfice car on lui fait cadeau de deux actions gratuites par action souscrite. Et, en effet, il peut vendre ses droits de souscription et peut se procurer ainsi un gain immédiat, ne

31 Such that, at an interpretive level, it already suggests, *ex abrupto*, a point of view partly *alternative* to that expressed by our friends Pier Francesco Asso and Marcello de Cecco (1987, p. 35) according to whom "in the last few years [of Albert Hirschman's work] that elapsed between the writing *National Power* and the essays on Italy [in the Marshall Plan period] the methodological break came about to which the latter writings testify."

32 That is, the institution of a 10% levy on the capital of Joint Stock Companies: "*la mesure de beaucoup la plus importante au double point de vue financier et économique*." See below; emphasis added.

s'apercevant pas trop de la diminution de valeur en capital que ses actions ont subie ou subiront en conséquence de l'impôt."[33]

To conclude his studies, Hirschman had to present (and discuss in a public graduation session) a thesis and two additional papers.[34] The first of these latter, in economic geography[35] (under Prof. Giorgio Roletto), was entitled "Whether and in what way the economic element was a determining factor in the Philippine Islands' independence." The second, in statistical science (under Prof. Pierpaolo Luzzatto-Fegiz), had the title "Two methods for constructing marriage-rate tables," and clearly echoed the "Note" that Hirschman had published six months earlier in the *Giornale degli Economisti*.[36]

The "centerpiece" of Albert's degree, however, was of course his thesis, supervised by Jewish-born Prof. Renzo Fubini (later tragically killed at Auschwitz). The title was *The Poincaré Franc and its Devaluation*.[37] It is through this work, finally, that I will approach a third and more important professional horizon that appeared to open up for Hirschman during his time in Trieste.

To get an idea of this, however, it is necessary to take a step back; and almost to go back over the reasoning *ab ovo*. It is first of all necessary to take into account—as I have already mentioned—that Hirschman's early cultural and political development had taken place within a German cultural context (including, of course, the influence of a labor movement which, in its various components, claimed to be the beating heart of a great process of

33 Cf. below. Scrolling through the text, one can certainly sense the attraction that the technical prowess (not just economic in the strictest sense!) of Italian civil servants exerted at the time on the young scholar—as if to reveal *ante litteram* an attitude that would characterize him in the future. "D'une manière générale," Hirschman concluded, "la finance italienne à une longue et fameuse tradition fait rendre à la technique tout ce qu'elle est an état de rendre. Ceci n'empêche pas que le montant actuelle des dépenses militaires et d'investissements doit être considéré comme exceptionnel et que la continuation indéfinie de cet effort créerait un appauvrissement et une désagrégation du système économique et monétaire qu'aucune science financière si habile qu'elle soit ne saurait conjurer."

34 Finzi (2004, p. 129).

35 Economic geography "a la français," a friendly subject for Albert ever since he had attended Albert Demangeon's classes at the HEC in Paris (see Hirschman, 1995, p. 116).

36 Cf. below, Ch. 2 and above, n. 12.

37 Cf., Ch. 4. Hirschman graduated with a score of 110 (although, much to the dismay of some commissioners, it was not deemed worthy of honors). "At this point," the author stated retrospectively (1998, p. 68), "Ursula, Eugenio and I went for a brief vacation to Selva di Val Gardena in the Dolomites. It was July and immediately afterward I left for Paris. Eugenio was arrested with a great deal of fanfare as soon as he returned to Trieste."

social emancipation on an international scale).[38] It is true, moreover, that contemporary political events had pushed Ursula and Albert onto a path of rapid politicization—such that Albert later recalled that "in my last year in Germany I was mostly occupied with political activity."[39]

On the other hand, Albert had from a very early age shown a notable attraction for French culture, and had even in a sense experienced a premonitory "friction" between the two cultures. In 1931–1932, in fact, while attending the Fronzösische Gymnasyum in Berlin, he took part in a group working on "Hegel's *Phenomenology of the Spirit* and spent a summer writing an interpretation of a passage that Hirschman admits today is incomprehensible. 'Perhaps,' he observed[40] 'the torment of having to make sense of Hegel had an unintended side effect later in France: to make me fall in love with the French moralists of the 17th century, such as Pascal and La Rochefoucauld; they seemed to me just as deep, but in a marvelously easygoing manner.'"[41]

In Paris, this early philosophical attraction for French culture began to "expand" to literature, poetry and the arts, and especially to statistics and economics, which Albert was engaged with at the time. Inevitably, in fact, he had again encountered the effects of the Great Depression (less severe in France than in Germany, but getting worse). Understandably, therefore, Hirschman's wish was (probably) to become a public economist, engaged in government activities, and his first choice for training would therefore have been the École libre des sciences politiques (SciencesPo).

Instead, he was authoritatively dissuaded,[42] and ended up enrolling at the HEC, a sort of *ante litteram* business school devoted mainly to accounting and

38 In this regard, I would say that Christian Fleck (2020, pp. 383–394) is right to maintain that biographical reconstructions of the beginnings of Albert's life and work (including my own) do not sufficiently take account of his youthful politicization the two-way relationship it had with his early way of thinking. Cf. Adelman (2013, Ch. 2 and Ch. 3 passim.).

39 Clearly linked to his interest in Marxism, classical economics and economic crisis theory. In fact, among many activities, he and his sister Ursula participated in a conference held by Otto Bauer on the "long Kondratieff cycle" (Adelman, 2013, p. 66)—a theme that not coincidentally would reappear later in Hirschman's work (but in a self-subverting vein) at the beginning of *Shifting Involvements* (1982).

40 Hirschman (1984, pp. 2–3); Meldolesi (1995, p. 4).

41 "This 'falling in love' which extended to Montaigne and Diderot and 'the whole eighteenth century' is perceptible in the first chapter of the *National Power and the Structure of Foreign Trade* (1945), and is further manifested in *The Passions and the Interests*" (Hirschman, 1990, p. 155; Meldolesi, 1995, p. 217, n. 2).

42 Hirschman (1995, Ch. 8).

the rudiments of engineering. His disappointment was very great.[43] And yet, viewed retrospectively, this two-year experience had the double advantage of opening Albert's eyes to the world of private business (which would later stand him in good stead, above all in the second part of his postwar adventure in Colombia), and at the same time not preventing him from pursuing his goal of becoming an economist dealing with public policy.

Actually, "it was during his years at HEC that Hirschman developed an interest in statistics and applied economics—a certain kind of inductive applied economics (intelligently presented factual reconstruction) that was nurtured by the Parisian ambience. It is important to remember," I observed on this point,[44] "that several features, for a series of reasons generally left aside, were peculiar to French economics at the time. These include an inclination toward practical descriptions of economic facts, a fair degree of tolerance for various schools of thought (liberal, historical, social, mathematical, sociological etc.), and a marked interest in the political aspects of economics [. . .]. This, together with HEC courses on money and banking [. . .], probably made up the breeding ground of Hirschman's research projects on French monetary policy from the 1920s to the 1930s, conceived in London and completed as a graduation thesis in Trieste."

"I had some excellent teachers in economic geography, and in money and banking such as Albert Demageon and Henry Pomméry," said Albert Hirschman while receiving an honorary degree in economics in Nanterre. Moreover, as he added later on, "from the point of view of my intellectual formation, it was very important to understand what was then happening in modern economics. For me this [1935–1936] was a decisive year, even though the London School was not at all Keynesian. It was rather anti-Keynesian—in fact Lionel Robbins and Friedrich von Hayek were among its principal teachers. I took some of their courses. But there were also some younger people, about my age, who had fled from Germany or Hungary. [. . .] They were all Keynesians and had been to Cambridge to hear the master. Among them there was a brilliant young economist, already well-known, by the name of Abba Lerner, and some excellent teachers of international trade."[45]

43 Mainly because Albert had no intention of going into business or even one of the liberal professions (although, at one point he had to consider a job in banking, which he nevertheless managed to avoid).

44 Meldolesi (1995, pp. 6–7). Cf. Dumez (1985) and Meldolesi (1991).

45 Hirschman (1998, p. 59). In June 1919, as Giorgio La Malfa (2023) has recently recalled, Keynes, who had worked at the British Treasury during the First World War and had "participated in the Paris peace conference as a representative of the ministry, resigned in

One can sense from this passage the attitude that Hirschman was beginning to develop toward economics. His idea was to learn the various theories and thoroughly weigh their utility for his own purposes (as witness his adopting a Keynesian position on various occasions)—but without "taking sides," without fully embracing the veracity of such theses, nor pushing himself to theorize further by perhaps joining one of the various currents that advocated them, claiming that they were "self-contained" (and bomb-proof!).[46] And without (even implicitly) asserting their validity at the expense of different knowledge from other disciplines or experiences (but rather, on the contrary, seeking to appraise by degrees the eventual combination of one with the other).

At the same time, as Hirschman later pointed out,[47] "I didn't follow a regular plan of studies [at the LSE] since I already had my French [HEC] diploma. I decided to study for my own account[48]—in particular, a special problem of recent French economic history: the economic reform of 1925–1926 and the history of the "franc Poincaré." At the time, this was an important topic for

disagreement with the stance that the U.S., Britain. and France intended to take toward the peace treaty. Following this he published *The Economic Consequences of the Peace*, his indictment against reparations—that they were senseless and would create such resentments that a new war would ensue 'before which the horrors of the late German war will fade into nothing.'" In addition, in 1923 he published *A Tract on Monetary Reform*, translated into Italian by Piero Sraffa in 1925, in which he wrote that "fortunately for the Italian taxpayer and Italian business, the lira does not listen even to a dictator and cannot be given castor oil." Finally, as is well known, Keynesian polemic towards the traditional recessionary policies of neoclassical economics had taken the path of high theory.

46 "It was a great relief," Hirschman indeed declared retrospectively (1995, p. 118), "to realize that one could do tolerably competent work in economics without having to resolve whether Keynes, whose *General Theory* I had bought in London in the year of its publication (1936) and then taken along to Italy for study, had all the right answers."

47 Hirschman (1998, pp. 59–60). Employing his typical way of "saying and not saying" something—which allowed him, often and quite willingly, to sidestep arguments that he judged as too challenging or that he otherwise . . . did not wish to address.

48 Even choosing to take some LSE courses that were likely to help him in this endeavor. It is also likely that through their opposition, the (not always accurate) criticism of French economic policies that came from British government and financial circles played a significant role. Albert had seen this when he arrived in London. From then on, as de Cecco rightly observed (2004, p. xii)—"Hirschman seems to have resisted the tendency to turn economic theory and practice into orthodoxy and was apparently conscious of the legitimacy of those who appealed to both theoretical and practical pluralism. There are many roads that the financial organization that accompanies the development of capitalism can take and just as many that those who study it can tread. The English way is only one of many."

the French, and since I had lived in France and was convinced I would return there, I decided to study some problems of recent French economic history. I started a research project in this field under the supervision of Professor Barrett Whale, a fine teacher in international economics at the London School. This was in effect the project I developed later in my dissertation in Trieste."

It seems to me important to highlight this point. Albert had undertaken this work on recent monetary history *for the French market*, thinking he could establish (and prove) himself in Paris. It was only later that he used it to get his degree in Italy. The paper, in fact originally written in French, was translated into Italian (and perhaps further developed), and in the end became his graduation thesis.

In this regard, I think Marcello de Cecco was right to argue that *The Poincaré Franc and its Devaluation* is not really a thesis in the usual sense of the term,[49] but rather an "economic report"—as if it had been commissioned by a public authority. "It is a report of very high quality, firstly because it avoids any redundancy, dissecting the subject matter with elegant parsimony, but also because, from the very first page, it places the reader 'in medias res,' mixing facts and theories without any rigidity in a relentless search for convincing explanations of French economic policies in the turbulent two decades between the World Wars."[50]

It is here, I would add, that our author's style gets its start—a style that is sober, free, professionally (and culturally) competent, pared down, sometimes ironic, and captivating. The layout of this thesis-report follows the temporal sequence of the issue as observed from different points of view: "Some thoughts on French monetary policy after the de facto stabilization of the franc"; "French monetary history from 1930 to the first devaluation of the franc"; "The franc from an economic viewpoint (1931–1937)."

49 In fact, Marcello continued (ibid., pp. vii–viii), "anyone reading Hirschman's thesis will immediately realize that it does not follow any of the canonical rules of Italian dissertations." That is to say, it does not adhere to "the tried-and-true template resulting from centuries of experience, in which the writer usually begins with a critical review of the literature" by which "he or she hedges against the possibility that the personal analysis of the thesis topic, which usually comes immediately after the review, is unoriginal. Normally, the main purpose of the thesis is academic—you want to show that you know the theories and can connect them to the facts, which are of interest only because they prove one or another alternative theoretical hypothesis." Obviously this was not Albert Hirschman's purpose!

50 Ibid., p. viii.

The socio-political background "is sketched out in brief but effective hints and references. But the heart of the analysis deals with the economic policy problems of French governments, and the aim is to report on them as an economist—one who has at his disposal the most up-to-date panoply of analytical tools; including, of course, those that Keynes had just set forth in the *General Theory*, which Hirschman makes effective utilization of in his work."[51]

Back in Paris (and under the circumstances forced to remain there[52]) Hirschman cleverly put to use the *expertises* he had now acquired. "I was able," he later affirmed, "to establish myself as an expert on the Italian economy, writing quarterly reports on it for a newly founded Institute on Economics and Social Research directed by Charles Rist and Robert Marjolin." He met Jack Condliff, who was working at the time for the League of Nations. He wrote a paper highly critical of Fascist monetary policy, "Histoire de la Lire de la rivalorization au contrôle des changes," which remained unpublished.[53] He was commissioned to write a proper report: "*Mémoire sur la contrôle des changes en Italie*."(Paper written for the "XIIéme Session, Bergen 1939, Conference permanente des hautes études internationales," "Conference generale d'études sur les politiques economiques et la paix," Institut International de Coopération Intellectuelle, Société des Nations, Paris, June.)[54] Finally, he prepared an "Étude statistique sur la tendence du commerce exterieur vers l'equilibre et le bilateralisme" for the same session of the "Conference" (which never managed to attend)[55]—just before he was absorbed, *toto corde*, by the

51 "Hirschman," de Cecco finally observes (ibid., pp. ix and xv), "is aware of the necessity, in his thesis, of having to remain on the high road of economic analysis in order to show his professionalism, without giving away too much to the other social sciences. Fortunately for the reader, this strict intent is sometimes betrayed by the young author."

52 Cf. above, n. 37.

53 It is an essay that, at the behest of its author, did not appear in "Albert Hirschman's Works"—the bibliography I had painstakingly put together (Meldolesi, 1995, p. 293). Probably Albert had not even shown it to Asso and de Cecco, the editors of Hirschman (1987).

54 In this report, as in the thesis, as de Cecco observes (2004, pp. x and xiii) "Hirschman's analyses and judgments have stood the test of time. The self-assurance with which he offers his own viewpoint on the political, economic and social dilemmas of the 'Latin sisters' in the decades between the two wars is equaled only by their ability to endure at a distance." And again, "those familiar with Hirschman's output [. . .] cannot help but notice [...] his special attention to the interweaving of economics, psychology, sociology and politics—something that has consistently fascinated our author."

55 With the author's consent, the "Indices of Bilateralism" it contains would later be published in fine print by Jack Condliffe in 1940, p. 283. Moreover, it is with this text that

political-military efforts of the World War, which, after his voluntary enlistment in the French army, led him to his exploits in Marseille as Varian Fry's assistant,[56] and to his emigration to the United States.

In Algiers in 1944, having eventually enlisted in the U.S. Army, Hirschman learned of Eugenio Colorni's assassination at the hands of the Nazi-Fascists. It was "a terrible blow."[57] At that point he recognized the indelible role Eugenio had played in his intellectual and political education. Furthermore, the memory of his "Trieste period" appeared to him as a fruitful, if irreproducible, parenthesis within a tragic era.[58] And over time Colorni's intellectual, political and moral teaching ended up taking an increasingly significant inspirational role in Hirschman's own work.

Luca Meldolesi

Note This volume contains all of Albert Hirschman's writings from the period 1937–1939—that is, preceding his emigration to the United States. Photocopies of each were given to me personally by the author in the late 1980s. The indispensable (and accurate) translations from Italian into English were done by Michael Gilmartin. At the same time, in order to maintain the authentic original flavor of these *Early Writings* for the attention of an educated audience, the all the papers (the French texts included) have simply been transcribed from the original copies.[59]

Hirschman began the exploration of a fourth professional horizon, the statistical-economic study of international trade that would play a significant role in the genesis of *National Power* (1945).

56 Cf. above, the first epigraph of this introduction.

57 Cf. above, the second epigraph.

58 And the source, if I am not mistaken, of the first of Albert Hirschman's "half-truths" (1986, pp. 4–5). He always maintained, in fact that his degree from Trieste had been a PhD, while in fact it was a BA: formally this is undoubtedly true. But in actual substance? His reading of *The Poincaré franc* shows that his claim contains an element of truth. This is my understanding. And I would add that in my own small way, I had a similar experience as a young man in the United Kingdom.

59 All the texts have been slavishly followed step by step. Only a few obvious "slips in the pen" have been corrected. The Index of names alone was added. (Ch. 4 and Ch. 7 of this book appeared previously in Italian, in Albert Hirschman—2004 and 1987, respectively).

Bibliography

Adelman J. (2013) *Worldly Philosopher. The Odyssey of Albert O. Hirschman*, Princeton (N.J.), Princeton University Press.

Alachevich M. and Asso P.F. (2023) "Albert O. Hirschman at the Federal Reserve 1946–1952", in Albert O. Hirschman, *The Postwar Economic Order* cit.

Asso P.F. e de Cecco M. (1987) "Introduzione," Albert O. Hirschman, *Potenza nazionale*, cit.

Bobbio N. (1975) Introduzione a Eugenio Colorni, *Scritti*, cit.

Colorni E. (1937) "La spontaneità è una forma di organizzazione", *Nuovo Avanti!*, 12 giugno; English tr. in Eugenio Colorni, *Critical Thinking*, cit. 2019.

Colorni E. (1975) *Scritti*, a cura di Norberto Bobbio, Firenze, La Nuova Italia.

Colorni E. (2019) *Critical Thinking in Action. Excerpts from Political Writings and Correspondence, vol. I*. Luca Meldolesi and Nicoletta Stame eds., New York, Bordighera.

Colorni E. (2019a) *The Discovery of the Possible. Excerpts from Political Writings and Correspondence, vol. I*. Luca Meldolesi and Nicoletta Stame eds., New York, Bordighera.

Colorni E. (2023) *Il compromesso Leibniz*, a cura di Luca Meldolesi, Soveria Mannelli, Rubbettino.

de Cecco M. (2004) "Prefazione" a Albert O. Hirschman *Il Franco Poincaré* cit.

Dumez H. (1985) *L'economiste, la science et le pouvoir: la cas Walras*, Paris, PUF.

Ferraresi F. (1987) "Laudatio", Laurea Honoris Causa del prof. Albert O. Hirschman, 12 novembre 1987; in Albert O. Hirschman, *Tre Continenti*, cit., 1990; English tr. in Albert O. Hirschman, *Three Continents*, cit., 2022.

Fleck C. (2020) "The Context of Otto Albert's politicization", in Luca Meldolesi and Nicoletta Stame eds., A *Passion for the Possible*. cit.

Finzi R. (2004) "Postfazione. Uno studioso studente a Trieste: Otto Albert Hirschmann", in Albert O. Hirschman *Il Franco Poincaré* cit.

Hirschman A.O. (1958) *The Strategy of Economic Development*, New Heaven Conn., Yale University Press.

Hirschman A.O. (1970) *Exit, Voice, and Loyalty: Responses to Decline in Firms, Organizations and States*, Cambridge (Mass.), Harvard University Press.

Hirschman A.O. (1981) *Essays in Trespassing: Economics to Politics and Beyond*, Cambridge, U.K., Cambridge University Press.

Hirschman A.O. (1984) "Erinnerung an das Fronzösische Gymnasyum", mimeo.

Hirschman A.O. (1984a) "A Dissenter's Confession: Revisiting the *Strategy of Economic Development*", in G. M. Meier and D. Seers eds., *Pioneers*, cit.; now in Albert O. Hirschman, *Rival Views* cit. 1986.

Hirschman A.O. (1986) *Rival Views of Market Society and Other Recent Essays*, New York, Viking.

Hirschman A.O. (1987) *Potenza nazionale e commercio estero. Gli anni Trenta, l'Italia e la ricostruzione*, a cura di Pier Francesco Asso e Marcello de Cecco., Bologna, il Mulino.

Hirschman A.O. (1987a) *L'economia politica come scienza morale e sociale*, con un saggio e a cura di Luca Meldolesi, Napoli, Liguori.

Hirschman A.O. (1987b) ["Io, detective dell'economia fascista"], *Laurea Honoris Causa* del prof. Albert O. Hirschman, 12 novembre 1987; in Albert O. Hirschman, *Tre Continenti*, cit., 1990; English tr. in Albert O. Hirschman, A *Propensity*, cit. 1995; and *Three Continents*, cit., 2022.

Hirschman A.O. (1990), *Tre Continenti. Economia politica e sviluppo della democrazia in Europa, Stati Uniti e America Latina*, a cura di Luca Meldolesi; English tr. Albert O. Hirschman, *Three Continents*, cit., 2022.

Hirschman A.O. (1994) *Passaggi di frontiera. I luoghi e le idee di un percorso di vita*, a cura di Carmine Donzelli, Marta Petrusewicz e Claudia Rusconi, Roma, Donzelli.

Hirschman A. O. (1995) A *Propensity to Self-Subversion*, Cambridge Mass., Harvard University Press.

Hirschman A. O. (1998) "Trespassing: Places and Ideas in the Course of Life. An Interview with Carmine Donzelli, Marta Petrusewicz e Claudia Rusconi", in Albert O. Hirschman, *Crossing Boundaries. Selected Writings*, New York, Zone.

Hirschman A.O. (2004) *Il Franco Poincaré e la sua svalutazione*, a cura di Giorgio Gilibert, Roma Edizioni di storia e letteratura.

Hirschman A.O. (2022) *Three Continents. Political Economy and Development of Democracy in Europe, the United States and Latin America*, Luca Meldolesi ed., New York, Peter Lang.

Hirschman A.O. (2023) *The Postwar Economic Order. National Reconstruction and International Cooperation*, Michele Alachevich and Pier Francesco Asso eds., New York, Colombia University Press.

La Malfa G. (2022) *Keynes l'eretico. Vita e opere del grande economista che ha cambiato l'Occidente*. Milano, Mondadori.

Meier G.M. and Seers D., eds., (1984) *Pioneers in Development*, Oxford, Oxford Univ. Press.

Meldolesi L. (1987) "Alle origini del possibilismo: Albert Hirschman 1932–52," in Albert O. Hirschman *L'economia*, cit.; French tr. *Revue française de science politique*, n. 3, 1993.

Meldolesi L. (1991) "Durkheim, Simiand e la riforma dell'economia", in François Simiand, *La moneta realtà sociale ed altri scritti*, a cura di Luca Meldolesi, Napoli, ESI.

Meldolesi L. (1994) *Alla scoperta del possibile. Il mondo sorprendente di Albert O. Hirschman*, Bologna, il Mulino; Spanish tr. México, Fondo de Cultura Econòmica, 1997.

Meldolesi L. (1995) *Discovering the Possible. The Surprising World of Albert O. Hirschman*, Notre Dame, University of Notre Dame Press.

Meldolesi L. (2013) "Eugenio Colorni e Albert Hirschman a Trieste (1937–'38)", in Luca Meldolesi *Imparare ad imparare. Saggi di incontro e di passione all'origine di una possibile metamorfosi*, Soveria Mannelli, Rubbettino.

Meldolesi L. (2023) "Introduzione" a Eugenio Colorni, *Il compromesso* cit.

Meldolesi L. and Stame N. eds. (2020) A *Passion for the Possible. Excerpts from the Third Conference on Hirschman Legacy*, A Colorni-Hirschman International Institute and Berlin School of Economic and Law, Berlin 24th–25th October 1919; Rome, Ide.

· 1 ·

FERTILITY OF ITALIAN WOMEN BY AGE AND NUMBER OF CHILDREN BORN: SOME OBSERVATIONS*

1. Prof. Mario de Vergottini's article "Table of Fertility of Italian Women by Age and Number of Children Born," which appeared in the February issue of this journal [*Giornale degli Economisti*], is, to the best of our knowledge, the first attempt to consider women's fertility as a function of their prolificacy, that is, the number of children they have borne. This problem, along with others, was noted by Knibbs under the title "Unexplored elements of fecundity."[1] It does not seem strange, therefore, that the methods of the first exploration of a hitherto almost unknown demographic terrain should elicit criticism and suggestions for improvement.

2. In the first part of his article, de Vergottini very clearly notes the lack of comparability between the two statistics that need to be compared, namely

* Mimeo, March 1937.

1 See *Mathematical Theory of Population*, pp. 368–369. "To distinguish between the effect of previous births and age upon the frequency of maternity, of twins etc., more comprehensive data are required than at present exist for Australia." I would disagree with this last statement, given that the research requires only that the census provide statistics for women regarding age and number of children borne, and that birth statistics show births classified by mother's age and birth order. Both of these statistics exist for Australia in 1911.

1) the distribution, at a certain date, of married women according to age and the number of children they have had, and 2) the distribution of births according to birth order and the age of the mothers at the time of delivery. The author elects to calculate fertility quotients by comparing, for example, all legitimate ordinal births (k+1) for mothers aged 15–50 with the number of all women married once or more from ages 15 to 50 who had k children. But since the birth order indicated in the statistics under "Population Change" considers only births from existing marriages and not legitimate or illegitimate children born previously, while the figures in the "Women's Fertility Survey" take all births into account, the calculated quotients are erroneous with respect to the theoretical quotients that would result if the statistics for births by birth order were similar to those for women based on the number of children they had borne.

The error, while perhaps not terribly important, presents two disadvantages noted by de Vergottini himself: 1) it does not affect all the quotients equally, since for low-order births the quotients are distorted upward, while they are distorted downwards for high-order births, and 2) the magnitude of the error cannot be assessed.

Now, by narrowing the field of observation to only "pure births"—that is, to fertility based on the number of children born to women who had no children before their present marriage, we can eliminate, if not the error itself, at least the two disadvantages mentioned. By comparing the statistics for pure births by birth order with that for women married once, it can be shown, in fact,[2] that the calculated quotients are all distorted downward to the same extent by comparison with the theoretical quotients, in the narrower sense that these come to acquire.

Furthermore, a comparison of the statistics for all births with those for women married only once produces a new series of quotients, and it can be shown that these represent the *upper* limit of the theoretical quotients for which it is possible to adopt the averages of the two very close series found by calculation. The error of the figures in Table 1 averages 2/3 per thousand, and almost never exceeds five per thousand.

3. If, as it would appear, the above method produces more precise figures, the overall differences, however, turn out to be small. The second criticism we

2 For details, see the footnote at the bottom of the article.

have to advance on de Vergottini's article, on the other hand, if correct, has consequences for his figures that are much more serious.

In demography, the necessity and concurrent difficulty of comparing figures resulting from censuses and annual statistics have given rise to the distinction between probabilities and frequency ratios. In general, probability (of death, childbirth, marriage, etc.) is the *measure* of the phenomenon studied, but the frequency ratio accounts for it with satisfactory accuracy. Thus in particular for general and specific fertility, the probability that a woman of age x will give birth before reaching age x +1 is given by the formula

$$n_x = \frac{N^{x/x+1}_{z/z+1}}{P^{x/x+1}_{z+1/2} + 1/2\, D^{x/x+1}_{z/z+1}} \qquad (1)$$

where $N^{x/x+1}_{z/z+1}$ indicates the number of births for mothers aged x/x+1 in the period z/z+1, $D^{x/x+1}_{z/z+1}$ the number of women who died at age x/x+1 in the period z/z+1, and $P^{x/x+1}_{z+1/2}$ the number of women aged x/x+1 surveyed at moment z + 1/2. Now $D^{x/x+1}_{z/z+1}$ is very small compared with $P^{x/x+1}_{z+1/2}$ especially during women's reproductive years, and disregarding it yields the usual specific fertility quotient.

If we now consider the probability that a married woman aged x who has had k births will have ordinal birth k+1 before reaching age x+1, we must (disregarding women who have died or become widows) apply the following formula:

$$n^{k+1}_x = \frac{{}_{k+1}N^{x/x+1}_{z/z+1}}{{}_kP^{x/x+1}_{z+1/2} + 1/2\left({}_{k+1}N^{x/x+1}_{z/z+1} - {}_kN^{x/x+1}_{z/z+1}\right)} \qquad (2)$$

where k or (k+1) expresses the ordinal of the birth or the number of births. The explanation of this formula is similar to that of the formula generally adopted for the construction of mortality tables: married women with k births who report being aged x in the census have an average age of x + ½. Since the time they were exactly x years old, their number—which we are trying to reconstruct—has been *diminished* by the death of some and by the death of the husbands of others, facts that we have disregarded because of their minor importance. But it has also been diminished by the fact that some had a new birth between ages x and x + ½. On the other hand, their number has been *increased* by the fact that some women with (k – 1) births at age x have had a birth ordered k in the age interval x/x + ½. Assuming that the number of women giving birth at age x/x + ½ is equal to the number of women giving birth at age x + ½ – x + 1,[3] in order to reconstruct the number of married women with k births at the age of x, we must add to the census figure half the births ordered (k + 1) and subtract from it half the births ordered (k).

A special case is the probability that a married and childless woman will give birth for the first time. Here the number of births ordered k – 1 (= 0) by mothers aged x/x + ½ is replaced by the number of childless women married at age x/x + ½,[4] so that we should write

$$(3)\qquad n\frac{1}{x}=\frac{{}_{1}N^{x/x+1}_{z/z+1}}{{}_{0}P^{x/x+1}_{z+1/2}+1/2\left({}_{1}N^{x/x+1}_{z/z+1}-M^{x/x+1}_{z/z+1}\right)}$$

The weighted average of the values of n_x, from $n\frac{1}{x}$ to $n\frac{\omega}{x}$, will be the probability of a legitimate birth for a woman aged x, however many children she has had, and will be given by the formula

$$(4)\qquad n\frac{l}{x}=\frac{{}_{l}N^{x/x+1}_{z/z+1}}{{}_{c}P^{x/x+1}_{z+1/2}-1/2\,M^{x/x+1}_{z/z+1}}$$

while the usual legitimate fertility quotient is satisfied by the ratio $\frac{{}_{l}N^{x/x+1}_{z/z+1}}{{}_{c}P^{x/x+1}_{z+1/2}}$

4. The practical application of formula (2) (possible only for five-year age classes) encounters only one difficulty, namely that the statistics give us the distribution of women according to the number not of deliveries, but of

3 The errors that this assumption will cause us to make for the values for births ordered k and k + 1 will be partially offset between them by the fact of consecutive addition and subtraction.

4 For their determination see the note [at the bottom of the article].

children they have had. Nor is the birth order established according to the actual succession of births.[5] A birth by a woman who has had two children will be classified as a third birth, for example, whether the children she has come from one birth or two. Disregarding triple or quadruple births, the probability that a woman aged x with k children will have an additional birth is given by the formula

$$(5) \qquad n^{k+1}_{x} = \frac{{}_{k+1}N^{x/x+1}_{z/z+1}}{{}_{k}P^{x/x+1}_{z+1/2} + 1/2\left({}_{k+1}N^{x/x+1}_{z/z+1} - {}^{sing}_{k}N^{x/x+1}_{z/z+1} - {}^{double}_{k-1}N^{x/x+1}_{z/z+1}\right)}$$

A woman can in fact become the mother of k children either through a simple birth ordered k or a double birth ordered (k – 1).

For ease of calculation, however, I have used formula (2), since the difference between the correct denominator in formula (5) and the incorrect one in formula (2) is extremely small.[6] Only for the probability of giving birth for a woman with one child have I used formula (5), which takes the form

$$(5a) \qquad n^{2}_{x} = \frac{{}_{2}N^{x/x+1}_{z/z+1}}{{}_{1}P^{x/x+1}_{z+1/2} + 1/2\left({}_{2}N^{x/x+1}_{z/z+1} - {}^{sing}_{1}N^{x/x+1}_{z/z+1}\right)}$$

It is evident that the application of the probability formulas shown above will give entirely different values from the simple frequency ratio $\frac{{}_{k+1}N^{x/x+1}_{z/z+1}}{{}_{k}P^{x/x+1}_{z+1/2}}$ used by de Vergottini (and which he nonetheless calls probability, see p. 105).

The inadequacy of this ratio for measuring a woman's fertility according to the number of children she has had is especially apparent when one considers that not only does its denominator sometimes differ significantly from the denominator of the probability ratio, but it is also lower or higher than the

5 See "*Population Change*" 1931, p. 55.

6 $1/2\left({}^{double}_{k-1}N^{x/x+1}_{z/z+1} - {}^{double}_{k}N^{x/x+1}_{z/z+1}\right)$ that is, half the difference between the double births of two successive orders of birth.

denominator depending on whether the value of $\left({}_{R+1}N^{x/x+1}_{z/z+1} - {}_{R}N^{x/x+1}_{z/z+1} \right)$ is positive or negative; therefore, the frequency ratio will itself be lower or higher than the probability and will not even present a reliable index of the trend in the problem under study.

5. After proportionally allocating married women with an unknown number of children[7] and births both of unknown order and to mothers of unknown age, I calculated the probability of a woman with k children having another birth. As shown in sec. 1, such probabilities apply only to women who have not had children before their current marriage. The differences between the figures found by de Vergottini (see. p. 105 of the cited article) and those below, however, can be explained almost entirely by the difference between frequency ratio and probability.[8]

A glance at the two tables immediately reveals the great discrepancy, especially with regard to women of young ages, but for intermediate ages as well. The maximums in the horizontal rows (fertility of women with a certain number of children across different age groups), are shifted—always to the left—very frequently, six times to be precise: for women with no children and women with 1, 7, 8, 15 and 17 children. One especially interesting and significant result is the shift in the maximum for married women without children from age class 21–24 to class 15–20. In fact, it is most likely that the fertility of childless married women aged 15 to 20 is higher than that of childless women aged 21 to 24, for a number of reasons: women who marry before age 20 are among the most prolific; the protogenesic interval increases, as we know, as the mother's age increases; for very young women, marriage is more likely the consequence than the cause of their fertility.

The total probability of legitimate fertility calculated using formula (4) is much higher than the usual quotient in the first two age groups. Thereafter, the number of women getting married is only a small fraction of the women already married so that the quotient is no longer substantially altered.[9]

7 That is, those not classified in the *Women's Fertility Survey*.

8 To clarify: it is not that the quotients calculated by de Vergottini are "wrong," but only that their use is not justified in this case, since they deviate substantially from the fertility probabilities, which give the true picture of the phenomenon under study.

9 For ages below 15 years (essentially the age of 14), formulas (2) and (4) are not applicable because the assumption of equal distribution of marriages and births between ages 14–14½ and 14½–15 is false.

Table 1.1. *Probability of a Birth, by Age and Number of Live Births, for Married Women Who Have Not Had Children before Their Present Marriage (1931, per thousand)*

Number of live births	15–20	21–24	25–29	30–34	35–39	40–44	45–49	Total
0	843	701	419	169	63	17	1,3	333
1	231	288	263	181	102	33	3,4	201
2	151	230	235	175	107	36	3,3	157
3	162	209	241	216	145	51	5,1	159
4	91	186	225	240	179	69	7,8	157
5	32	189	211	240	208	82	8,7	146
6		156	198	230	205	96	10,5	128
7		95	202	226	211	109	11,4	116
8		77	158	199	194	111	14,4	99
9		15	126	182	207	127	17,4	98
10			107	175	179	115	15,5	79
11			68	198	216	132	20,3	86
12			86	123	184	115	17,5	67
13				94	170	123	19,8	67
14				112	153	106	17,9	56
15				48	130	122	17,5	59
16				83	138	104	19,9	54
17					114	105	18,5	52
18					135	61	7,4	29
Total	520	388	271	203	150	71	9,0	180

6. A third observation regarding de Vergottini's article relates to the elaboration and interpretation of his results. Noting that the reliability of fertility quotients is greatly compromised by the fondness for round figures, de Vergottini proceeds first with a graphical equalization, followed by an algebraic interpolation of the equalized series. If, however, the inaccuracy of the reports of birth order and number of live births (an inaccuracy that, as de Vergottini rightly notes, is cumulative) is the only justification for the interpolation procedures, equalization and interpolation should have begun no earlier than the fertility quotients for women with 8 children. In fact, these quotients are too small, because the number of births of the ninth order of generation (numerators of the above quotients) is reduced by a fondness for the number 10.

There is in fact *no evidence* of false reporting before number nine, either of birth order or number of children. The irregularities encountered in the trend of fertility quotients therefore extend as far as women with 8 children—irregularities that *actually exist in reality* and need to be explained, rather than being made to disappear by equalization.[10]

The equalizations and interpolations mentioned thus deprive de Vergottini of a very interesting lesson he could have drawn from his research, one that shows up more clearly from the probabilities calculated here. This is the surprising fact that the fertility of women with three children is higher than that of women with two children, both overall and for individual age groups, with the sole exception of women aged 25 to 29. And there is the additional fact that, as total, the fertility of women with four children is the same (157%) as the fertility of women with two children.

Considered from a physiological standpoint, the general female fertility curve (for all ages) by number of children delivered ought to descend regularly, since increasing average ages correspond to a higher number of children.[11]

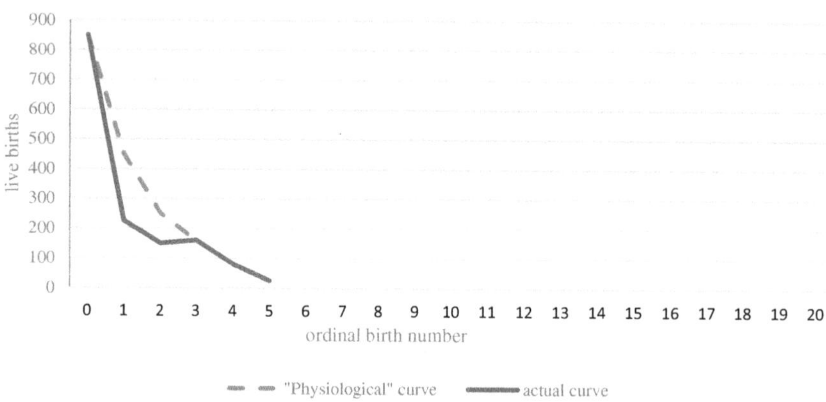

Table 1.2a. *15–20 Years Old: Space between Curves due to Human Factors (Voluntary Restriction)*

10 Mortara, in his article "Tavola di fecondità dei matrimoni per l'Italia (1930)," [Table of marriage fertility for Italy (1930)] *Giornale degli Economisti*, 1934, p. 175, rebukes Gini in the same way about the halt in the descent of the fertility curve in marriages from the second to the third year of marriage, a halt that is by no means fortuitous.

11 Except for women from 15 to 50 years of age with 0 or 1 child. But the reasons why the fertility of married women without children must be much higher than that of women with 1 child are obvious.

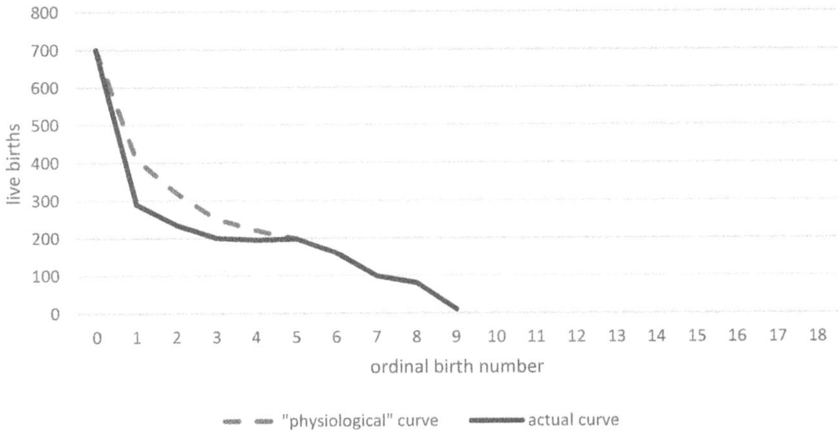

Table 1.2b. *21–24*

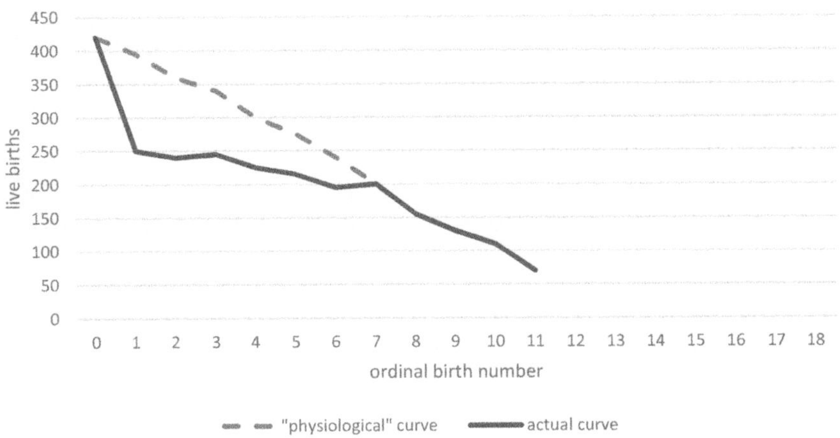

Table 1.2c. *25–29*

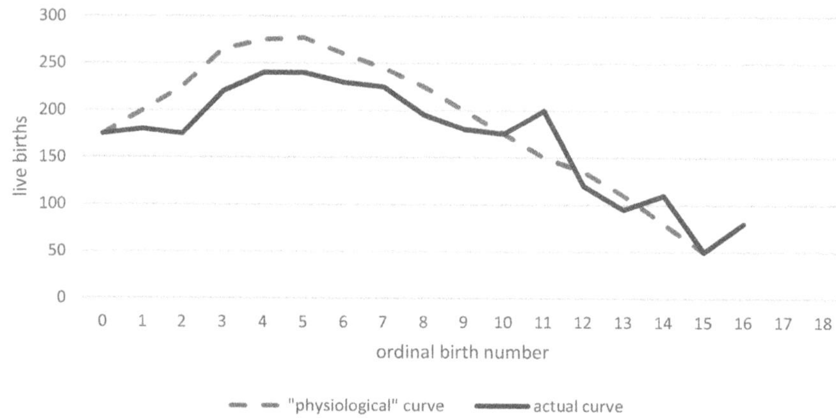

Table 1.2d. *30–34*

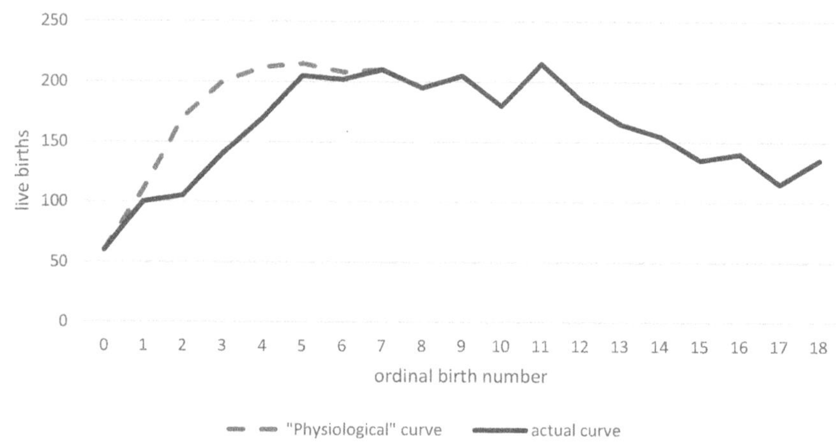

Table 1.2e. *35–39*

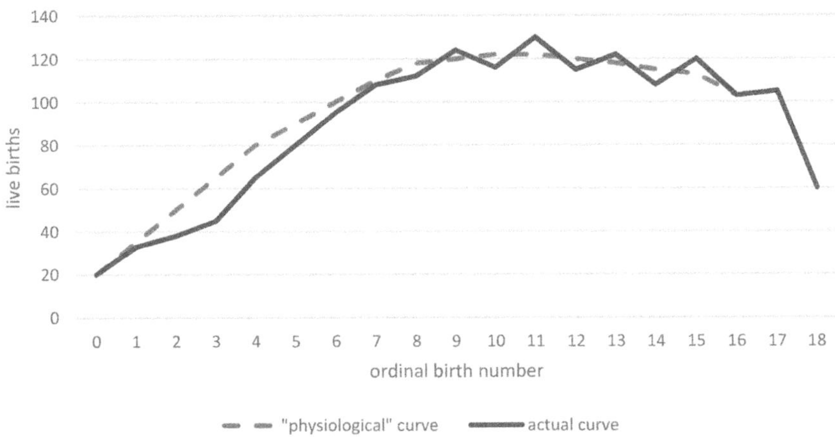

Table 1.2f. *40–44*

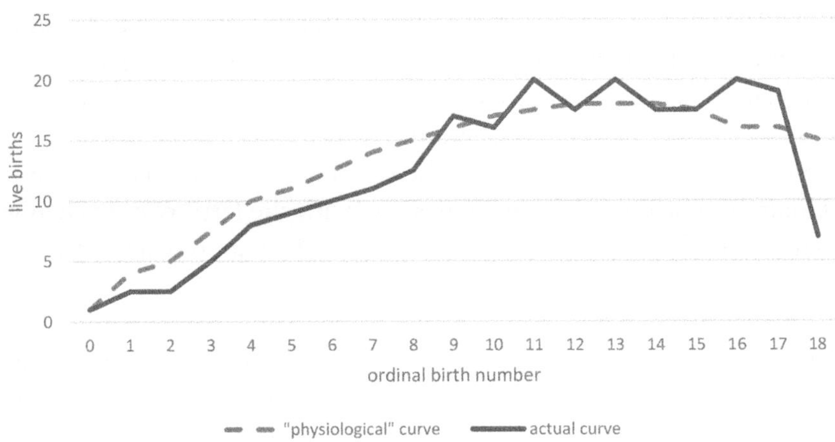

Table 1.2g. *45–49*

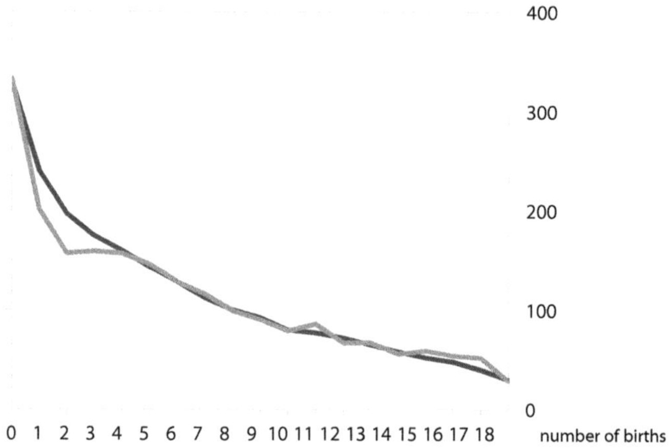

Table 1.2h. *Total*

Now if all women, regardless of how many children they have, voluntarily limited their births to the same extent, the fertility of all of them would be decreased in the same measure without harming the regularity of the curve. But since, as we know, voluntary restriction mostly occurs among women with 1, 2, or 3 children, it is the fertility of these women, and especially those with two children, that is reduced in comparison with the fertility of women with 4 and more children, who have not restricted and do not restrict births to any significant extent.

If one wishes to make an interpolation after these considerations, it can be done by making the interpolating curve look "natural" or "physiological." Assuming that in the fertility of women with 0 children[12] and with 5, 6, 7, and more children, social factors are not or almost not relevant, a continuous curve can be drawn,[13] so that this fertility can be linked. The fertility of women with 1/4 children will be below this curve. Now the difference between the ordinates of the natural curve and the ordinates of the actual curve will give a rough idea of the reduction in physiological fertility due to voluntary limitation.

12 Lenti ("La fecondità legittima della donna Italiana secondo l'età e l'ordine di generazione," [The legitimate fertility of Italian women by age and birth order]—this journal, 1935, p. 846) confirms this hypothesis for Italy (though not for some provinces).

13 Note that the concept of the continuous curve is somewhat problematic in our case, because the variable itself (number of live births) is discontinuous.

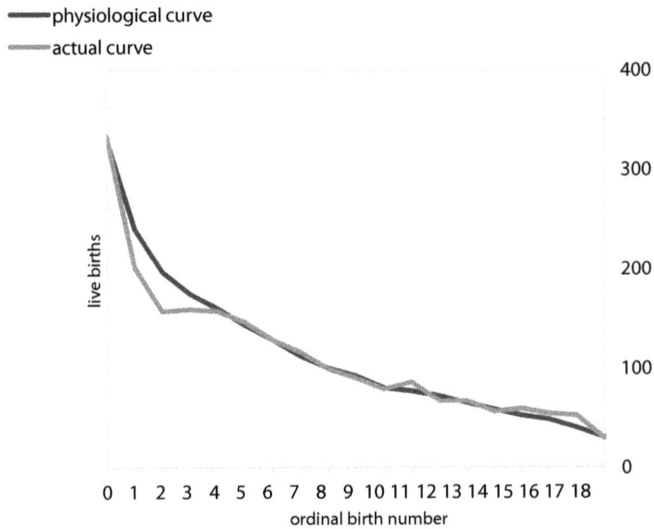

Table 1.3. *Fertility Curve by Number of Live Births for all Married Women of Reproductive Age*

The facts detected are perhaps one of the characteristic manifestations of voluntary limitation and differential fertility. They show the tendency toward the "Zweikindersystem" already being powerfully felt in Italy in 1931 and should be corroborated by more specialized investigations into the demographic conditions of the different provinces.

7. If we now consider the general trend of the problem, we see that the quotients calculated by de Vergottini and our probabilities considered by vertical columns—i.e., for the fertility of women by number of live births in a given age class—show the same trend despite the very important disparities for the individual values. The figures in the previous table also decrease—with the noted irregularity—for the three first classes (15–20, 21–24, 25–29), while for the age groups that follow they first increase and then decrease.

According to de Vergottini, this trend shows that in the younger groups a "high level of prolificacy" results in "a serious detriment to current fecundity" (p. 106 art. cit.) while for older ages more "robust" current fertility "no longer inversely correlates with prolificacy."

We repeat here what we said at the beginning—that we are in almost unknown territory, ignored up to now by demographers, and we must therefore proceed very cautiously in our deductions. We do know for certain one statistical law about women's legitimate fertility—that it physiologically diminishes and is exhausted with age. The question that arises is whether such physiological exhaustion occurs for women not only with advancing age, but as the number of children they have increases—and *independently* of exhaustion with age.

The answer to this question based on the figures and curves obtained is unquestionably negative. In fact, if there were a "law of physiological exhaustion of women as the number of children they bear increases," women's fertility curves by prolificacy should fall regularly in *all* age groups, and not only in the younger ones. We see on the contrary that in the age classes 35–39, 40–44, and 45–49, for example, the fertility of women with 17 or 18 children is much higher than that of women with 0 or 1 child. For this reason, attempts to explain the curves as a function of greater or lesser exhaustion resulting from prolificacy should be abandoned.

Now, if de Vergottini, with his notions of the weakness and robustness of current fertility in terms of prolificacy, meant to say that the lower fertility of a 20-year-old woman with 4 children as compared with a woman of the same age with 1 child is determined by physiological exhaustion—which would suggest that this woman will also be less fertile than other women in the future—it seems to me that he has made an inference that his figures do not allow. Such a deduction would be permissible only if women with 4 children and those with 1 child were in the same position regarding the time elapsed since the last birth. On the contrary, the lower fertility of women in their twenties with 4 children can be explained precisely by the fact that they are on average not yet *fertilizable* or have been so for a very short time, whereas for women with 1 child, fertilizability will have been re-established on average for much longer.

From this point of view, in my opinion, the different aspects of the fertility curves can largely be explained as a function of the number of live births for the different age groups. Considering the fertility of women with one child or more as *a function of the elapsed interval since the last delivery*, gives us a curve whose values are zero for the first nine months and then begin to rise, only to fall again after a certain period.[14] Now young women with few children and older women with many are likely to be in the interval corresponding to maximum fertility in relation to the last delivery; while young women with many

14 V. P. Luzzatto-Fegiz, "La stagionalità delle nascite" [The seasonality of births], *Metro*, Volume V. 4, 1925, p. 14.

children or older women with few will be in an interval corresponding to the minimum ordinals at the beginning or end of the curve. This assumption cannot be verified by current statistics, but it is nevertheless fully consistent with common sense and solves the problem in a most satisfactory way.

8. The purpose of this article was to demonstrate the benefit of a thorough study of the problem first raised by de Vergottini. I will attempt in the near future to show how the probabilities found here can be used to calculate, assuming a stationary population, the probability that a newborn female will have a certain number of children at any given age and, in general, over the course of her lifetime.

Appendix

Note on the calculation of fertility quotients and the probability of an additional birth for a married woman with k children, for women who were childless before the current marriage.

We shall consider only fertility quotients and not the probabilities resulting from formula (2).

The numerator of the quotients is given to us by the birth statistics based on birth order and mother's age for parents who presumably had no children before the current marriage. This numerator errs slightly on the low side insofar as it also excludes births to fathers who had children prior to the current marriage. But since the statistics likely cannot eliminate all "impure" births, we can consider the figures provided by *Population Change* as approximately correct.

The denominator required for a rigorous calculation should contain:

1. The number of women married once who have had k children from their current marriage without having had illegitimate children before the marriage.
2. The number of women married more than once who have had k children from their current marriage without having had either legitimate children from their previous marriages or illegitimate children.

In contrast, the denominator provided by the statistics of the *Women's Fertility Survey* (for women married once) contains:

1) The number of women required by group 1) of the theoretical denominator,
2) The number of women married once having 1 or 2 illegitimate children but (k – 1) or (k – 2) legitimate children.

Group 2) of the theoretical denominator is very small,[15] especially for high values of k, whereas group 2) of the actual denominator has to be a fairly large fraction (perhaps 5%) of the actual denominator, which is therefore larger than the theoretical denominator. The calculated quotients will therefore be smaller than the theoretical quotients. (Quotient ac < quotient at).

If we now want to calculate the fertility quotients with the order number for the current marriage including women who had illegitimate children before this marriage, it will be found through similar reasoning that the quotients obtained by dividing the figures in the table relating to *all* births by those in the table of women married once show values that are too large, or approximately equal to the theoretical values. (Quotient bc ≥ quotient bt).

We also see from the calculation that quotient ac < quotient bc, and since we know that rate at has to differ slightly from rate bt, it follows that the theoretical quotient for pure births (at) lies between the two rates ac and bc, calculated by means of statistics. The average of these two rates is the value we gave to the theoretical rate sought. Application of the probability formula (2) leaves the above inequality intact.

A special case is the fertility of women without children. The theoretical denominator of the fertility quotient has to contain:

1) the number of women married once without children;
2) the number of women married more than once without children.
   Both groups are provided by the *Survey* statistics, and the fertility quotient can therefore be calculated with all the accuracy desired. The difficulty here lies in the application of probability formula (3), where we want the number of *pure* marriages—that is, of women who had no children before the marriage they are about to enter into. An approximation of this figure can be achieved by the following method:

Since the statistics distinguish women who marry by whether they are single or widowed, one can subtract from the married widows the proportion of

15 See the table of women married more than once in the *Survey*.

those who already have children, assuming that among them the proportion without children is the same as that among all widows counted in the Survey. This will suffice for the older ages (35 and up), where "impure" firstborns come mostly from women married for the second time. For the younger ages I have assumed that the relation between pure firstborns and pure marriages is the same as that between all firstborns and all married women. The number of pure marriages found in this way (258.911 out of a total of 271.744 marriages for women aged 15–50) is perhaps still somewhat high, but it seems to us accurate enough for our purposes.

R. University of Trieste,
O. A. Hirschmann.
Institute of Statistics.
March 1937

· 2 ·

NOTE ON TWO RECENT TABLES OF MARRIAGE RATES IN THE ITALIAN POPULATION*

Summary:

1. Two basic types of theoretical formulas; 2. Probability concepts corresponding to the two types of formulas; 3. The formulas as used in practical calculation; 4. Cases of the use of one type of formula; 5. Cases of the use of the other type of formula and criticism of recent tables of elimination of bachelors; 6. Conclusion

1. Two different tables of calculated marriage rates have recently appeared side by side in the *Annali di Statistica.*[1] Both surveys made use of the mortality tables by marital status calculated by Galvani, which were published in the

* *Giornale degli Economisti*, January 1938.

1 P. Medani, Tavole di nuzialità italiane per celibi e nubili, 1930–1932, in *Annali di Statistica*, serie VII, vol. 1; S. Somogyi, *Tavole di nuzialità e di vedovanza per la popolazione italiana, 1930–1932*, ibid.

same volume of the *Annals*[2] and predated the *Italian Statistical Compendium* of 1935.[3] The discrepancy in the results of the two studies—conducted independently of one another—can be explained not only by differences in the details of the calculations, but by a *fundamental* difference in the calculation of the probability of marriage.

At bottom this is a theoretical problem of great scientific and practical significance: the determination of the probability of exit from a statistical set, when this exit may have more than one cause. The probability that a single man of age x will die or marry before reaching age x +1 is a very clear example of such an exit probability, since a man can cease to be single through death or marriage.

Let us consider for the purpose the well-known Lexis scheme, which allows the analytical depiction of statistical sets entering formal population theory. In a system of Cartesian axes, Lexis reports time periods on the x-axis and ages on the y-axis, so that a person's life is represented by a segment parallel to the y-axis. This "lifeline" begins at a point on the x-axis corresponding to the time of birth and ends at a point—called the death point—that has as its ordinate the age at death. The lifeline of a bachelor—as a bachelor—may terminate at either a death point or a marriage point.

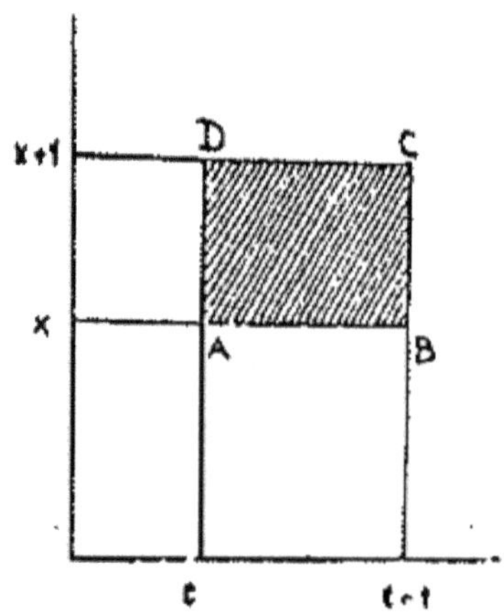

Fig. 2.1.

2 L. Galvani, *Tavole di mortalità della popolazione italiana, 1930–1932*, ibid., pp. 29–45 and 78–83.

3 *Compendio statistico italiano*, 1935-XIV, pp. 59–60.

Figures 2.1 and 2.2 are based on these briefly recalled fundamental notions. The sum of all the lifelines of bachelors that, in Figure 2.1, cross-segment *AB*, expresses the number of bachelors at precise age *x*, born in a given year *t*/*t* +1, a number we will designate as *c*(*AB*).

Similarly, let *c*(*DC*) be the number of members of the same unmarried generation at the precise age *x*+1. It then follows from the method of representation described that we will find in the rectangle *ABCD* death and marriage points equal in number to the difference between *c*(*AB*) and *c*(*DC*). We designate as *d*(*ABCD*) the sum of the death points, and as *m*(*ABCD*) the sum of the marriage points found in the rectangle *ABCD*.[4]

It is evident from this that the overall probability of exiting from the set of bachelors—that is, the probability of *not remaining bachelors*—is given by the formula:

$$u_x = \frac{d(ABCD) + m(ABCD)}{c(AB)}$$

At first glance it seems obvious that this overall probability of exit can be split into two special probabilities: the probability of exit *caused by death*, viz:

$$d_x = \frac{d(ABCD)}{c(AB)}, \tag{1}$$

and the probability of exit *caused by marriage*, that is:

$$m_x = \frac{m(ABCD)}{c(AB)}. \tag{2}$$

The sum of these two probabilities gives precisely the total probability of exit. Indeed, it is this last formula that Medani[5] used to construct his table of marriage rates.

4 Leaving aside that the actual statistics do not make available to us the sets we are talking about. See § 3.

5 Medani, *op. cit.*, p. 297, formula (1).

On the other hand, however, we see that Galvani[6] and Somogyi[7] used two quite different formulas. For the probability of death for bachelors, Galvani uses the formula:

$$d'_x = \frac{d(ABCD)}{c(AB) - 1/2m(ABCD)}, \qquad (3)$$

and for the probability of marriage Somogyi uses the parallel formula:

$$m'_x = \frac{m(ABCD)}{c(AB) - 1/2d(ABCD)}. \qquad (4)$$

How can this difference be explained?

The reasoning leading to the adoption of these last two formulas is as follows, as regards the calculation of the probability of death. The aim is to find the number of bachelors who are actually susceptible to death *throughout the year*. Now if we assume—and this generally fits with reality—that cases of marriage are uniformly distributed over the entire year, then bachelors who married at age $x/x + 1$ were at risk of death *as bachelors* for only half a year on average. This is the same as saying that only half of the married bachelors were exposed to the risk of dying unmarried during the entire year. For this reason, the initial number of bachelors is decreased by half the number of marriages. The same reasoning leads to the reduction by half of the dead bachelors in the denominator of the formula for the probability of marriage.

2. Comparing the two sets of formulas, it is immediately apparent that it is impossible to say which of them is correct and which in error. Both are probabilities of death and marriage for bachelors, but they represent totally different concepts of probability.

The probability of marriage in formula [4] expresses the probability that a bachelor will get married *if he doesn't die*—that is, the probability of exiting the set of bachelors as a result of marriage *not considering the risk of death*. Formula [2], on the other hand, shows the probability of marriage without

6 Galvani, *op. cit.*, p. 34, formula (*a*).

7 Somogyi, *op. cit.*, p. 220, formula (1).

this reservation—the probability, that is, that a bachelor will not remain a bachelor and will not die as a bachelor.

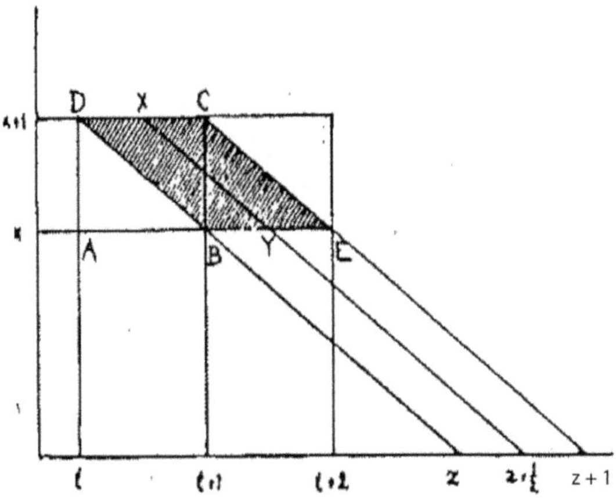

Fig. 2.2.

Similarly, formula [3] expresses the probability that a bachelor will die, not considering the risk of getting married, and formula [1] the same probability, but taking this risk into account.

This distinction is not new. Mortara included it in his *Lezioni di statistica metodologica* [Lessons in methodological statistics] (Città di Castello, 1922).[8] Indeed, his formula [4] of lesson 8 (p. 61) and [2*e*] of lesson 29 (p. 289) correspond exactly to formulas of types [1] and [2] of the present paper; while [3] of lesson 8 (p. 60) and [10] of lesson 29 (p. 291) can easily be reduced to formulas of types [3] and [4] as explained above.

Mortara, who simultaneously considers the case of *entrances* into the community—something in any case not essential to the argument being made—also assigned to these formulas their precise meaning, saying (p. 291) that formulas of the first type measure "the frequency per element of eliminations that would result from the particular cause of elimination under consideration in a group where no entries occurred and *all the observed causes of elimination* operated with the intensity ascertained." Formulas of the second type, on the other hand, measure "the frequency per element of the

8 Mortara prefers to speak of "elimination indices," believing that these are not true probabilities, given the inevitable artifice involved in determining the number of "equally possible cases."

eliminations for a supposed closed group where *only the elimination cause specifically under consideration* would operate."[9]

3. We shall now look at the formulas that can be derived from the above theoretical formulas and contain sets that can be observed in the actual statistics. In the text cited, Medani shows on p. 298 how, with the admission of certain simplifying assumptions, formula [2] above becomes, in a variation of the graphical representation adopted above (see Figure 2.2):

$$m_x = \frac{m(BECD)}{c(XY)+1/2d(BECD)+1/2m(BECD)}. \qquad \text{(2a)}$$

In this formula $m(BECD)$ and $d(BECD)$ are respectively the number of bachelors who married and died at age $x/x+1$ during the course of solar year $z/z+1$, while $c(XY)$ is the number of bachelors aged $x/x+1$ present at the moment of a census carried out halfway through the year. All the sets in formula [2*a*] are given by the statistics (at least for five-year age groups).

Similarly, formulas [1], [3] and [4] become, respectively:

$$d_x = \frac{d(BECD)}{d(XY)+1/2d(BECD)+1/2m(BECD)}, \qquad \text{(1a)}$$

$$d'_x = \frac{d(BECD)}{c(XY)+1/2d(BECD)}, \qquad \text{(3a)}$$

$$m'_x = \frac{m(BECD)}{c(XY)+1/2m(BECD)}. \qquad \text{(4a)}$$

9 Mortara pointed out the same distinction using the same expressions in his earlier work *Elementi di statistica* (Roma, Athenaeum, 1917), note on pp. 256–257; see also *ivi.*, pp. 36–37.

Mortara, in his demographic study of the larger Italian cities at the beginning of this century arrives at formula [2*a*] through straightforward reasoning, and uses it to calculate marriage probabilities,[10] opposing it to the formula proposed by Benini and here designated [4*a*], which basically corresponds to Somogyi's formula. Instead, Mortara uses [3*a*]—and not [1*a*] parallel to [2*a*]—which corresponds to the formula employed by Galvani [3], for calculating the probability of death. Somogyi and Galvani did not have to pass through the approximate formulas [4*a*] and [3*a*], since they had very complete statistical data at their disposal.

4. In the concrete task of measuring a phenomenon, it can be inferred from the conceptual distinction in § 3 which cases call for one and which for the other type of formula (Type [1] and [2] or type [3] and [4]).

As for the probability of death for bachelors, this is useful mainly to compare with the probabilities of death for married people and widows, or with the probability for single women or with bachelors in other populations. Clearly in these cases only the use of formula [3] fully achieves the intended purpose.[11] We would like to know, for example, the mortality rate for a 30-year-old who is and remains a bachelor *during the entire year*, as compared with the same rate for a 30-year-old who is and remains married until the age of 31. For the bachelor we must therefore eliminate the risk of marriage, and for the married man the risk of becoming a widower. For both probabilities, formulas of type [3] should therefore be used. For the same reason, when probabilities of marriage for bachelors are to be compared with the same probabilities for widowers or unmarried women or with the marriage probabilities for bachelors from another population, only formulas of type [4] should be used.

Another purpose of calculating the probability of death is to show the evolution of the risk of death for bachelors according to age. Here again it would seem that preference should be given to formulas of type [3]. Let us suppose by way of example that at the two different ages a and b we have, out of 1000 initial bachelors, 20 cases of death at both age $a/a + 1$ and age $b/b + 1$, and 100 cases of marriage at age $a/a + 1$, and 50 at age $b/b + 1$. Under this assumption, formula [1] gives us the same probability of death for both ages

10 G. Mortara, *Le popolazioni delle grandi città italiane al principio del secolo XX*, in "Bibl. dell'economista," series V, vol. XIX, p. 519 and p. 523, formula (β).

11 Cf. Mortara, *Lezioni di statistica metodologica*, p. 299 (note).

$\left(\frac{20}{1000}\right)$. In reality, however the mortality rate cannot be the same at both ages, because at age *a*/*a* +1, 50 more bachelors escaped the risk of death than at age *b*/*b* +1. Precisely for this reason, formula [3] gives us a probability of death at age *a* of $\left(\frac{20}{1000-50}\right)$, greater than the probability of death at age *b*, which is $\left(\frac{20}{1000-25}\right)$.

If we want to construct the mortality curve for bachelors, we need to remove bachelor marriages as a disturbing element just as we remove migratory movements when constructing a general mortality table. Just as such a table would conclusively show us the extinction rate for a generation for which no migration is assumed, the bachelor mortality table will need to show us the progressive extinction rate for a generation of bachelors who never marry. And—we would add—the marriage table calculated by applying formula [4] shows us the transformation into husbands of bachelors who never experience death—at least for the time they remained unmarried.[12]

5. The two tables constructed from formulas [3] and [4], those of Galvani and Somogyi, thus give us the pure—that is, artificially isolated—concept of the mortality and marriage rates of bachelors. They are therefore preferable in all investigations dealing with mortality and marriage rates in isolation. They are useless, however, for another and no less important task assigned to tables of marriage and death rates by civil status. This is the construction of a *table*

12 The hypothesis of a generation of bachelors disappearing only through marriage is very artificial—much more so than that of a generation of bachelors going extinct only through death. But adopting the above hypothesis is justified, in my opinion, because it can teach us something.

Assume, for example, two populations of bachelors, and that for a certain age the probability of marriage in one population is smaller than in the other, the marriage probabilities having been calculated using [2]. This may be due primarily to a *lesser attractive force from marriage* or to a *greater attractive force from death.*

(Depending on which of these is the case, demographic policy directives, for example, will have to be different. In the former case they will be oriented more toward encouraging marriage, in the latter more toward fighting death).

Now the use of [4] allows us precisely to measure in isolation the force of attraction of marriage, so that by means of the formula we will be able to identify the two potential factors in the given population's deficiency in the area of marriage.

of elimination for bachelors—the representation, that is, of the life of a generation of bachelors from the dual perspective of their deaths and marriages. From such a table very important biometric indices can be derived.

We have already seen that the probability of exiting from the group of bachelors by reason of death or marriage is without doubt provided by the formula $\frac{m(ABCD)+d(ABCD)}{c(AB)}$, and it is quite clear that for any age the values resulting from this formula will have to coincide with the sum of each pair of probabilities of death and marriage. This is true only for formulas [1] and [2], which can therefore be regarded as partial elimination rates; their sum then gives us the total elimination rate.[13]

The addition of [3] to [4], on the other hand, gives an overall elimination rate for bachelors that is higher than the real figure, and therefore the use of these formulas is inadmissible for constructing a table of survival and marital status changes. For this reason the tables calculated by Somogyi[14] cannot be accepted. As for Medani's[15] corresponding tables, these are compiled using marriage probabilities as per formula [2], but added to Galvani's probabilities of death calculated according to formula [3]—so that the total elimination of bachelors thus found is also higher—although to a much lesser extent than Somogyi's—than the elimination rate actually observed.

It may seem that the same error should be imputed to the table of survival and variations in marital status for bachelors and single women given by Mortara for Milan and Italy for 1899–1902,[16] since Mortara indeed calculates the probability of marriage according to formula [2*a*], but the probability of death using formula [3*a*] rather than [1*a*]. But this is not the case. In fact, Mortara cautions on pages 524–525 of his study that while he applied the probability of marriage to the number of survivors at the beginning of each year of age, he applied the probability of death *not* to the same number of survivors (as Medani did), but to the number of survivors at the beginning of each year of age *reduced by half the number*—previously calculated—*of newlyweds during that year*.

13 In the sense given to these terms by Mortara, *Lezioni cit.*, p. 61.

14 Somogyi, *op. cit.*, pp. 244–253.

15 Medani, *op. cit.*, pp. 311–312.

16 Mortara, *Le popolazioni*, etc. pp. 553–556.

It is easy to see that this method of Mortara's leads to the same result that would have been obtained by the direct use of formula [1] or [1*a*].[17] Thus the rate of elimination of bachelors found by Mortara for the stationary population corresponds to the rate actually observed in Italy and Milan in 1899–1902.

6. To conclude. When the aim is to study the probability of death for bachelors *in isolation*, one must consider death and disregard marriage, and, conversely, when one wants to study the probability of marriage in isolation, one must disregard mortality. On the other hand, when we set out to consider *the two phenomena together* in their effect on the fate of bachelors, we must use probabilities of death that take into account the risk of marriage and the probabilities of marriage that take into account the risk of death.

Therefore, two different tables of marriage and mortality rates for bachelors should be constructed and consulted according to the type of investigation to be undertaken.

As mentioned at the outset, the case of bachelors is merely a clear and simple example of the general case of exit from a statistical set due to multiple causes. It would be easy, in fact, to generalize the whole of the above reasoning. But it would thus lose even what little concreteness I have tried to give it.

Trieste R. University

17 Recall that formulas [1*a*], [2*a*], [3*a*]. and [4*a*], which are usually used in practical calculus, are nothing more than approximate versions of the theoretical and scientifically exact formulas [1], [2], [3] and [4].

· 3 ·

LES FINANCES ET L'ÉCONOMIE ITALIENNE. SITUATION ACTUELLE ET PERSPECTIVES*

Sommaire**

* Société d'études et d'informations économiques. Supplément au Bulletin quotidien, n. 123 du 1re Juin 1938. ["Écrit en Italie et envoyé à Paris fin de mars 1938"—Albert Hirschman's handwriting].

** Sources principales: *Bollettino Mensile di Statistica dell'Istituto Centrale di Statistica; Bollettino di Notizie Economiche; Rivista Bancaria; Rivista di Politica Economica; Giornale degli Economisti; Rassegna Economica del Banco di Napoli; il Sole; The Economist.*

Les finances et l'économie italienne

Les finances et l'économie italiennes sont de plus en plus difficilement pénétrables. Rares sont les chiffres publiés. Pour avoir une idée approximative de ce que peut être la situation financière du Royaume, on en est réduit à une méticuleuse compilation des quelques communiqués officiels du Conseil des Ministres et du Grand Conseil du Fascisme, des exposés fort peu explicites du Ministre des Finances à la Chambre et au Sénat, des études toujours très discrètes parues dans les journaux et les revues de la Péninsule.

Cependant, en comparant ces données, en les complétant les unes par les autres, on arrive à dresser un tableau, un schéma, plutôt, de ce que peuvent être actuellement les finances et l'économie italiennes. C'est ce travail de reconstitution, reposant sur une base solide—(la documentation utilisée est indiquée avec le sommaire)—ou l'hypothèse est réduit à la plus juste mesure, que l'on trouvera ci-après.

I. Les finances publiques

Dans les trois dernières années, la vie économique italienne a été profondément imprégnée par trois facteurs essentiels: la guerre abyssine, le réarmement et les efforts tendant vers l'autarcie. Ces trois phénomènes qui ont des origines politiques communes ont eu des conséquences économiques et financières identiques dont une des plus importantes est la part de plus en plus–large–prise par l'État dans le système économique. D'après des évaluations tout à fait grossières, les dépenses totales de l'État et des collectivités publiques atteindraient pour cette année avec 50 milliards des lires 50% du revenu national estimé tout aussi sommairement à 100 milliards—tandis que cette même proportion était évaluée à un tiers avant la crise.

1) Budget

Essayons d'abord, malgré le manque de renseignements, de donner un tableau des finances de l'État qui nous permette au moins de fixer approximativement les idées.

L'année financière en Italie va du 1er juillet au 30 juin. En combinant les exposés du ministre des Finances à la Chambre des Députes et au Sénat, les communiqués officiels du Conseil des Ministres et du Grand Conseil du Fascisme et l'article certainement inspiré de V. Gayda dans le *Giornale d'Italia* du 17 décembre 1937, on peut établir le tableau suivant du budget ordinaire et extraordinaire pendant les années 1935–1936 et 1936–1937:

Tableau 3.1. *Dépenses (en millions de lires)*

	Ordinaires	Extraordinaires	Total
1935/1936	21.929	11.136	33.062
1936/1937	23.413	17.519	40.932
	45.339	28.655	73.994
	Recettes budgétaires	Déficit	
1935/1936	19.970	13.092	
1936/1937	23.053	17.879	
	43.023	30.971	

Le total des dépenses non couverts normalement atteint donc près de 31 milliards de lires. Remarquons que la conquête de l'Abyssinie a englouti moins d'argent que, par la suite, les dépenses pour sa mise en valeur et pour les dépenses extraordinaires d'armement.

2) Couverture du déficit

Les moyens par lesquels le déficit a été couvert peuvent être groupés en trois catégories principales: l'emprunt à long terme, l'emprunt à court terme et l'inflation. Mais nous allons voir qu'il n'est pas toujours facile de préciser leurs parts relatives et en outre, il y a eu des recettes ne rentrant dans aucune des catégories habituelles.

a) Emprunts à long terme

α) En 1935, on émit un grand emprunt amortissable 5% qui devait être souscrit en majorité par les propriétaires des titres de rente perpétuelle 3½% datant de la grande opération de conversion de 1933. La mutation de 3½% en 5% eut lieu par le versement à fonds perdu de 15 lires par 100 lires de capital nominal. Cette opération jointe aux souscriptions à proprement parler donna un produit de 6.805 millions de lires.

β) La deuxième opération de crédit à long terme fut en 1936/1937 l'emprunt amortissable 5% qui devait être souscrit par tous les propriétaires d'immeubles dans la mesure de 5% de la valeur de l'immeuble. Par la combinaison avec un impôt de 3.5% sur la propriété immobilière par lequel les propriétaires d'immeubles payaient à eux-mêmes les intérêts de l'emprunt celui-ci prit l'aspect d'un véritable impôt sur le capital. Ceci fut d'ailleurs confirmé par la stipulation qu'au lieu de souscrire à l'emprunt amortissable en 25 années, on pouvait racheter en une fois l'impôt immobilier (payable lui aussi pendant 25 années) en le capitalisant aux taux de 7%, ce qui donne environ le montant dû à titre d'emprunt.

Dans la prévision que les propriétaires d'immeubles n'auraient pas suffisamment de fonds liquides disponibles, on leur créa dans des limites bien déterminés des facilités d'emprunts hypothécaires auprès des Banques qui à leur tour pouvaient se rembourser auprès de la Banque d'Italie. Il va sans dire que ce circuit revient à une inflation indirecte au profit de l'État avec cette différence importante pour l'inflation opérée directement par l'État, que sa résorption est affaire des particuliers qui remboursent leurs dettes avec relativement plus d'empressement que l'État.

Nous connaissons le produit que l'emprunt immobilier a donné jusqu'au 31 avril 1937, date à laquelle les opérations étaient achevées sur presque tout le territoire. Les souscriptions avaient donné 4.260 millions de lires, les rachats de l'impôt immobilier 1.117 millions, chiffre que nous avons inclus parmi les recettes budgétaires de l'année 1936/1937. En outre, le Ministre des Finances précisa devant le Sénat que la Banque d'Italie a financé l'emprunt par ses avances pour la somme de 1.542 millions qui devrait donc entre inscrite parmi les moyens inflationnistes.

b) Emprunts à court terme (dette flottante)

Depuis la conversion forcée des bons du Trésor en emprunt Littorie en 1937, il n'y avait plus en Italie d'émissions de Bons. La dette flottante était représentée par des avances en compte courant portant intérêt près la Cassa Depositi et Prestiti, organisme correspondant à la Caisse des Dépôts et des Consignations et près le Banco di Napoli. Ces avances furent utilisées pendant les deux années sous revue jusqu'au 30 avril 1937 à concurrence de 2.422 millions pour la Cassa Depositi et Prestiti et de 1.285 millions pour le Banco di Napoli.

Mais il était devenu nécessaire d'utiliser plus largement les ressources du marché monétaire et ainsi on reprit en 1936 l'émission des Bons du Trésor dont la circulation au 30 avril 1937 se montait à 4.713. Il faut cependant diminuer ce chiffre de 2 milliards qui servaient de garantie à de nouvelles avances de la Banque d'Italie au Trésor.

Le tableau ci-dessous indique la progression de la dette intérieure entre 1929 (30 juin) et 1937 (30 avril).

Tableau 3.2. *Dette publique intérieure (en millions de lires)*

	consolidée	flottante	totale
1929 (30 juin)	84.624	2.510	87.134
1934 (30 juin)	91.997	10.625	102.622
1937 (30 avril)	101.241	20.065	121.306

c) L'Inflation

C'est là un premier moyen inflationniste auquel nous ajouterons tout de suite un autre milliard d'avance temporaire. En outre, le Gouvernement italien a utilisé pour ses besoins courants le "profit" de la réévaluation de l'encaisse or opérée après la dévaluation de 1936. Ce profit fut de 1.649 millions de lires et son utilisation pour les besoins du Trésor n'est autre chose qu'une forme d'inflation.

Nous avons déjà parlé du financement de l'emprunt immobilier par la Banque d'Italie. Enfin le Trésor a émis des billets d'État pour un montant total de 1.350 millions.

d) Moyens divers

Dans une rubrique a part il faut énumérer: l'or donne a la Patrie (401 millions, montant de la première tranche, la seule précisée) et le produit de la vente de titres étrangers ou de titres italiens émis à l'étranger (2.807 millions).

Nous arrivons ainsi au tableau suivant:

Tableau 3.3.

1.	Emprunts à long terme:		
	Rente amortissable 5%		6.805
	Emprunt immobilier:		
	- Souscriptions	4.260	
	- Avances de la Banque d'Italie	1.542	
		2.718	2.718

			9.523
2.	Dette flottante:		
	Avances en C/C Cassa Depositi & Prestiti		2.422
	Avances en C/C Banco di Napoli		1.285
	Bons du Trésor	4.713	
	- dont près la Banque d'Italie	2.000	

		2.713	2.713

			6.420
3.	Moyens à caractère inflationniste:		
	Avances de la Banque d'Italie sur bons du Trésor	2.000	
	Avances temporaires de la Banque d'Italie	1.000	
	Produit de la réévaluation de l'encaisse-or	1.649	
	Financement de l'emprunt immobilier par la Banque d'Italie	1.542	
	Billets d'État	1.350	

			7.541
4.	Moyens divers:		
	Or donné a la patrie (1ère tranche)	401	
	Titres étrangers réalisés	2.207	
			2.608

	Total des recettes extraordinaires		26.092

Nous pouvons ainsi analyser en détail par quels moyens l'État s'est procuré 26 milliards d'un total de 31 milliards de besoins exceptionnels pendant les deux années sous revue. Le recours à l'inflation a été maintenu dans des limites assez modestes (25% du total).

Quant' aux 5 milliards inexpliqués, on peut considérer en se basant sur des allusions des récents comptes-rendus des banques qu'ils ont été couverts en grande partie par de nouvelles émissions de bons du Trésor. Ceci vaut de même pour l'année courante ou le recours à l'inflation a dû être minime à en juger d'après le montant presque inchangé de la circulation de billets sur laquelle nous reviendrons tout à l'heure.

Pour l'année financière 1937/1938, on a en tout et pour tout le communiqué du Conseil des ministres du 15 décembre dernier. Il nous indique que le budget ordinaire sera de 25 milliards de lires, ce qui est un chiffre record pour l'Italie. Mais nous ne possédons aucune donnée sur la marche des finances de l'État pendant les derniers mois ni sur le budget extraordinaire qui, on l'a vu, représentait en 1936 plus de 40% de dépenses totales.

On sait d'autre part qu'en octobre dernier le gouvernement a pris de nouvelles mesures fiscales en augmentant le taux de la taxe sur le chiffre d'affaires (Tassa sugli scambi) de 2,5% à 3%.

3) L'impôt sur le capital des Sociétés par action

Mais la mesure de beaucoup la plus importante au double point de vue financier et économique fut l'institution d'un prélèvement de 10% sur le capital des sociétés par action. Voici ses caractéristiques principales. L'assiette de l'impôt est donnée par le capital et les réserves des Sociétés moins les exemptions suivantes:

1) Les titres d'autres sociétés figurant dans l'actif pour éviter la double imposition;
2) La part de l'actif de la société qui a déjà été assujettie à l'emprunt immobilier;
3) Les titres d'État possédés par la Société, pour ne pas contrevenir aux engagements assumés par l'État lors de l'émission de ces titres.

En outre, les établissements de crédit sont entièrement exempts de l'impôt.

Le paiement de l'impôt a lieu en 15 semi-mensualités pendant les années 1938, 1939, et 1940. Mais on favorise le paiement immédiat de tout l'impôt par un escompte de 8% et par son financement par le Banques et la Banque d'Italie jusqu'à concurrence de 80% du montant dû à titre d'impôt. Voilà donc créé un nouveau circuit inflationniste similaire à celui de l'emprunt immobilier; la masse de crédits qui naitra ainsi devra cependant être résorbée jusqu'en 1940.

Si les sociétés ne peuvent pas faire face à l'impôt—et c'est là le cas de l'immense majorité—par leurs moyens de trésorerie, la loi leur indique deux possibilités pour se libérer: d'abord elles peuvent décider de payer la moitié de l'impôt en décidant une augmentation de capital pour ce montant et en remettant à l'État les actions ainsi créées; il ne parait pas que beaucoup de sociétés aient fait usage de cette possibilité.

La grande majorité des sociétés importantes a suivi l'autre voie indiquée par la loi en faisant appel à leurs actionnaires pour se procurer les sommes nécessaires par le moyen d'augmentation de capital. Mais pour rendre ce sacrifice moins dur aux actionnaires, les sociétés peuvent réévaluer, en abrogation d'un décret intérieur, leur actif sur la base de la nouvelle valeur de la lire et distribuer gratuitement cette plus-value apparente sous forme d'actions gratuites jusqu'à concurrence du double du montant souscrit en espèces.

L'opération, il faut bien le dire, est magistrale. L'actionnaire en réalité paie l'impôt pour la société, mais non seulement il ne s'en aperçoit presque pas puisqu'il reçoit une action en échange, mais il croit même réaliser un bénéfice car on lui fait cadeau de deux actions gratuites par action souscrite. Et, en effet, il peut vendre ses droits de souscription et peut se procurer ainsi un gain immédiat, ne s'apercevant pas trop de la diminution de valeur en capital que ses actions ont subie ou subiront en conséquence de l'impôt.

Au milieu de l'année dernière, la Bourse avait même escompté, par une baisse préventive, des mesures financières beaucoup plus sévères de sorte que lors de la publication du décret instituant l'impôt le marché fut agréablement surpris et s'orienta vers la hausse qui dura jusqu'en janvier dernier. Depuis les marchés ont de nouveau baissé considérablement, soit à cause des augmentations de capital devenues effectives, soit à cause de la situation économique moins encourageante.

En outre, la distribution des réserves et des plus-values résultant de la réévaluation de l'actif a d'autres avantages. C'est qu'elle permet la distribution de dividendes plus élevés sans que leur taux soit augmenté, ce qui permet d'esquiver l'impôt progressif sur les dividendes; en plus, elle consent que des sommes plus élevées soient allouées à l'amortissement en exemption de l'impôt sur les bénéfices industriels et commerciaux.

C'est donc ce mode de paiement qu'ont choisi la majorité des sociétés et ainsi nous sommes actuellement en présence d'un nombre formidable d'augmentations de capital. Selon une compilation récente pour 37 sociétés importantes (*Il Sole* du 14 avril 1938) totalisant un capital de 9.844 millions de lires, c'est-à-dire environ un quart du capital total des sociétés soumises à l'impôt, ont déjà procédé à des augmentations pour 2.455 millions de lires dont 1.263 millions d'actions gratuites et 1.192 millions d'actions souscrites en espèces. Ces augmentations sont à elles seules presque égales à l'augmentation nette du capital de toutes les sociétés par actions (2.889 millions) de 1937, année d'investissement par excellence.

Le rendement de l'impôt est évalué à une somme de 5 à 6 milliards de lires.

La brève description des mesures financières des dernières années montre que non seulement on a essayé de réduire l'inflation autant que possible, mais encore qu'on n'a pas voulu peser trop sur le marché des capitaux; c'est pour cela qu'on s'est adressé de préférence à des catégories spéciales d'épargnants en marge du marché général. En outre, la volonté d'éviter un gonflement démesuré de la dette publique qui mènerait tôt ou tard à l'inflations apparaît évidente. L'alternative: inflation ou impôt sur le capital posée par Keynes en 1924 est pour la première fois peut-être résolue partiellement en faveur de l'impôt sur le capital.

D'une manière générale, la finance italienne restant fidèle à une longue et fameuse tradition fait rendre à la technique tout ce qu'elle est en état de rendre. Ceci n'empêche pas que le montant actuelle des dépenses militaires et d'investissements doit être considéré comme exceptionnel et que la continuation indéfinie de cet effort créerait un appauvrissement et une désagrégation du système économique et monétaire qu'aucune science financière si habile qu'elle soit ne saurait conjurer.

oOo

II. La politique monétaire et bancaire

Le fait le plus remarquable de l'évolution monétaire italienne récente est sans doute la stabilité extraordinaire de la circulation des billets. Elle a été de 16.297, 16.325 et de 17.468 millions de lires aux fins respectives de 1935, 1936 et 1937; en même temps les comptes courants créditeurs à vue qui sont de l'ordre d'un milliard n'ont presque pas varié. On voudra trouver tout de suite une contradiction entre ces chiffres et les 7 milliards et demi d'inflation opérée au profit de l'État que nous avons calculée plus haut. En fait, il ne s'agit que de 6 milliards, puisque l'inflation causée par l'émission des billets d'État n'apparaît pas dans le bilan de l'Institut d'émission. En tenant compte ensuite de l'augmentation de la circulation d'un milliard, il nous reste à expliquer pourquoi une création de billets de 5 milliards de la part de l'État n'a pas conduit à une augmentation correspondante de la circulation totale.

Nous avouerons tout de suite que c'est là une énigme que nous ne saurons résoudre que partiellement. Pendant l'année 1936 il s'est produit dans l'économie italienne un processus de déthésaurisation et de désendettement qui a permis aux banques d'augmenter leur liquidité et de réduire leur recours à l'Institut d'émission; celui-ci a vu par conséquent se dégonfler son actif d'effets et d'avances aux banques, au commerce et à l'industrie d'environ trois milliards. Dans le bilan de fin 1936, nous voyons se substituer le Trésor pour cette somme aux débiteurs privés.

Le fait de la réduction des besoins de l'industrie et du commerce pendant l'année 1936 ne doit pas nous surprendre. Depuis 1934, l'Italie se trouvait engagée dans une reprise économique et par le contrôle des changes institué alors, on essayait d'assurer le "Circuit fermé" de la richesse. Il est normal que durant les premiers stades de la phase ascendante du cycle économique, la demande et l'offre de capitaux augmentent parallèlement. Or, en 1936, année où les sanctions firent sentir tous leurs effets sur l'industrie par le manque de matières premières et la fermeture des marchés extérieurs, la demande de capitaux d'investissement et de roulement de la part de certains secteurs de l'industrie privée baissa brusquement. En même temps la loi de septembre 1935 qui défendait en général la distribution de dividendes supérieurs à 6% contribuait à la formation de réserves qui ne purent être aussitôt remployés et vinrent ainsi grossir les trésoreries des entreprises. De tout ceci résultait une réduction générale de l'endettement de l'industrie auprès des banques qui de leur côté ne renouvelaient point les avances ou les réescomptes auprès de la Banque d'Italie.

Les sanctions ont ainsi eu un effet certainement imprévu par leurs auteurs: elles ont assuré la liquidité des entreprises et des banques et aidé puissamment à drainer le crédit disponible vers les caisses du Trésor, qui put ainsi couvrir ses besoins extraordinaires sans inflations totale notable.

Mais ces conjonctures étaient exceptionnelles. Dès le milieu de 1936 les sanctions furent levées et après l'alignement de la lire, l'industrie italienne reprit fortement dans toutes ses branches. L'indice de la production industrielle, qui était descendu de 102,4 (1928 = 100) en 1935 à 95,5 en 1936 repartit en flèche et atteignit le chiffre record de 117,9 en septembre 1937. Toutes les industries participaient à cette montée, les industries d'armement et d'autarcie, étant de beaucoup les plus favorisées. Mais cette augmentation de l'activité industrielle et commerciale ne pouvait manquer d'avoir l'effet opposé du ralentissement de l'année précédente.

Si dans une première période qui va de septembre 1936 jusqu'au debout de 1937, l'accroissement de l'appareil productif put être financé en grande partie par les réserves propres des entreprises, les appels à l'épargne et au crédit bancaire devinrent bientôt nécessaires pour soutenir le rythme des nouveaux investissements. Le compte-rendu récent de la Banque d'Italie pour l'année 1937 déclare qu'en plus de l'émission des bons du Trésor et des avances en relation avec l'emprunt immobilier, "les besoins augmentés de l'activité industrielle et sa transformation dans le sens autarcique expliquent les modifications intervenues dans les opérations des établissements de crédit qui se résument dans le développement de l'actif par une utilisation plus intense des moyens liquides disponibles et par un recours plus large au réescompte et aux avances passives; recours facilité par la possession d'effets déclarés en partie réescomptables et par l'amplitude d'investissements en titres d'État effectués par les banques dans les dernières années."

Le seul poste de l'actif du bilan de la Banque d'Italie que nous connaissions, celui des avances, a augmenté selon les indications du compte-rendu de 1.599 millions à 4.507 millions de lires. On doit s'attendre, toujours d'après le même compte-rendu, à un accroissement parallèle du portefeuille effets. Donc, même en supposant, ce qui paraît pour le moins douteux, que les avances au trésor n'aient pas augmenté depuis décembre 1936, on ne s'expliquerait pas comment les engagements à vue de la Banque d'Italie se seraient gonflées d'un milliard seulement. Nous sommes donc portés à ajouter peu de foi aux chiffres officiellement donnés de la circulation fiduciaire, auxquels on est probablement arrivé grâce à quelque artifice (par exemple en déduisant de la circulation totale la réserve en lires de l'Institut pour les échanges avec l'étranger, qui joue ici un rôle analogue au Fonds de Stabilisation).

Quoi qu'il en soit, il est bien évident que ce que le gouvernement fasciste craint le plus dans la situation actuelle, c'est l'inflation fiduciaire, ainsi qu'il ressort du passage suivant du rapport de la Banque d'Italie: "L'Institut d'Émission considère cette politique (restriction de l'émission de billets) comme le moyen essentiel de la défense de l'épargne constituée et d'encouragement à la formation de l'épargne nouvelle qui, en s'investissant dans les emplois offerts par l'État et dans les entreprises privées, permet le développement de l'appareil productif et la satisfaction des besoins des finances publiques."

La tendance de circonscrire l'inflation au strict minimum ne se restreint pas seulement à la circulation de billets. Il ressort de l'évolution des dépôts dans les banques qu'on a voulu également éviter dans toute la mesure du possible l'inflation de crédit. Voici les chiffres principaux à cet égard:

Tableau 3.4. *Dépôts et c/c créditeurs près les Établissements de crédit et les Caisses d'Épargne ayant une masse de dépôts supérieurs à 5 millions*

	Dépôts	c/c Créditeurs	TOTAL
1935	31.786	15.545	47.331
1936	34.550	17.768	52.318
1937	35.766	18.282	54.048

L'accroissement des dépôts, très sensible en 1936, s'est donc sensiblement ralenti en 1937. Ceci ne veut pas dire que le rythme du crédit bancaire ne se soit point intensifié en 1937. On a déjà dit que la liquidité des banques s'était renforcée pendant l'année 1937; ainsi, de fin 1935 à fin 1936, les avoirs en caisse des deux plus grands établissements de crédit, la Banca Commerciale Italiana et le Credito Italiano, étaient passés de 724 à 1.237 millions de lires.

Il est donc probable que pendant l'année passée, les banques ont puisé dans leurs ressources de caisse anormalement gonflées et d'autre part, on a déjà rappelé l'importance des avances passives et du réescompte; enfin, toujours selon le compte-rendu de la Banque d'Italie, la vitesse de circulation des dépôts a fortement augmenté, fait généralement observé en période de reprise économique.

Toujours est—il qu'on perçoit clairement la volonté du gouvernement agissant sur le système bancaire par l'"Ispettorato pour la défense de l'Épargne et l'exercice du crédit" de ne pas laisser se développer des conditions de boom. Ceci apparaissait déjà dans la loi de 1935 sur la limitation des dividendes, remplacés en 1936 par l'impôt progressif sur les dividendes distribués; en outre, dans la défense faite aux entreprises de procéder après la dévaluation a la réévaluation de l'actif pour rendre possible des distributions gratuites d'actions. On voulut éviter ainsi une fièvre spéculative et une déviation des moyens d'action des entreprises vers les consommateurs.

Toutes les ressources des particuliers, des entreprises et des banques devaient être employées à satisfaire les besoins considérés impératifs, c'est-à-dire ceux de la défense nationale, de l'autarcie et—dans une moindre mesure peut-être—ceux de l'industrie exportatrice. Les autres secteurs de l'économie sont délibérément remis au deuxième plan: nous constatons ainsi la réduction des travaux publics, la stagnation voulue des industries du bâtiment et surtout le retard dans la production de biens de consommation.

Les augmentations de capital actuellement en cours sont encore un exemple saisissant de cette politique de crédit et d'investissement dirigé. On a déjà expliqué qu'elles servent surtout à procurer aux sociétés les sommes liquides nécessaires au paiement de l'impôt sur leur capital. Ainsi l'épargne qui, dans la période de reprise industrielle—elle ne donne que tout dernièrement les premières signes de fatigue—déserte les emplois à rendement fixe, trouve moyen de s'investir dans des valeurs industrielles et d'alimenter en même temps le Trésor.

Nous pouvons donc résumer la politique monétaire italienne sous les trois chefs suivants:

1) Restriction au strict minimum de l'inflation de billets.
2) Modération dans l'attribution de crédits bancaires.
3) Encouragement et appels variés à l'épargne pour la réalisation d'un programme d'investissement établi sous le contrôle et avec la participation de l'État (autarcie) ou exécuté directement par lui (armement).

oOo

III. Les prix et la consommation

Ce sont probablement les préoccupations relatives à l'évolution des prix qui ont été responsables de la modération de la politique monétaire. Il importait avant tout de freiner autant que possible la hausse des prix: 1°) pour ne pas affaiblir la capacité de concurrence de l'exportation; 2°) pour ne pas mécontenter le monde ouvrier et ne pas devoir s'engager dans ce qu'on appelle en France la "course infernale des salaires et des prix."

Ici on se trouve pour la première fois sur un terrain où l'état des statistiques permet plus que des conjectures plus ou moins vagues. L'Institut Central de Statistique calcule et publie mensuellement de longues séries de prix de gros ainsi qu'un indice national du coût de la vie.

Tableau 3.5.

	Prix de gros				Coût de la vie
	Matières brutes	Matières semi-ouvrées	Produits finis	Indice général	
1934	57,3	66,6	62,5	62,0	71,0
1935	65,6	74,9	68,3	68,2	73,4
1936	76,2	89,7	72,8	76,4	80,9
1937	89,5	101,3	84,0	89,1	91,7
Décembre 1937	93,9	109,4	91,8	96,4	98,2
Janvier 1938	92,1	110,9	91,7	95,2	99,1
Février	89,1	110,4	91,6	93,7	99,2
Mars	89,4	110,5	91,4	93,8	99,2

Les prix avaient atteint leur niveau le plus bas en 1934. Cette année-là, la tendance expansionniste de la politique économique et financière triomphait définitivement de la tendance orthodoxe et déflationniste. En même temps, on fut d'ailleurs forcé d'établir le contrôle des changes à cause des difficultés croissantes d'équilibrer la balance commerciale. La hausse des prix devait être ultérieurement renforcée par la guerre abyssine et ses conséquences. Nous avons vu que du côté financier, les conditions créées alors se sont perpétuées depuis; il en est de même pour l'évolution des prix, dont la continuité n'a pas été notablement altérée par la dévaluation d'octobre 1936. Son influence s'expliquant par des achats spéculatifs et par le renchérissement automatique des importations, a été un facteur certainement secondaire de la hausse des prix qui distingue l'économie fermée italienne d'une manière si désavantageuse de l'économie fermée allemande.[1]

La hausse a été provoquée par divers facteurs; l'inflation limitée qu'on a essayé de chiffrer, ainsi que l'augmentation certaine de la vitesse de circulation de la monnaie, y ont leur part naturelle. Du côté de l'industrie les frais ont été augmentés par les augmentations de salaires (v.p.l.) et par la politique essentiellement coûteuse de l'autarcie. En outre, il est probable que les phénomènes de la dernière phase du boom, l'utilisation progressive de machines à moindre rendement, le manque de main-d'œuvre spécialisée, sont apparus très vite dans les branches les plus favorisées. La semaine de 40 heures, introduite sans augmentation du salaire horaire pendant la crise pour repartir le travail disponible sur un plus grand nombre d'ouvriers, a probablement contribué à créer une certaine pénurie de main-d'œuvre. On sait toutefois que de larges dérogations au régime des 40 heures ont été admises partout où des "intérêts supérieurs" étaient en cause.

Du côté des biens de consommation on observe le phénomène de l'"épargne forcée." A l'augmentation des revenus ne correspondait pas une disponibilité plus grande de biens de consommation, tout l'effort de l'économie italienne ayant été dirigé vers les industries de biens de production ou vers des dépenses "improductives." Ceci est d'ailleurs explicitement affirmé dans le rapport de la Banque d'Italie qui explique la hausse du coût de la vie par le fait que "l'orientation d'une partie de la production vers des biens instrumentaux et vers des produits d'exportation a contenu l'afflux de biens de consommation sur le marché intérieur."

Le phénomène de l'épargne forcée se produit généralement au début de la conjoncture; ce qui est grave c'est que non seulement la consommation ne s'est pas accrue pari passu avec la production mais qu'elle a indubitablement baissé en quantité et en qualité ainsi que le démontrent les chiffres suivants:

Tableau 3.6. *Consommation de viandes dans 94 chefs-lieux de province*

	Veaux	Autres bovins	Porcins	Volailles	Chevaux	Viandes conservées	Poissons conservée
	(en milliers de quintaux)						
1935............	1.282	1.688	673	205	135	196	228
1936............	1.192	1.656	646	221	134	211	179
1937............	1.046	1.601	525	218	139	213	236

1 L'Italie a d'ailleurs réduit en octobre 1936 plusieurs droits de douane pour atténuer l'incidence de la dévaluation sur les prix. Ces réductions ont été maintenues depuis pour la majeure partie.

Tableau 3.7 *Indice du volume des ventes au détail des denrées alimentaires à Milan —*

(Janvier 1934 = 100)
• Janvier 1935 95,9
• Janvier 1936 78,9
• Janvier 1937 78,5
• Janvier 1938 72,0

Parmi ces chiffres qui ne permettent aucun doute, on notera en particulier l'augmentation de la consommation de viande de chevaux, de conserves et de poissons—nourritures bon marché—par rapport à la diminution des autres colonnes. La diminution totale montrée par l'indice du volume des ventes à Milan est de 28% depuis 1934 ce qui est évidemment inquiétant eu égard au standard de vie déjà traditionnellement bas de l'Italie.

C'est là le point le plus faible peut-être de l'économie italienne en ce moment. En toute vraisemblance on touche aujourd'hui une limite qu'on ne saurait dépasser sans de graves dangers. Une preuve qu'on en est pleinement conscient c'est la défense, toujours prorogée depuis 1936, d'augmenter les prix des loyers, de l'eau, du gaz, de l'électricité, des transports municipaux et autres prix mi-publics. On ne se soucie point de l'état d'infériorité dans lequel sont mises les industries productrices desdits biens ou services qui ont vu leurs coûts s'élever comme toutes les autres entreprises.

Il n'existe pas d'indice de salaires satisfaisant. Mais nous savons que les salaires ont été relevés à deux reprises, en aout 1936 de 8% en moyenne et en mai 1937 de 10%; ces augmentations cependant ne compensent pas la hausse du cout de vie qui de 1934 a aujourd'hui atteint 34%.

Relevons que l'amélioration du standard de vie est en grande partie un problème du commerce d'importation. Il s'agirait d'importer moins de fer et de pétrole et plus de viandes et de matières grasses. Et il n'est pas difficile de discerner les obstacles qui s'opposent à un tel changement.

oOo

IV. La production et l'état actuel de la conjoncture

C'est dans l'évolution de la production qu'on retrouve mieux qu'ailleurs les traits fondamentaux de la phase économique que l'Italie traverse actuellement. Pour pouvoir l'étudier concrètement il faudrait faire une étude détaillée de l'autarcie ou plutôt une série de monographies sur les tendances vers l'autonomie dans tel ou tel produit de base. Il nous suffira ici de rappeler par quelques chiffres l'orientation fondamentale vers les industries lourdes et vers la substitution des matières premières étrangères. Dans beaucoup de cas, on doit se contenter de remplacer l'importation du produit ouvré par celle du produit brut (il en est ainsi pour beaucoup de minerais qui sont maintenant traités en Italie ainsi que par le pétrole brut qui remplace à l'importation de plus en plus les divers produits de raffinerie).

Tandis que l'indice général de la production industrielle, calculé sur la base 1928 = 100, monte de 73,0 en 1932 à 117,9 en septembre 1937 pour retomber en janvier 1938 à 105,2, nous trouvons pour ce dernier mois les indices suivants: industrie chimique 127,6, énergie électrique: 167,7, industrie mécanique 132,8, aluminium 574,5, zinc 343,3, plomb 208,5, manganèse 314,2, combustibles fossiles 229,0, huiles minérales 310,3, etc.

L'orientation de la production vers la mise en valeur des colonies et surtout de l'Empire d'Éthiopie ressort de l'excédent des exportations de la métropole sur les importations coloniales (en million de lires):

Tableau 3.8.

• 1934	166
• 1935	622
• 1936	1.561
• 1937	2.232

En revanche l'indice des travaux publics tombe de 188 en 1933 à 98,1 en 1937, celui des constructions de 162,3 en 1935 a 95,9 l'année dernière. Dès septembre 1935 on avait extrêmement réduit le nombre de permis de construire pour ne pas laisser dévier de ses buts le courant d'investissements qu'on était en train de créer. L'industrie textile, qui avait été particulièrement éprouvée par les sanctions, a repris l'année dernière à 83,7 contre 70,1 en 1936, mais elle se trouve toujours à un niveau très bas par rapport aux autres branches malgré le développement prodigieux de l'industrie de la rayonne (indice 1937: 457,5).

On ne doit pas s'attendre à une diminution de tension des prix au moment où les nouveaux investissements seront "mûrs." C'est en effet une conséquence même de l'autarcie que les biens fournis par ces investissements se substituent aux produits importes jusqu'alors, de sorte que la totalité des biens disponibles sur le marché italien ne se trouve pas augmentée. A cause du déficit de la balance commerciale il est improbable que les économies de devises ainsi réalisées puissent avoir une contrepartie dans des augmentations d'autres achats à l'étranger, a moins d'un relèvement simultané des exportations.

Ainsi l'unique remède contre la continuation de la hausse des prix paraît être le ralentissement général du rythme des investissements en un partage de l'économie en deux secteurs plus prononcé encore aujourd'hui c'est-à-dire un État où le secteur protégé et le secteur non protégé différeraient non seulement par le degré mais par les sens même de leur développement. L'examen des possibilités de financement conduit lui aussi à la conclusion que l'expansion de la production italienne, exception faite pour les produits d'intérêt national, subit en ce moment ou subira bientôt un coup d'arrêt. Après les récentes augmentations de capital dont on a donné la raison et qui, en fait, n'ont pas apporté de nouveaux moyens aux entreprises, il ne sera plus possible, pour longtemps, de faire appel aux actionnaires.

D'autre part nous avons vu que la politique monétaire et bancaire était nettement hostile à la création de crédit qu'elle circonscrit dans d'étroites limites. Elle a justement pour but de combattre la hausse des prix. Enfin l'état des marchés extérieurs fait prévoir une réduction du pouvoir d'achat et une concurrence plus âpre. D'autre part l'économie italienne n'est pas encore suffisamment isolée du reste du monde pour ne pas se ressentir des contrecoups matériels et psychologiques de la conjoncture mondiale.

Dans cet ordre d'idées, nous relèverons en premier lieu que les prix sont devenus stationnaires depuis plusieurs mois. Une légère baisse de l'indice de prix de gros (v. p. h.) s'explique par celle des matières agricoles d'origine animale qui avaient dès le début été l'objet d'une hausse antérieure, certainement anormale; mais les autres prix sont immobilisés, presque sans exception, aux niveaux atteints vers la fin de 1937. L'indice du cout de la vie, à son tour, ne bouge plus depuis janvier.

Ce sont là des signes éminemment favorables, quoiqu'on aurait peut-être pu s'attendre à plus après la baisse des prix mondiaux. Mais le corollaire en est que l'activité productrice donne, elle aussi, des signes de stabilisation, sinon même de régression.

L'indice de la production industrielle qui avait atteint 117,9 (1928 = 100) en septembre dernier, a subi depuis une baisse, jusqu'à 105, en janvier, qui paraît être plus que simplement saisonnière et qui est de toute façon beaucoup plus importante que celle de l'année précédente. En particulier on constate des tassements importants dans certaines industries lourdes: ainsi la production d'aluminium baisse de 882 en août 1937 à 573 en janvier, celle du cuivre de 242 en juillet à 160 en janvier, celle des automobiles de 194 en juillet à 168 en janvier. L'indice général de l'industrie métallurgique baisse de 127,2 en juin 1937 à 105,3 en janvier 1938 c'est-à-dire de près de 25%.

Dans les compartiments énumérés ce n'est certainement pas le défaut de commandes de la part de l'État qui est responsable de la chute des indices mais le ralentissement des investissements et des commandes de l'industrie privée.

Ainsi nous entrevoyons pour l'Italie aussi la possibilité d'une évolution déjà constatée ailleurs: C'est que l'activité des industries d'armement auxquelles nous devons ajouter les industries essentielles au point de vue de l'autarcie devienne peu à peu, au lieu d'un stimulant supplémentaire et puissant du boom; un facteur d'atténuation de la dépression, suivante.

D'ailleurs le marché boursier a déjà tenu compte de cette situation par une baisse continue et importante depuis janvier-février, baisse qui ne saurait s'expliquer uniquement par les opérations d'augmentation de capital déjà décrites. Ainsi l'indice général Guarneri était revenu de 121 (1922 = 100) en février à 113 en mars et a dû fléchir depuis dans des proportions plus importantes encore. Particulièrement frappés sont les titres des industries hôtelières, textiles et d'automobiles.

oOo

V. Le commerce extérieure et la balance commerciale

L'impression que l'expansion industrielle ne pourra pas continuer au rythme de l'année dernière est renforcée par l'examen sommaire du commerce extérieur.

Tableau 3.9.

	Importations	Exportations	Déficit	Variations de l'encaisse-or
	(en millions de lires)			
1934	7.582	4.965	2.617	- 1.514
1935	7.562	4.488	3.074	- 2.488
1936	5.882	3.831	2.053	- 1.021[2]
1937	13.489	7.849	5.640	+ 7[3]
Janvier-Mars 1937	2.860	1.702	1.158	
Janvier-Mars 1938	3.081	1.907	1.174	

2 Lires-or 1927.

3 Lires actuelles. Total de l'encaisse-or de la Banque d'Italie en lires actuelles: 4.029 millions de lires.

Tableau 3.10. *Indices des valeurs, des quantités et de prix du commerce extérieur (1929 = 100)*

	Valeurs		Quantités		Prix	
	Import	Export	Import	Export	Import	Export
1934	35,0	32,6	75,5	73,1	46,4	44,6
1935	34,9	29,5	73,1	65,9	47,7	44,8
1936	27,1	25,1	46,1	49,9	58,8	50,3
1937	62,3	51,5	67,9	80,9	91,8	63,7

Tous ces chiffres se rapportent au seul commerce avec l'étranger à l'exclusion du commerce avec les colonies.

Après la dévaluation on a pu dire d'une manière grossière que les prix italiens étaient quelque peu inférieurs aux prix étrangers, avantage qui s'est d'ailleurs vite reperdu. L'exportation italienne libérée alors des sanctions et de la surévaluation de la lire compensée péniblement par le régime bureaucratique des primes, repartit vigoureusement. Mais, dans la course, elle fut vite distancée par les importations sorte que l'année 1937 laissa en définitive un déficit exceptionnel et inquiétant de 5,6 milliards de lires.

Les facteurs qui pendant l'année passée ont pesé sur les balances commerciales de tous les pays industriels d'Europe, c'est-à-dire le renchérissement des matières premières importées par rapport aux produits fabriqués exportés, ont joué à plein pour l'Italie (V; indices des prix). En outre, on peut expliquer le déficit par l'accroissement des approvisionnements en matières premières de la part de l'État et de l'industrie; par la reconstitution des stocks épuisés pendant les sanctions; enfin, pour un milliard de lires environ, par la défectueuse récolte de blé de 1936 qui a conduit à une importation exceptionnelle. Ce dernier fait a tant effrayé les autorités qu'elles ont ordonné en décembre dernier l'addition de 10% de farine de maïs a toutes les farines panifiables, malgré la récolte suffisante de 1937.

On admet généralement que le déficit a pu être couvert jusqu'à concurrence de trois milliards par les revenus du tourisme, les frets et les remises des émigrants.

L'augmentation de l'endettement commercial extérieur tel qu'il apparaît dans la situation des clearings rend compte d'un autre demi-milliard environ. Le solde de tous les clearings, créditeurs à la fin de 1936 pour la somme de 274 millions de lires, était devenu débiteur de 330 millions en décembre 1937.

Pour le reste du déficit, on doit supposer que des réserves cachées ont été entamées puisque le stock d'or de l'Institut d'Émission défendu selon les termes de M. Guarneri, ministre des Échanges et de Devises, "avec les ongles et les dents," montre même un léger accroissement de 7 millions. C'est probablement en première ligne l'Institut pour les Échanges avec l'étranger ou sont concentrées toutes les opérations en monnaies étrangères et qui dispose en outre d'une réserve en métal et en titres étrangers qui a dû soutenir le choc.

Les résultats du commerce extérieur pendant les premiers mois de l'année courant ne donnent point de signes d'amélioration. Malgré la suppression de l'importation de blé en raison de la bonne récolte de 1937, le déficit pour les trois premiers mois est, avec 1.174 millions, légèrement supérieur au déficit de la période correspondante de l'année précédente (1.158 millions de lires). Les chiffres ont été particulièrement décevants en janvier (déficit supérieur de 125 millions au déficit de janvier 1937) et se sont améliorés substantiellement en mars (déficit inférieur de 125 millions à celui de l'année précédente).

De fin décembre 1937 à fin avril 1938 le solde débiteur des clearings montre une nouvelle augmentation de 330 à 539 millions. Il est évident qu'une telle progression ne saurait continuer indéfiniment. Au contraire les exportations italiennes devront sous peu payer les dettes du passé au lieu de balancer les importations courantes. C'est à cela que tend entre autres l'accord commercial franco-italien récent, la France étant créditrice de plus de 110 millions de lires en compte de clearing.

Que faire pour réduire le déficit qui mène à une perte de substance difficilement supportable a la longue? On a trouvé que la relation de prix entre produits fabriques et matières premières commence à se renverser et qu'ainsi la cause principale du déséquilibre pourrait disparaître.

On parait donc souhaiter une hausse au moins relative des prix des produits exportés. Mais d'autre part on lit tout aussi couramment qu'en raison de la hausse des prix intérieurs et de la baisse des prix mondiaux l'exportation risque de se trouver de nouveau en difficultés. Voilà donc qu'une baisse des prix à l'exportation est préconisée pour remédier au déficit. Dans l'état actuel des choses les partisans d'une hausse relative des prix nous paraissent être dans le vrai, l'Italie a poursuivi, à en juger d'après les indices des prix et des quantités cités plus haut, une politique d'exportation à tout prix en oubliant que l'important pour la balance commerciale ce n'est pas la quantité exportée mais le produit de la quantité et du prix.

De tout façon, on se préoccupe beaucoup de l'exportation en ce moment, après l'avoir peut-être un peu oubliée dans le programme autarcique.

M. Guarneri a lancé aux industriels "l'impératif catégorique: Exporter!" et de plus en plus l'institut pour les échanges fait dépendre l'attribution de devises, pour l'achat de matières premières, d'une exportation de produits finis au moins équivalente. On essaie aussi de libérer le commerce d'exportation de certaines formalités et de réveiller l'initiative privée des industriels et commerçants trop confiants jusqu'ici dans la conjoncture intérieure.

Citons quelques passages significatifs du *Sole* qui mettent en relief certaines difficultés d'une économie mi-privée et mi-étatique: "dans le secteur des importations où tout risque est désormais éliminé et où par contre on a la certitude d'une discrète marge de profit, les initiatives ne manquent pas, au contraire, elles abondent. Aujourd'hui tous sont prêts à faire les importateurs jusqu'à ceux qui hier encore étaient des employés à la Loterie ou des professionnels de la chiromancie mais la situation est bien différente quand il s'agit d'exporter..." (*Il Sole*, 1er février 1938). Avant de se lancer vers de nouveaux marchés, l'initiative privée attend que l'État lui garantisse le milieu économique le plus adapté à ce but, et l'administration publique, de son côté, demande que l'initiative privée donne, d'abord, des preuves de son efficacité. (*Il Sole*, 14 février 1938).

Mais ce sera déjà une belle réussite de cette campagne si dans l'état actuel de l'économie mondiale l'exportation italienne peut se maintenir au niveau de l'année dernière. Une réduction substantielle [du déficit] ne pourra donc prévenir que d'une diminution marquée des importations.

Cela est confirmé d'une manière éclatante par la balance commerciale de mars qui montre pour la première fois depuis plus d'une année une amélioration par rapport à l'année précédente. Or, depuis que pour février la comparaison des importations avec les résultats de 1937 avait fait ressortir un accroissement de 74 millions, on observe pour mars une diminution de 71 millions et c'est uniquement ce facteur qui est responsable de la réduction du déficit.

Mais, sauf pour le blé, la réduction des importations ne saurait porter en proportion notable sur les articles d'alimentation, la consommation étant déjà diminué dans la mesure que l'on sait. On sera donc amené à limiter l'approvisionnement de l'industrie en matières premières importées. Il est en effet facile de réduire l'importation en freinant le développement des investissements nouveaux et c'est de ce côté surtout que l'analyse du commerce extérieure nous conduit aussi à une vue pessimiste de la conjoncture italienne.

Il y aurait cependant un autre moyen de résoudre les difficultés de la balance des comptes et de permettre ainsi la continuation de la reprise ainsi que l'accélération de la mise en valeur de l'Abyssinie. Ce serait l'importation—favorisée par un décret récent—de capitaux étrangers. Mais, a cet égard, l'assurance de leur intangibilité, même en cas de guerre, et les exemptions et dégrèvements fiscaux dont ils ont été l'objet sont d'une efficacité plutôt douteuse; la conditions nécessaire et probablement suffisante d'une reprise des migrations de capitaux est l'établissement d'une nouvelle atmosphère de détente et de collaboration internationale si heureusement ébauchée par la signature de l'accord anglo-italien.

oOo

VI. Conclusion

La première observation qui se dégage de cette étude est l'importance croissante de la part de l'État dans la vie économique italienne. D'après une évaluation grossièrement approchée, les dépenses totales de l'État et de collectivités publiques atteindraient, rapidement chiffrées, pour cette année, 50 milliards de lires, c'est-à-dire 50% du revenu national estimé sommairement à 100 milliards. Cette proportion ne devait pas atteindre 33% avant la crise.

Le rôle des finances publiques à l'intérieur du système économique italien devient, en conséquence, de plus en plus important. L'habilité des techniciens a été mise à l'épreuve. On sait quelle est leur réputation. Ils n'y ont pas été inférieurs. Les subtilités de l'impôt sur le capital des sociétés anonymes témoignent d'une véritable virtuosité.

Mais la technique ne saurait suffire à tout. Le montant considérable des dépenses militaires et des investissements non rentables n'a pu qu'appauvrir le Royaume. Le déficit qu'il a fallu combler pour l'exercice 1935–1936 et l'exercice 1936–1937 atteint au total 31 milliards de lires. L'effort accompli—considérable—ne saurait continuer indéfiniment. Aucune science financière, si habile soit-elle, ne saurait conjurer la désagrégation finale du système tout entier.

La stabilité extraordinaire de la circulation officielle des billets reste une énigme. On verra comment elle peut être—en partie seulement—expliquée par le phénomène de déthésaurisation. On s'efforce d'éviter les effets de l'inflation que l'on redoute avant tout. On y est arrivé de justesse, jusqu'à présent, grâce à la restriction au strict minimum des crédits bancaires, a des appels répètes à l'épargne pour la réalisation du programme d'investissement et d'armement établi et contrôlé par l'État.

Mais si l'on peut agir sur les signes extérieurs—la monnaie et aussi, dans une certaine mesure, les prix, on ne saurait empêcher l'appauvrissement de se manifester en fin de compte. C'est ce qui apparaît dans les statistiques officielles de la consommation de viande et des ventes au détail des denrées alimentaires. On peut y observer la progression des aliments à bon marché dans la consommation italienne—viande de cheval, conserves et poissons. Quant à l'indice des ventes au détail—à Milan—il passe de 95,9 en janvier 1935 à 72 en janvier 1938, la diminution est donc de 28%.

La production s'est développée en raison directe des progrès de l'autarcie. Il y a, dans la plupart des cas, substitution à l'importation du produit brut au produit ouvré et l'ensemble reste essentiellement orienté vars les industries d'État et la mise en valeur de l'Éthiopie. Les chiffres cités à ce propos sont frappants. La diminution des investissements privés est manifeste. Pendant un certain temps les commandes officielles ont masqué la baisse, nouvel indice d'appauvrissement. Depuis quelques mois elle apparaît nettement, même dans les industries lourdes, industries d'État par excellence. La production d'aluminium est passée de 882% (indice) en aout 1937, à 573 en janvier. Celle de cuivre a 242 en juillet à 160 en janvier. Celle des automobiles de 194 en juillet à 168 en janvier. L'indice général de la production métallurgique baisse de 127,2 en juin à 105 en janvier soit de 25%.

Le commerce extérieur se traduit par un déficit qui pour les trois premiers mois de l'année dépasse 1 milliard de lires. Si l'on désire, ce qui paraît être le cas, combler ce déficit et en même temps conserver intacte la réserve d'or, en l'absence de rendement notable des autres postes de la balance des comptes, on ne peut qu'agir sur les importations ou sur les exportations.

C'est vers une diminution des importations que l'on s'oriente, comme il apparaît pour le mois de mars, étant donné l'impossibilité d'accroître les ventes à l'étranger. Là encore le phénomène d'appauvrissement est évident.

Ainsi les finances et l'économie italiennes, en dépit de prodiges techniques donnent une impression d'essoufflement. Le régime a jusqu'à présent réussi à vivre sur les réserves habilement exploitées, grâce à des expédients. Mais l'avenir s'annonce sous de sombres auspices. Sans doute les techniciens financiers du Royaume trouveront-ils encore quelques moyens subtils pour retarder l'échéance. Mais on ne voit pas comment elle pourrait être définitivement écartée et, en dépit d'une autarcie croissante, la nouvelle dépression mondiale ne peut que compliquer la tâche des dirigeants fascistes.

· 4 ·

THE POINCARÉ FRANC AND ITS DEVALUATION*

Introduction: The franc from the end of the war until stabilization

The crisis of the franc after the war reached its peak in 1926 when the pound was quoted at 240 francs. The different and interdependent causes of the decline of the franc after the end of the war were:

1. the termination of inter-ally credits that had supported it on an artificial course during the war;
2. balance of payments deficits due to the need to rebuild the French economy and particularly the areas that had been devastated;
3. government budget deficits where huge but purely fictitious sums owed by Germany as reparations had been entered as revenue;
4. finally, the suffocating state debt, and in particular the floating debt, whose repayments, like many other treasury payments, could only be guaranteed through "advances" from the Bank of France—in other words, through inflation.

* Tesi di laurea, June 27, 1938.

In July 1926, the implementation of the balanced budget combined with the creation of the Autonomous Fund for the Amortization of Public Debt (whose task consisted first and foremost of changing the *composition* of the public debt) very soon brought the franc back to 124 to the pound, at which time the Bank of France declared itself ready to buy and sell foreign currencies at this price. This was the beginning of the period of de facto stabilization of the franc, which lasted until 1928. The law of June 28, 1928, fixed the weight in gold of the "Poincaré franc" at approximately one-fifth (65,5 mg of gold at 900/1000) of its previous weight, and relations between the state, the Bank of France and the Autonomous Fund were realigned.

Here are the main features of the currency reform that defined the regime under which the franc existed until September 24, 1936:

1. The provisional formal establishment of the gold standard (prior to the imposed course, the franc existed under the regime of so-called halting bimetallism) without circulation of gold coinage, but with convertibility in gold of a minimum quantity of notes.
2. The obligation imposed on the Bank of France to maintain a gold reserve of at least 35% of its total cash liabilities.
3. The revaluation of the gold reserve of the Bank of France based on the new definition of the franc; the accounting benefit of this revaluation was allocated to the repayment of the state's debt to the bank.

oOo

Part One
Some Thoughts on French Monetary Policy after the de facto Stabilization of the Franc

I. The debate over French gold policy 1926–1930

1) Reproaches to France

French monetary policy from 1926 to 1936 was the subject of passionate controversy, attacks, and rebuttals. Especially in England, the policy followed by the Bank of France drew criticisms that were more-the-less harsh and objective. We will disregard the view held mainly by Dr. Einzig that the whole of French monetary policy at the time was merely a means for France to secure political hegemony through financial supremacy. From a more specifically economic point of view, three charges against France may be noted:

1. That the franc was stabilized at a level that was too low—at a level, that is, at which French prices were significantly lower than international prices; that an entirely artificial advantage was thus gained in the balance of payments; and that this had made it difficult if not impossible to re-establish the economic equilibrium in England that had raised the pound back to its old parity.
2. To this imbalance France was adding another by drawing in gold from England and contributing to a "poor distribution" of gold around the world, which would be one of the causes of falling prices. In fact, France did not increase its imports or make long-term capital loans abroad to a sufficient extent to absorb the surplus in its balance of payments; and the short-term deposits abroad made in 1928 and 1929 were more disturbing elements than balancing factors because of their sudden shifts and withdrawals.
3. Finally, France allegedly "sterilized" its gold in the vaults of the Bank of France, which due to the inelasticity of its credit policy and the maintenance of too high a discount rate prevented or at least delayed a rise in the domestic price level—a rise that would have eliminated the disparity in French and international prices and thus reversed or at least stopped movements of gold.

II. The French defense

1. Regarding the stabilization of the franc, defenders of French policy cannot deny that its level was below its purchasing power parity, as measured

through the different indexes of prices and salaries. But this level, chosen after lengthy deliberation, was not meant to benefit French exports at the expense of those of other countries. Exporters of course protested against the new rise in the value of the franc, but exporters would never have been favored over "rentiers" (the best proof of this is France's monetary policy in the following years) had there not been a compelling reason: as in 1924 an ill-considered rise in the franc would have called the balance of the budget into question and in this way the currency itself would again have been compromised. On the other hand, the stabilization crisis of 1927 showed that already at 125 to the pound, French industrial adjustment encountered not insignificant difficulties.

As for the two other charges made against French monetary policy—of attracting gold and then sterilizing—it is disputed that there ever was such a policy.

2. As early as 1929 the Bank of France had to convert a certain amount of its foreign exchange into gold to make stabilization possible by ensuring a coverage ratio of 40% to 45%. This gold came back to the Bank mainly from the United States and thus contributed to a better distribution of gold between Europe and America. But after this date the issuing Institution, merely accepting the gold that was sold to it through arbitrage rather than encouraging it, sought on the contrary to stop the inflow of gold, directly or indirectly.

Directly, in spite of its aversion to the "gold exchange standard," the B. F. did not liquidate its stock of foreign currencies, and proceeded to acquire foreign currencies to support their exchange rate in dangerous moments.

Indirectly, the B. F. generally followed other issuing banks when they lowered their rediscount rate but did not follow them when they raised it. Foreign securities were relieved of certain additional taxes and an attempt was made to organize an acceptance market in Paris. The purpose of all this was:

- to stop the influx of foreign capital and the repatriation of French capital,
- to encourage banks and individuals to employ their liquidity in foreign investment and the financing of international trade.

If this was not accomplished to the desired extent it was because the banks could not make long-term loans with the money deposited on demand and because private individuals had not yet forgotten the losses they had incurred as a result of Russian loans. In the end, the crisis in international trade prevented the development of the Paris marketplace as a monetary center.

3. Against the accusation of the so-called sterilization of gold, emphasis was placed on the aforementioned policy of cheap money, the various concessions at the Bank of France discount, the productive use of budget surpluses and treasury liquidity (financing a program of "*Outillage national*" and national defense projects), and finally the retail price increases that continued for more than a year after the onset of the crisis in other countries. If the expansion of credit was insufficient in relation to the influx of gold, the reason was not a policy of credit restriction but the insufficient credit needs of industry, which had to go through the stabilization crisis in 1927 and suffered shortly thereafter from falling wholesale prices.

Advocates of French policy are thus convinced that the influx and sterilization of gold were strongly resisted, and if they happened all the same the focus should be on the effects rather than the causes of the crisis.

II. Discussion of the flaws in French monetary organization

English critics, however, refuse to explain the ineffectiveness of Bank of France policy solely on the basis of the objective factors in the developing crisis and note two flaws in the French monetary setup:

1. The insufficient use of the *chéque* as a mean of payment in France—the relative importance, in other words, of note circulation in relation to bank deposits, so that too large a part of the country's overall means of payment appears in the Bank of France's liabilities and requires coverage in gold.

On the other hand, one might reply that this element of imbalance—if indeed there is one—has always existed and cannot be invoked as a particular reason for a crisis, because it represents a fact completely independent of the will of the government, which has granted every fiscal advantage and legislative safeguard to the circulation of *chéques*.

2. The second alleged flaw is the inelasticity of the Bank of France concerning its choice of assets due to the absence of an "open-market policy." The result is meant to be the same as above—an expansion of credit would very soon require gold shipments when it could easily have been financed through purchases of government securities on the open market.

The French rebuttal seeks to show that such a policy would be of no benefit to the Paris money market. In the first place, contrary to what happens in London, banks make extensive use of the rediscount facility offered by the B. F.—the official rate is generally in close contact with the "*hors banque*" rate. For these reasons, what was given in the open market purchase would be recovered in the rediscount. Finally, Paris experiences neither the scale of the money market nor its enormous momentary and seasonal fluctuations—factors which necessitated the open market policy in London.

These are the main issues that split French and British economists. Alongside the differences in interpreting the facts there is a basic disagreement. This is that the British exalt while the French dispute the importance of the monetary factor in the economic system and the influence authorities can exert over it.

After 1930 it was plain that movements of gold were not determined by any policy of the B. F., but by alternate fluctuations between caution and confidence. In the face of these movements the B. F. remained neutral for many years, countering inputs and outputs by "classical" means alone.

III. The sterilization of currencies

In the light of certain current monetary phenomena, it is interesting to return to some of the problems that arose in France during the period of de facto stabilization.

While the basis for criticism of gold sterilization, as we have shown, is not terribly solid, it nevertheless cannot be denied that a sterilization of currencies on a large scale did take place between 1926 and 1928. Since the flows of capital constantly favored France, the B. F. bought currencies against the issue of francs throughout this period. It could not yet buy gold directly, and when it wanted to convert its currencies—mainly pound sterling—into gold, to avoid the duplication of credit, the Bank of England vigorously opposed it. Thus, between July 1926 and April 1928, the B. F. acquired currencies amounting to 28 billion francs, but at the same time the circulation of banknotes and private deposits only increased by five billion each. The remaining 18 billion were used not to increase liabilities, but to deflate the bank's unhealthy assets.

The four billion reduction in discounts and advances reflects the stabilization crisis and the fact that "the market was not in the bank." What interests us here is the 14 billion decrease in the Bank's advances to the state, 10 billion during the first six months of 1927 alone.

This is the consequence of the phenomenon known by the term "circuit." The francs created by the bank against the acquisition of foreign currencies were invested in National Defense Bonds or deposited with the Treasury, which functioned at the time as a true deposit bank yielding relatively high interest to depositors. The state then employed the money thus returned to its coffers to repay the advances that the Bank of France had granted it during the period of inflation. These reimbursements were later consolidated through the issue of medium- and long-term loans.

It is strange that the obvious similarity between these operations and those of the British Exchange Equalization Account has not captured more attention. In both cases we have the acquisition of currencies by the monetary authority without a corresponding extension in the internal volume of credit. In both cases this "sterilization" or "neutralization" is implemented because the Treasury withdraws newly created francs or pounds from the money market. In this way, the French circuit of 1927 can rightly be regarded as the precursor to the neutralizing policy of the British Fund.

Nonetheless there are significant differences between the two procedures:

1) With regard to the procedure itself, the British fund immediately converts acquired currencies into gold. While the French circuit leaves the French and foreign credit structure intact, English neutralization leaves only the English volume of credit unchanged, while contracting the foreign volume.
2) As to purpose, the aim of the French circuit was solely the reduction of the state's debt to the B. F.—the elimination of the residue of the years of inflation; while the purpose of the English Fund is actually what we have shown to be the common outcome of both procedures—the neutralization of capital inflow.
3) As for the voluntary nature of the two proceedings, in France the newly created francs flowed spontaneously into the state coffers because the ailing private economy could not absorb them. In England, on the other hand, the E. E. A. intervened in the market with sales of Treasury Bills and thus forcibly withdrew the availability it deemed excessive.

In the second half of 1927, when the policy of consolidating the floating debt increasingly shrank the volume of short-term National Defense Bonds in circulation, and the Treasury for its part decreased the rate connected to depositors, the circuit ceased to function fully. However, foreign currencies continued to flow, and since the money market was now deprived of any possibility of employing its short-term holdings, some thought was given to re-exporting capital abroad so as not to leave huge unproductive resources in the banks.[1]

Now for banks to allow their liquid assets to be invested abroad, they had to hedge against the always considerable risk of a rising franc by buying back the franc futures that they were spot selling. But under the conditions of the market, considerable carryovers would certainly have been quoted on franc futures, 1) because the interest rates were lower in France than abroad, and 2) because indeed a more marked appreciation of the franc was expected. In this way, through their coverage operations the banks would have lost more than they would have gained from investing their liquidity abroad. This is why the B. F. decided to intervene by buying foreign currency futures with backwardations that left French banks with beneficial margins.

1 This was the real reason for the policy to be outlined below, and not the wish to "oppose a monetary expansion and a reduction in the discount rate" as Dr. Einzig claims in his book *The Theory of Forward Exchange*, p. 351.

These B. F. operations were considerably extended in the first half of the year 1928, and by May the B. F. held 15 billion in foreign currency futures. After stabilization these operations, no longer required in response to urgent market needs, were discontinued, and the stock of currency futures was gradually liquidated.

The observer of monetary events is struck by the stark contrast between the situation in 1926–1928 and what has happened in recent years. In 1926–1928, there was an influx of capital such that it could not be incorporated into the economy, while in 1935–1937 its exportation has been such that—as we shall see—the gaps left by capital flight have had to be filled through inflation. In 1927–1928, the interest rate was lower in France than abroad and the carryover on the franc was such that the authorities intervened to keep it within normal limits and thus encourage overabundant capital to emigrate. In 1936–1937, the interest rate in France was higher than abroad and backwardation on franc futures was such that—and as we shall see later—the authorities again intervened to keep it within more reasonable limits and thus eliminate at least one of the many reasons for the export of capital.

oOo

Part Two
French Monetary History from 1930 to the First Devaluation of the Franc

I. The banking crises of 1930 and 1931

What distinguishes the French monetary crisis from most of the others is that the immediate cause is not to be sought in private credit difficulties, either from an international standpoint as in England, or from a domestic point of view, as in the United States especially and in Belgium.

Thanks to their prudent management, French banks had neither taken risks abroad nor invested their assets in the domestic economy in a way that would jeopardize the currency in the event of the insolvency of foreign or domestic debtors. The private debts of agricultural and industrial enterprises were limited, and where the French banking system had weaknesses, their elimination or the necessary adjustments were made fairly quickly during the two successive crises of late 1930 and late 1931.

The first of these, which opened with the fall of the Adam Bank, represented primarily a liquidation of losses incurred through stock market speculation. The second was more serious and culminated in the difficulties of the Banque Nationale de Crédit. While the other troubled banks were mainly old provincial banks or specialized banks, this was one of the large French credit unions. A general run on the banks was foreseen, and the state was forced to guarantee the liabilities of the Banque Nationale de Crédit through a 2 billion advance and to help the Bank of Alsace and Lorraine with a sum of 900 million.

These crises had significant repercussions. On the one hand, the banks that had been less prudently managed or had specialized in one of the areas or trades hit hardest by the crisis were eliminated. On the other, seeing the difficulties of generally reputable establishments, the extreme sensitivity of the public, and the insecurity of their assets abroad, all other banks redoubled their vigilance, liquidating their foreign assets. Since this coincided with inflows of foreign capital, they were able to secure huge liquid assets at the beginning of the crisis, which enabled them to withstand the sharp decline in deposits in the years that followed and at the same time respond to the state's demands for credit.

These developments are reflected in the changes in liquidity ratios (ratio of cash on hand at the B. F. to demand liabilities) for the four major credit institutions:

Table 4.1.

end 1929 – 8,2	end 1932 – 26,1	end 1935 – 13,9
end 1930 – 10,8	end 1933 – 19,7	end 1936 – 11,1
end 1931 – 33,2	end 1934 – 19,0	

(Figures taken from *Société des Nations*, *Banques Commerciales* and *Bulletin Quotidien*, *les Banques françaises en 1936*).

II. Public finance

The effect of the economic crisis on the franc thus came through the public debt crisis rather than the private credit one. This is in the purest French tradition, whose history demonstrates the paramount importance of the situation of public finance for the overall life of the nation.

Let us look first at the successive deficits in the state budget:

Table 4.2.

1930–1931	4,917	1934	8,813
1931–1932	5,484	1935	10,383
1932–(9 months)	4,628	1936	9–10 billion for the ordinary budget alone
(000.000 of francs)			

What were the financial and economic policies of successive governments in the face of this situation?

1) The budget up to 1933

In 1932 and 1933 the radical governments employed a variety of means to cover the deficits. On the fiscal side there were some tax increases and the strengthening of fiscal control. In addition, a multitude of exceptional resources were marshaled, principally the abandonment of contractual depreciation at the Autonomous Depreciation Fund and the National Lottery, along with benefits from the minting of silver coins, and there were major savings on expenditures, estimated 5,5 billion francs.

In addition, the Herriot government undertook an extremely important conversion in 1932, which included 85 billion in capital consisting of the following values: *rentes* 5% 1915–1916, Treasury bonds 6% 1920 and 7% 1927 would be converted into an amortizable Loan at 4½%. Although it could have been completed in 1931 on much more favorable terms if it had gained the approval of the Chamber at the end of its legislature, this conversion nevertheless relieved the budget of an annual interest burden of 1,5 billion. And taking new subscriptions into account, the repayment claims were insignificant (2% of the total), but from an economic point of view, in contrast to the concurrent conversion in England, the effect was nil—the fall in the nominal rate was more than offset by the fall in the rate of the annuities newly introduced on the stock exchange.

During 1932 and 1933 the French crisis didn't seem as bad as in other countries. Indeed, beginning at the end of 1932 there were observable signs of recovery, and a halt in the decline of economic indexes in 1933 seemed to mark the end of the crisis. The government's general policy was therefore limited to seeking to balance the budget, albeit through nonrenewable resources, and assisting the classes most affected by the crisis—the agricultural sector, where a minimum price for grain was set, and the unemployed, through public works. It pursued a policy of waiting for the better times that were expected to come in the automatic nature of the business cycle, with no overall plan to take the national economy in any particular direction.

2) Deflation in 1934 and 1935

The Doumergue government had emerged from the great political crisis at the beginning of 1934, which was also the first crisis of the franc. The budget deficit was threatening, the economic crisis was deepening, and the debate surrounding the franc opened with a speech by Paul Reynaud to the Chamber in June 1934. All this obliged the government to adopt a principled attitude regarding the proposed remedies. The government's first act was strict budget deflation through legislative decrees. The 4 billion deficit was to be fully recovered through expenditure reduction.

The government's intention was that this financial deflation be accompanied by general economic deflation—by a decrease in production costs: tax relief through fiscal reform, lower short- and long-term interest rates, and a reduction in the cost of living and consequent lower wages. But the only real achievement of the government was reducing the short-term interest rate, marking the easing of the money market thanks to a "return of confidence." This reduction was only very marginally followed by the long-term rate and the bond market in fact remained hesitant, concerned with the state's constant appeals for savings and the uninspiring outlook for public finance.

As for a drop in the cost of living, this really happened during 1934, but it was mainly due to a drop in agricultural prices which was the last thing the government wanted.

On the other hand, under the double influence of the elevated level of French prices (as we shall see, the overvaluation of the franc was at its maximum just at the beginning of 1934) and the official policy of deflation, economic activity contracted sharply and France was thereby detached from the pace of the world crisis. This inevitably led to a reduction of financial revenues—made worse by the tax reform—so that ultimately the compression of expenditures was nowhere near enough to balance the budget.

Thus, the year 1935 promised to be even more difficult. Financial shortfalls, borrowing needs for various projects to rehabilitate the agricultural market and increased expenditures for National Defense were such that some political opposition effectively nullified the interest rate reduction policy that the Flandin government (see p. 91) had attempted to implement as an alternative to deflationary policy.

From a financial point of view as well as from the standpoint of state intervention in economic life, the July 1935 legislative decrees were the key event of the year.

Under the influence of the crisis of the franc at the end of May there was growing recognition that the problem was not only financial but primarily economic, that the only choice really was either devaluation or deflation. This framing of the problem was reflected in the legislative decrees that applied a 10% reduction not only to all state, local government and concessionary service expenditures (excluding armament and assistance expenditures, but including interest payments on public debt) but also to rents, mortgage debts and bonds, gas, electricity, coal and sugar prices. Once again, financial deflation was expected to spread into the economic sphere, reducing the costs of industry and trade.

However, just when the government embraced "penance" with such energy, we see the beginning of a price rise due almost exclusively to the increase in agricultural prices—the success, that is, of the protectionist and agrarian policies of consecutive governments. The fall in agricultural prices in July and August had reduced the disparities between French and foreign prices. Beginning in August 1935 these disparities increased once again, undermining the deflationary effort at the economic level, an effort which shortly thereafter was destroyed on the purely financial side as well by spending increases for armaments and by political developments.

3) The 1936–1937 "reflation"

Already the 1936 budget adopted in December 1935 was balanced only thanks to the creation of an emergency budget of 6,5 billion to be financed by loans, which included exceptional expenditures on armaments and public works. New revenue shortfalls on the one hand and significant increases in expenditures on the other (the abolition of several legislative decrees of 1934 and 1935, new works and armaments, the constitution of an "*office du blé*," etc.) led to a new deficit, which the new finance minister, Vincent Auriol, estimated in June at 7 billion francs for the current year. Ultimately it was approximately 9 billion for the ordinary budget alone.

The financial policy of the Blum government, part of a general economic policy geared toward "reflation," was to make a balanced budget conditional on economic recovery. Spending widely, increasing the purchasing power of the population, it was believed, would stimulate economic activity, which would in turn bring the budget back into balance through increased revenue.

Without a devaluation at the beginning of this policy, the imbalance between French and foreign prices, a fundamental cause of the prolonged depression in France, was increased. When devaluation finally became necessary, in September 1936, it was carried out in such a way that it did not lead to the large repatriation of capital that would have brought a noticeable improvement in the financial and economic situation.

The failure of the Blum government's financial policy (to be explained in detail below) has turned the current government back to the idea of balancing the budget as the main goal of financial policy. Substantial increases in taxes and tariffs (at a total value of 19,5 billion) should now bring about a balancing of the ordinary budget, while the squeeze on expenditures for public works, local communities and railways is aimed at easing the Treasury's burden. Thus, the aim is to move in stages toward the goal stated in the resignation letter of the Stabilization Fund experts—to get to the point where only exceptional armament expenses would be covered and these through loans.

4) The development of the public debt from 1930–1936 and the rise in the interest rate

The state financial deficit caused by the economic crisis and reinforced by the need to rearm weighed entirely on the Treasury, which had to finance it through loans. The contribution provided by savings can be measured by the following table, which shows the total French public debt in 1930 and 1936, without repayment premiums and not including the debt carried by departments, municipalities and railroads:

Table 4.3.

	December 1930	September 1936
Perpetual debt	95,8	50,5
Amortizable debt	106,3	191,4
Medium- and short-term debt	22,1	32,5
Floating debt	37,5	69,6 (including the debt to the B.F.)
PP. TT. debt	2,7	10,6
National Bank of Agric.	–	2,3
Total	264,4	356,8

The overall increase in the public debt, which between 1929 and 1930 had been reduced by 34 billion francs, was thus over 92 billion. At the same time, we see the transformation of the composition of public debt into the most burdensome and dangerous forms.

We note that the state has increasingly monopolized the capital market during recent years, as reflected in the following table of issues:

Table 4.4.

Year	Total issues	Direct or indirect state loans	
	in 000.000 Fr.	in 000.000 Fr.	in % of total
1931	28.283	8.147	29
1932	31.217	23.393	75
1933	26.205	20.657	79
1934	24.545	20.040	83
1935	21.579	18.816	87
1936	18.120	16.992	94

The growth of the public debt coincided with an increasingly pronounced contraction of the capital and monetary markets resulting from the hoarding and exportation of capital and in this way provoked a short- and long-term interest rate increase. Along with the industrial production index, it was the trend in interest rates that conflicted most with the economic development of countries where a successful devaluation had eased the economy. A correlation has recently been calculated (by Lhomme in a book of little value, *L'intéret et l'évolution économique (1919–1935)*, appendix) between interest rate changes in France and England from 1911 to 1935, which constructs general theoretical interest rates using the most significant rates from the two markets. The result was an extremely strong negative correlation of 0,987.

The rise of the interest rate in France can be considered as one of the deeper evils of the French economy, as it goes against recovery investments and the cost reductions, while also working against decreasing the interest burden of the public debt. It is precisely the interest rate problem that leads us from the financial aspect to the monetary aspect of the French crisis.

III. The monetary market and capital movements from 1930 up to the devaluation of 1936

Developments between 1930 and 1936 can be divided into two distinct periods—the foreign monetary crises and the crises of the franc. For both periods, it is particularly interesting to note the interdependence of events abroad and domestic in France, whether established through links of cause and effect or by mere coincidence.

1) The period of capital inflows, 1930–1932

The first year of the crisis, 1930, saw a considerable influx of gold (12 billion francs) into the coffers of the B. F. Since the income balance (*balance des revenus*, comprising the balance of trade, income from tourism and shipping, and interest payments) stood at a surplus of only 300 million, and reparations payments were on the other hand almost offset by foreign debt payments, the gold receipts that occurred only in the second half of the year must be explained by the repatriation of French assets from abroad, either in the form of foreign securities or in the form of simple deposits. The main causes were the steeper fall in values abroad than in France, uncertainty about the political and monetary future abroad and, after October 1930, the first French banking crisis. This incited banks to liquidate their foreign portfolios, which at the time were yielding less at the interest rates than their French portfolios.

That year marked a complete reversal of the composition of the balance of payments under the guise of the continuation of gold shipments. Whereas in 1928 and 1929 these were caused by gains in the income balance and by reparations, and were taking place in spite of considerable short-term capital exports, in 1930 these gains were disappearing and what was causing the gold receipts were capital movements towards France. This trend established itself more clearly and intensely during the following two years. In fact, the income balance went heavily into debt (3 billion in 1931, 4,8 billion in 1932), reparations ceased with the Hoover moratorium, and despite this, massive gold imports took place. The B. F. gold reserve increased by 14,9 billion in 1931 and 14,6 billion in 1932. But apart from this, there were major purchases of gold by banks and individuals. These imports can only be explained by capital movements due to the central European crisis, the English devaluation and the French banking crisis of October 1931. The crisis abroad and foreign trust in French currency coupled with the lack of French trust in their banks contributed to the same result—an influx of liquidity into the French market.

If 1931 was the year of mass inflows of private French and foreign capital, in 1932, with the near liquidation of private French assets abroad and the recovery of the pound, it was the redemption of foreign exchange held by the B. F. and the Treasury that determined the gold inflows. This year was marked throughout Europe by the liquidation of the gold exchange standard, since after the losses incurred due to the English devaluation (2,4 billion francs by the B. F. alone) and because of the uncertainties surrounding the dollar, all issuing European banks sold their foreign currencies, which instead of a reserve of collateral had become a source of losses for them.

It appears from this analysis that foreign currencies and French banking crises were what led to the imports of capital and gold. Their effect on the money market was clearly to further reinforce the abundance of liquidity that the crisis alone was already causing. The domestic hoarding of banknotes in this period was largely offset by this. For the most part, there were only shifts of deposits to the large banks and a slowdown in these deposits' rate of circulation. Thus, short-term interest rates were extremely low until mid-1933 although the first issues of treasury bills, which were to multiply very soon, rebounded in mid-1932. Because the official rate was kept at a level much higher than the rate on the open market—from late 1931 until 1933 the official rate was 2½%, while the *hors banque* rate hovered around 1%—rediscounts at the B. F. were very low and at the same time private deposits increased.

The long-term interest rate curve—measured by the rate of return on fixed-income values—had been rising since late 1931 influenced mainly by political factors, and the 1932 conversion could not stop its upward march, which was to reach its first peak in February 1934.

Except for the redemption of its foreign exchange stock, the Bank of France throughout this first period of the crisis took a position of total passivity. It noted in its annual reports that gold only came in through arbitrage and that it "saw its control of the market taken away." This is precisely what Ch. Rist reproached it for—not sufficiently reducing its discount rate when this was possible and thus failing to provide serious aid in support of the state's financial restoration and economic recovery.[2]

2) The period of the crisis of the franc: 1933–1936

Gold receipts were determined by French and foreign capital imports in 1930 and 1931, and by B. F. foreign currencies sales in 1932. In the following

2 *Revue d'Economie Politique*, May–June 1935; La France économique, Introduction.

years it would again be invisible movements of capital that would condition the precious metal's entries and especially its outflows. Thus for 1933 the deficit of 2,9 billion in the income balance (considerably reduced compared to 1931 and 1932) was covered by the liquidation of the B. F.'s foreign exchange inventories, an almost complete liquidation spread evenly over the whole year, while the changes in the gold reserve coincided exactly with the invisible movements of capital. The same was true for 1934 and 1935, when the income balance deficit became less significant (1,2 billion in 1934 and 400 million in 1935) as did visible capital exports and imports. In 1936 and 1937, the increase in the budget deficit indeed put additional pressure on the franc, but it was still capital movements that determined the monetary situation.

Three periods can be distinguished: early 1933 saw the beginning of the run-up to the franc crisis of February 1934; a year of calm followed, succeeded by a period of more or less acute crises for the franc that finally culminated in the devaluation of September 1936.

a) The year 1933 and the first crisis of the franc in February 1934

The year 1933 was marked from the start by the American banking crisis and the devaluation of the dollar. It is significant that on balance Paris did not benefit from the international movement of capital that was produced on this occasion. During the first part of the year French and foreign capital left Paris for London, and for the first time the Exchange Equalization Account had to purchase significant sums of francs, which it immediately converted into gold at the B. F. The cause of this movement was multifaceted: the improving situation in England, the rise to power of National Socialism, and the discouraging financial prospects in France. At the same time there was a noticeable internal increase in the hoarding of notes and of gold, which—and this was repeated several times later—was partially transferred to London, taking refuge in the shelter of English legislation. All this led to a contraction in the long- and short-term capital markets, particularly inopportune at a time when the Treasury was facing, in addition to the budget deficit and seasonal cash shortages, massive repayments of medium-term debt. Thus, the free market rate very soon approached the official rate still maintained at 2½%, and private deposits at the Bank of France, like deposits in the banks, declined under the threefold effect of note hoarding, withdrawals of capital, and issues by the Treasury, which was in fact obliged to borrow 30 million pounds from London.

Between July and October 1933 this trend was interrupted by events entirely unrelated to the intrinsic French situation. Worries, or rather expectations concerning a fall in the pound caused a lot of capital to return to Paris, and British banks invested significant sums in French Treasury bonds, which provided them with high interest at a time when they were quoting carryovers on franc futures. But as the drop in the pound had occurred, this exceptional aid disappeared, and all the unfavorable fuel already mentioned was compounded by political unrest from October to February 1934. The acute Treasury crisis that followed was the result not only of budget deficits but also of demand for the redemption of circulating bonds. It appeared that the only choices left were those of the inflation years—stopping Treasury payments or printing B. F. notes. Events abroad made the situation still more delicate: the temporary stabilization of the dollar caused capital that had taken refuge in France to flow back to the United States. In February, the discount rate had to be raised to 3% and the capitalization rate for fixed-income securities exceeded 6%. The B. F. lost 3 billion francs in gold, but overall since the beginning of 1933 more than 9 billion had left its coffers.

b) Money market affluence and the Flandin government's attempt at "reflation"

Tensions persisted during the month of March, when the Treasury contracted a 100 million guilder loan at Amsterdam, and eased only with the "psychological shock" of the April legislative decrees. From that point on the market situation was quite comfortable; substantial capital returned to Paris and was made available to the Treasury. Certain foreign events such as the silver policy of the United States and the weakness of the pound in the fall of 1934 or early 1935—it was then worth only 70 francs—also contributed to the gold inflow. This easing of the money market until almost the middle of 1935, making possible a reduction of the discount rate to 2½% as early as June 1934, was contrasted with a very patchy rise in yields and the difficulties the Treasury subsequently experienced in issuing long-term securities.

To the Flandin government's credit, attention was focused on the interest-rate question. Observing the progressive drying up of the capital market this government proposed looking closely to the money market for a time. But in order to get businesses and banks to subscribe widely to the Treasury bills, they had to be given the assurance that they could move them easily. The government first obtained authorization from Parliament for a new issue of 5 billion in bonds, over and above the 10 billion already in circulation. More difficult, however, was obtaining the cooperation of the B. of F.: despite having replaced the governor, it stubbornly refused to allow the bonds into its portfolio except with such precautions and conditions as to make the government's request aid unrealistic. The government was striving for a very broad rediscount in terms of maturity and quantity. Indeed, it wanted to have the bank itself take the initiative in these transactions, which would thus have looked like open market policy. However, the bank would only grant "pensions" at a maximum of 30 days on public notes with maturities not exceeding two years.[3]

The orthodoxy of the B. F. leadership thus led it to reject a money market easing that presented no danger to the currency at a time when public credit was out of the question. As of December 1935 it saw itself obliged to resort in large measure to the policy it had rejected a few months earlier, but under infinitely more dangerous conditions and forms, and after 20 billion francs in gold and capital had left France. Faced with the B. F.'s refusal, the Flandin government had to turn once again in March-April 1935 to the capital market—which ensured the checkmate of its fleeting attempt at reflation.

c) The crisis of the franc from May 1935 to June 1936

The crisis of February 1934 had brewed intermittently for a period of months. This second crisis of the franc, in May–June 1935, is notable for the rapidity of its development under the coinciding influence of a wide variety of factors. Here is a list of them according to Mr. F. Jenny ("Chronique Financiére" in *Revue Politique et Parlamentaire*, June 1935):

1. Encouragement of speculation from profits realized in the fall of the Belgian franc;
2. Repatriation of Belgian funds deposited in France during the crisis in Belgium;
3. A worsening financial imbalance and refusal of the Chambers to grant full powers to the government;
4. Devaluationist propaganda;
5. Communist successes in municipal elections.

The outflows of gold during this crisis reached 11 billion francs, a not inconsiderable part of which to convert banknotes into gold, the first indicator

3 The difference between these "pensions" and ordinary bond advances was (1) a much lower interest rate, approaching the rate on the open market; (2) the amount of the advance which, after deducting interest, represented 100% of the bond.

of the public's loss of faith in the currency. The means used by the B. F. to curtail speculation were raising the discount rate to 6%, suspending advances on ingots and some degree of technical oversight of the market to prevent the credits granted from being used for speculation on futures. But neither during this nor the crises to come, up to September 1936, was any obstacle placed on the free convertibility of notes into gold.

After a period of relative calm following the legislative decrees, the end of November 1935 saw a new crisis caused by the political and financial uncertainties in France and a first Wall Street boom that was attracting European capital. The crisis was not as serious as the previous one (losses in gold amounted to 6 billion francs), but the discount rate, which had in the meantime been reduced to 3%, had to be brought back up to 6%. The increase in rediscounts at the B. F. was greater than in May, and the portfolio reached 11 billion as compared to 3,5 billion a year earlier, which revealed the growing contraction of the money market.

The fact that the fall of the Laval government in January 1936 was followed by losses in gold of no more than a billion francs led many to believe that the capital available for export was by now exhausted. Shortly thereafter events themselves disproved this view. Actually there were still considerable sums of hoarded banknotes in France, consisting partly of unused deposits in savings institutions and banks. Despite the sharp reduction in the volume of internal exchange, the increase in deposits and the circulation of banknotes since 1929, especially in denominations of 500 and 1.000 Fr. was testimony to the slowing speed of currency circulation (of banknotes and deposits) of which hoarding is merely the limiting case.

By the beginning of 1936, there was no longer any question of taking out a long-term loan, mainly because of political uncertainties; but in addition, the money market was exhausted because of repeated capital exports—or in any case its rate of around 5% was prohibitive for the state. The Treasury therefore turned to London, where it finalized a 9-month, £40 million (3 billion French franc) line of credit with a consortium of British banks in February. The credit was secured by the gold at the B. F., which put the credit balance in francs at the Treasury's disposal by gradually buying francs with the pounds granted in opening the line of credit. For the entire duration of the transfer, set at six weeks, this credit supported, therefore, the French exchange rate—particularly handy at a time when the serious international crisis caused by Germany's denunciation of the Treaty of Locarno was about to cause a new exodus of French capital. From February 8 to March 29, the reserve of the

B. F. amounted to only 600 million, revealing a capital outflow of 2.400 million francs for this period.

The English loan transfer had just been completed when new hemorrhages of gold began to occur. This was no longer a crisis as such, but rather a continuous state of crisis that lasted from the end of April to the end of June, and during these two months the gold loss was 11,7 billion francs and the discount rate, closely followed and sometimes even preceded by the *hors banque* rate, was again raised to 6%.

More than ever, political factors can be cited as the cause of the crisis. First of all there was the general fear—unjustified, by the way—that the election results had inspired in capitalists and savers—fear of disorder and anti-capitalist measures that was strongly reinforced by the June strikes. And then there was the conviction—this time justified—that the economic and social policy outlined by the new government would fatally lead to devaluation or exchange controls, since the new social laws coupled with inflation were bound to accentuate the disparity between French and foreign prices. This conviction was further reinforced among the public by the fact that economists like Ch. Rist and the ex-Finance Minister Germain-Martin had come around to devaluation as the lesser evil compared to exchange controls.

In May–June 1936, there were numerous French citizens who personally went to London to open accounts there with packages of bank notes or gold bars in their suitcases. The circulation of Bank of England notes was strongly affected by the demand for them on the part of French savers preferring to put in their "*bas de laine*" the white paper of the Bank of England instead of the colored paper of the B. F.

d) Inflation and the 18 June 1936 agreement between the Treasury and the B. F.

One monetary reason for the general crisis of confidence alluded to above was the concealed inflation recognizable in the swelling of the B. F.'s portfolio entry. After the yield of British credit had very quickly been exhausted by the new expenditures on armaments and partial mobilization, the Treasury had no other recourse but to turn to the issuing institution for money. In the last session of the outgoing legislature, the Sarraut government obtained authorization to issue an additional 6 billion in treasury bonds and it was clear that only the B.F. would be able to underwrite them as a last resort. P. Reynaud correctly noted that this was when the inflation officially began, pointing out the significant fact that the deflationary legislature of 1932 had on the last day of its existence come around to opposing the policy it had followed for four years, thereby admitting that deflation had been completely checkmated.

At this time the B. F. was already holding a substantial quantity of treasury bonds, certainly more than the Flandin government had wanted it to accept a year earlier.[4] Facing the risk of endangering the entire French banking system and jeopardizing the solvency of the Treasury, the Bank of France had to abandon its prior intransigence. But until February 1937 this rediscount had retained its character as treasury relief for the bond-holding banks. What took place from March to June 1937 and brought the Bank's portfolio, in repeated surges, from 10 billion to 21 billion, was simply the purchase of bonds by the B. F. through the brokerage of the banks. The latter in fact had taken the bonds only to immediately redeem them, thus acting as mere mediators between the Treasury and the B. F.

New Finance Minister Vincent Auriol was certainly right to suppress this unnecessary brokerage. The agreement between the Treasury and the B. F. of June 18, 1936, stipulated that Treasury and National Defense bills that had been rediscounted were to be removed immediately from the commercial portfolio. They amounted to 14 billion francs, which would form a new entry—"portfolio of public bills." At maturity dates, direct, interest-free advances were to take the place of the bonds listed in this account. This was the liquidation of the past. It was still necessary to secure the future, however, and for this purpose the same agreement provided that new temporary advances could be granted by the Bank to the Treasury up to an amount of 10 billion francs. At the same time, the government was granted permission to issue 10 billion in new Treasury bonds. But it was expressly stipulated that only one or the other of these borrowing options could be exercised. The government was to try to issue the bonds; only in the event that it could not place them, and only for the amount that separated the bond issuance from the 10 billion granted, could it resort to advances from the B. F. In this way the government was saying to the country that whether or not there is inflation is up to no one but you. If you come to me with your money I won't have to put the "*planche à billets*" into effect. And in order that its appeal would reach the greatest number of citizens, it went ahead with six-month and one-year bonds in small denominations

4 The issue raised was definitively resolved by Article 13 of the B. F. reform law, which stated, "All floating debt bills issued by the public Treasury and coming due within a space of three months at most, shall be admitted without limitation to the discount of the issuing institution unless for the profit of the public Treasury." This last phrase is a safeguard against the repetition of the indirect inflation process that ran from February to June 1936.

starting at 100 Fr. The Minister of Finance was surely expecting too much from this "democratization" of the money market, which in fact appealed primarily to the government's political supporters. Ultimately, "Auriol bonds" were issued for the certainly not insignificant sum of 4,5 billion. This was, however, nowhere near sufficient to meet the needs of the Treasury, which until September had to resort to advances from the B. F. in excess of 2 billion francs.

The end-of-June financial reorganization, the government's repeated declarations against devaluation, and finally some degree of political *détente* and the peaceful settlement of labor disputes restored a more favorable atmosphere during July and the first half of August of last year. Capital exports ceased and there were even some repatriations resulting from the obligation to declare assets abroad, translating into gold receipts of 900 million francs. The discount rate was allowed to fall to 3%. The high backwardations on the franc futures, however, denoted the market's deep conviction that the franc was "unsustainable."

IV. The devaluation of September 1936

In fact, the mediocre result of the issuance of Treasury bonds, the recommendation for devaluation by the Financial Committee of the League of Nations and rumors of conversations between the French, British and American monetary authorities about a "realignment" of the franc were enough to provoke a new flight of capital. This was less strong than the previous ones—between August 15 and September 25 the B. F. lost 4,7 billion in gold—2,6 in the week of September 18–25 alone—but it was fatal this time to the Poincaré franc.

The government had finally realized that defending the franc at its current level now made no economic sense. Also concerned for reasons of national security about the steady decline in the gold stock—on September 25 it was down to 50 billion (although mortgaged to the tune of 3 billion for the British loan), an amount designated by Poincaré as the minimum war treasury—the government obtained assurances from the Anglo-Saxon monetary authorities that the pound and the dollar would not be depreciated as a consequence of the fall of the franc. As soon as the pressure once again became heavy, it opted for devaluation.

1) Devaluation from a domestic monetary point of view

A September 26 legislative decree practically put an embargo on gold by raising the minimum amount of notes required for conversion into gold to an astronomical figure. A new agreement with the B. F. along with the Monetary Law of 1 October 1936 were to deeply alter the French monetary regime. Let us examine its main characteristics.

a) The "Franc Auriol"

The new franc was to correspond to between 49 and 43 mg of gold at 900/1000. This represented a devaluation of 25,19% at the least and 34,35% at the most with respect to the Poincaré franc, which contained 65,5 mg of gold of the same alloy.

This was the same method that had been used at the time of the devaluation of the Belgian franc. Under present international monetary conditions, this regime cannot generally be anything other than a transitional stage on the way to either definitive stabilization or the adoption of a currency completely detached from gold. There are two reasons for this. Either the devaluation percentage will be seen to have been chosen in order to restore the country's economic equilibrium, in which case the upward or downward margins that always represent ranges for speculation can be suppressed. Or it will be determined that the limits set are too tight and that they need to be removed so that the currency can find its level based on supply and demand, which a stabilization fund can regulate but cannot essentially change.

b) The re-estimation of the gold reserve

With this we arrive at the second characteristic of the monetary reform, which was the creation of a stabilization fund of 10 billion francs in gold from the re-estimation of the Bank of France's gold stock based on the value maximum (the new franc's 49 mg of gold). This re-estimation yielded 17 billion francs, which permitted not only the creation of the stabilization fund, but a notable reduction in the B. F.'s advances to the state. More will be said below about the stabilization fund.

c) Gold legislation

The third characteristic consisted of measures against speculation, the abolition of free trade in gold and the compulsory reporting of gold held by private individuals. This declaration was meant to lead to the transfer of this gold at the price of 65,5 mg per franc or the payment to the Treasury of the difference between its value at that price and the current gold-value of the franc. The justice—or at least the justification—of this measure could be argued at length, but what is indisputable is that its effect on the money market and on depositors was as disastrous as the effect of the other "measures against speculation" (mandatory declaration of foreign exchange futures transactions during September, a special 50% tax on the benefits of futures transactions contracted from September 21 to 26). Hoarders of gold of course went to impossible lengths to avoid declaring their holdings, which would deprive them of the benefits of the devaluation, in anticipation of which they had sacrificed huge sums in interests. Considerable masses of exported French gold remained abroad while an intensive clandestine gold export trade to Switzerland and Belgium developed in France. While one of the main benefits of the devaluation was supposed to be the repatriation of gold and prevention of its hoarding, the effect of the government's policy was the exact opposite. And since it is a mere step from requisitioning gold to obstructing the movement of capital, this measure also had a depressing effect on exported capital, which did not return at the rate seen in the other countries that had devalued and at the same time in Switzerland and the Netherlands.

The government recognized in stages the harm done by its own measures. The deadline for the declaration had been set at November 1, but on December 15 it was extended until February 1, 1937. A new bond was issued simultaneously, restricted to possessors of gold and "Auriol bonds." The bond was issued at a price of 100 Poincaré francs and was redeemable in 3 years with a redemption premium of 40 francs, corresponding approximately to the devaluation. In addition, from the moment it was issued, the bond would yield its redemption value upon partial payment (30%) of inheritance taxes. But this partial measure was not enough and, grappling with new monetary and financial difficulties, the government decided at the time of the issuance of the National Defense Loan in March 1937 to permanently and entirely waive all its gold legislation. Free trade in gold was restored and the Bank of F. was authorized to buy gold at the current market price without even asking the name of the seller. In this way a particularly unhappy financial episode was finally settled.

2) The devaluation from the international monetary point of view: "the tripartite agreement"

From an international monetary point of view the fall of the franc in September 1936 was especially important for the conclusion of the tripartite agreements between the monetary authorities of France, Great Britain, and the United States, joined shortly thereafter by Switzerland and the Netherlands.

The basis for these agreements was established by the joint declaration of the three governments on September 25. This statement essentially gave assurances that the pound and the dollar would not be depreciated as a result of the devaluation of the franc and no new obstacles would be raised to French exports that would tend to deprive France of the hoped-for benefits of devaluation. In addition, the governments stated that they would use the "appropriate means available to them to avoid, as far as possible, disturbances that might affect the new foreign exchange rate bases resulting from the planned adjustment." However, the obligations flowing from this passage are anything but clear since it is stated a little further on that "the government of the United States and the government of Great Britain must, of course, in their international monetary policy, take strict account of the needs of the domestic prosperity of the American Republic and the British Empire." So that even if the devaluation of the franc cannot be cited as the cause or pretext for another depreciation of the pound and the dollar, there is nothing to rule out the possibility of a depreciation for other reasons. The statement ends with an appeal for the restoration of international trade.

On the one hand, while the September 25 agreement thus aspired to at least relative exchange rate stability, on the other, the safest mechanism for maintaining this stability, the international gold standard, no longer existed. If each of the foreign exchange regulators could sell gold at the price they liked—that is, if they could at any time determine the exit point for gold, this was not the case for the entry point, since as of September 25, 1936, none of the three currencies in question was any longer convertible into gold. The dollar was actually convertible at its provisional stabilization rate, but only by countries applying the gold standard—to be precise, after September 1936, only by Belgium. Now it was technically impossible for all international gold movements to take place exclusively through the Brussels channel the way they had through Paris. Briefly, each government had the possibility to sell gold—to defend its currency against depreciation (or to oppose the appreciation of other currencies), but it could not defend itself against an appreciation of its own currency (or fight the depreciation of other currencies) without running the serious risk of accumulating a stock of foreign currencies.

A new agreement on October 13, 1936, neatly remedied this state of affairs, stipulating that the currencies held by each of the three countries' regulators could be freely exchanged against "earmarked" gold at regularly fixed rates. Like the previous agreement, this too was subject to reporting within a 24-hour period.

Thanks to this agreement, gold and capital movements remained free among the signatory countries, the automatic mechanism of the gold standard having been replaced by the more or less concerted action of stabilization funds. This action has undeniably exercised a stabilizing influence disturbed only by domestic monetary events in France. The difference separating the gold standard and the system in practice today, which is a sort of gold standard with flexible parity and voluntarily fixed gold points,[5] is surely less than the difference between the latter system and a hard currency whose course is set in the world market solely by supply and demand. The system thus devised is closer to the gold standard in that the interpretation of the freedom of movement granted to each of the parties under the agreements is more

5 See in this connection the interesting discussion of the advantages and disadvantages of gold point extension and a flexible parity monetary system by Prof. Gregory in *Reconstruction Economique Internationale*, edited by the International Chamber of Commerce—Paris 1936.

restrictive. The primary and decisive argument against a return to the gold standard, however, remains the existence of these floating masses of capital, which was one of the characteristics of the postwar monetary economy. Even if it were deemed appropriate to be bound again to the discipline of gold, it seems impossible at present to subject the nation's economy and domestic fortunes to these sudden and unpredictable shifts of capital driven largely by non-economic motives. Up to a certain point these movements can be offset by selling (in the case of an influx) or buying (if it is an exodus) treasury bills. But in addition to the fact that such a policy involves the always delicate distinction between normal movements whose effect on the domestic economy should not be hindered and abnormal ones whose effects should be nullified, it has limitations that mainly involve each country defending its gold reserve.[6]

The real raison d'être of stabilization funds is therefore not abnormal capital movements and the need to neutralize them. Such neutralization, it may be noted, could easily be undertaken by the issuing institution through an open market policy and the division of its gold reserve into one stock that is incorporated into the country's credit economy and another that is not. And it is notable as well that only the British fund and (starting in December 1936) the American fund practice this policy. The existence of the stabilization funds and the tripartite system in general is on the contrary justified by the expectation of a possible breakdown of this policy, in which case exchange rates would have to be set in motion again. In other words, the raison d'être of stabilization funds is the instability of the exchange rates, just as the raison d'être of the penal code is the existence of criminals.

6 See Cabiati, *Fisiologia e patologia economica negli scambi della ricchezza fra gli stati*, p. 555.

V. French monetary developments after devaluation. A comparison of the mechanisms and operations of the French and British stabilization funds

An excellent illustration of the operating constraints on a stabilization fund is offered by the activities of the French fund after September.

Let us therefore review the monetary developments of the last ten months. The devaluation was immediately followed by some return of capital and gold. The discount rate quickly fell from 6% to 2%, but this monetary recovery was short-lived. Following the general impression was that the 30% devaluation would not be enough to restore the balance, capital movements again became unfavorable to France shortly thereafter. The difficulties at the Treasury, growing inflation, and gold legislation contributed to new exports so that at the end of 1936 the discount rate had to be raised to 4%, and a major backwardation was again quoted on franc futures beginning in November 1936. Faced with mounting difficulties, and after contracting a new loan of 40 million pounds in London, the government proclaimed a "pause" on March 5, 1937, abolished gold legislation, and issued a highly successful 8 billion National Defense bond loan with an exchange guarantee, which was immediately underwritten. In addition, a committee of experts was appointed to direct the stabilization fund, and the franc was allowed to fall almost to its lower limit. These measures were followed by a temporary calm, but the new partial return of capital and gold was soon interrupted by new political disturbances, the April stock market crisis, and deepening financial and economic concerns. A new capital flight occurred in late June 1937, leading to a second devaluation of the franc. The lower limit of 43 mg was suspended and the pound rose from 111 francs to 128, and then 133, corresponding to a further devaluation of 15%. The overall devaluation of the Poincaré franc thus amounted to 44%—slightly more than the devaluations of the pound and the dollar from 1931 to 1933.[7]

In a new agreement the B. F. opened a new credit line to the state of 15 billion, and the re-estimation of the reserve at the price of 43 mg to the franc yielded an accounting benefit of 7 billion, which was allocated to a new fund for "*soutien des rentes*." This fund was supposed to help control and regularize the course of government bonds, which had fallen to an extremely low level.

7 Currently the franc, which has undergone new sharp declines, stands at 150 to the pound (October 15, 1937).

It is also noteworthy that France at the very time of the new devaluation confirmed its adherence to the tripartite agreements and has thus far been able to avoid exchange controls. America and England for their part recognized that the devaluation was necessitated by the internal French situation and did not react by altering the course of the pound and dollar.

Let us now see what part the stabilization fund played in these events. This entity was initially endowed with 10 billion in gold from the re-estimation of the gold reserve in September. This is its main difference from the parallel entity in Britain, whose resources initially consisted of Treasury bonds—i.e., potential pounds—transferred by the British Treasury. This difference is explained by the different origins of the two funds. The British fund was created in 1932 to defend the pound against a rise, and for this it had to be able to offer pounds. The French fund, on the other hand, had to protect the franc from falling further, so it had to be able to buy francs. The British fund would use the sterling resulting from the market sale of bonds to buy foreign currencies, which it immediately converted into gold. This in the case of buying pressure on the pound. Conversely, when the British fund wants to counter or limit a decline in the pound it sells the gold it holds against sterling, and with these pounds buys back the previously issued bonds. This in broad terms is the mechanism of the British fund—basically it sells treasury bills against gold, and gold against treasury bills. And it explains how it fulfills its main functions—avoiding violent swings in the value of the pound while not opposing fundamental trends, and neutralizing the effects of its own intervention in the money market, where it takes back with bond sales what it gives with the purchase of gold and vice versa.

Nothing like this applies in the case of the French fund, which does not in any way assume the second of these functions of its British counterpart. Indeed, it would have been impossible to create a new lending body under the guise of a stabilization fund when the state already had to turn to the issuing institution to cover a considerable part of its current expenses. The situation was also unlike the British one from a particularly important point of view, which is that while London was right not to want to incorporate the sums flowing into the City into its internal credit edifice because they came from abnormal movements, France had no reason not to reintegrate previously exported capital into its own economy. The export of this capital to London was "abnormal" as its repatriation would be "normal," and the issue was not to neutralize this repatriation which, on the contrary, was meant to restore the prosperity of the money market.

In order to procure francs for the purpose of countering any speculation on the currency's rise, the French Fund had to sell gold to the Bank of France against francs that it would resell against currencies to be promptly converted into gold. The issue of francs against gold from the stabilization fund is inflationary because the return is nothing but the *nominal* capital gain from the reestimation. But since these francs are to be used solely to purchase gold, what we have in the last analysis is the issue of francs against gold, and everything happens as it did under the old gold standard. On the other hand, if the fund is defending the franc against a decline, it sells the gold transferred to it and receives francs in return, which it deposits in a current account at the Bank of France. We thus arrive at a paradoxical result: if the B. F. were to sell its gold, it would reduce its liabilities at the same time by destroying the resold notes or debiting its creditor accounts. But if the stabilization fund sells the gold, the bank sees its liabilities increase because of the increase in the "private current accounts" entry—it might have been better not to bring the francs held by the fund onto the Bank's balance sheet, as had already been removed from this balance sheet the 10 billion in gold transferred to the fund. Apart from the fact that in this way the secrecy of the fund's operations would have been better preserved, the increase in the Bank's liabilities from the fund's gold sales is meaningless and has already led to all sorts of misinterpretations. If the fund has exhausted its gold, it can procure new gold at the B. F. and sell it back against francs. But the francs that gold sales have pulled from the market do not return to us as they do in England, and a monetary contraction will therefore follow, as under the gold standard regime.

It appears from this analysis that we have two indices for tracking the evolution of stabilization fund operations: (I) changes in the gold reserve, which will increase or decrease whenever the fund has exhausted its holdings in francs or gold, and (II) the entry "private current accounts" which, ceteris paribus, will change in direct proportion to the fund's holdings in francs.

When it came into existence the fund possessed nothing but gold. To cope with the favorable capital currents that materialized in October and the first half of November, it therefore had to procure francs by selling some of its gold to the issuing institution. It is therefore untrue to say that it would not have sold this gold if it had known that capital movements would again become unfavorable to France later—it was simply obliged to obtain currency so as not to allow the franc to revalue. So, the B. F.'s stock of gold went up to 2 billion on 9 October, and 5 billion on the 23rd. But already by the end of November, when the British loan of 40 million pounds came due, the fund was no longer able to repay it with its own gold. This sum therefore had to be transferred into it from the B. F., whose gold reserve shows a decrease of 4 billion francs on December 4. Finally, on January 29, the reserve again decreased by another 3 billion, thus restoring to the Fund the entirety of the gold previously ceded.

We also saw private current accounts swelling rapidly (especially starting in December) from 6,5 billion in September to 16,2 billion in March, an expansion attributable mainly to the increase in the Fund's reserves in francs. This figure fell to 13,1 billion in April because of the gold restocking that the Fund was able to do at the time of the capital repatriation caused by the National Defense loan and the official announcement of the "pause." In reality, the Fund's acquisitions of gold were probably greater than the amount of this decrease, since bank deposits at the B. F.—the other factor determining the aforementioned entry—had certainly gone up during the same period.

With the new franc crisis at the end of June the Fund's gold was rapidly depleted, and it had to ask the B. F. for 2,5 billion during the week of June 17–24 and 6 billion the following week, but this is not to say that this 8,5 billion was fully utilized. On the contrary, it is thought that thanks in part to new capital inflows, in July the Fund's 10 billion presently consists more of gold than francs.

The first ten months of the fund's existence have thus shown: 1) that keeping operations secret, although effective on a daily basis, is pointless in the long run under the French system given that the Fund's operations are reflected in the B. F. Complete secrecy would require suppressing the publication of the B. F.'s balance sheet.

In addition, 2) the Fund's stabilizing action will fail in the face of major capital movements, especially when these are unfavorable to the country affected by them because of gold losses that compel authorities to act.

Cabiati called this the confirmation of the economic limits of stabilization funds (p. 553). Indeed, some have even spoken of the complete checkmate of the French Fund. It must be said in response, however, that no one ever claimed that Fund action alone could maintain the value of the currency. All the elements that influence the value of a currency—balance of payments, capital movements, fiduciary circulation—maintain their determining importance. When the Fund is presented with impossible tasks such as keeping the national exchange rate within certain limits over an indefinite period with the help of 10 billion francs in gold, it's "complete checkmate" will hardly be surprising. English terminology was much more felicitous, modestly speaking of an exchange rate "equalizing" account and not a Stabilization Fund. All things considered, it appears that despite everything, the French Fund has fulfilled important functions, namely:

1) It has successfully taken on the task of regularizing the course of the franc detached from gold, protecting it against violent fluctuations due to speculation—its function of regularizing the course of the national currency.
2) It has made possible, in cooperation with other similar bodies, the inauguration of a new international monetary system based on the principle of flexible parity—its international monetary cooperation function.
3) Finally, it puts France on an equal footing with other countries (especially Britain) so that it can defend itself with equal arms against foreign monetary maneuvers—this is its function in defense of the national currency.[8]

8 The anonymous author of the article "Le marché monetaire et les changes" in the *Revue d'Economie Politique* of May–June 1936, writes on p. 699: "The rate at which the Equalization Fund decides to intervene, as much in buying as in selling, is actually the effective London to Paris gold point. It is doubtful whether in the long run free gold markets will not grow weary of being maneuvered in this way by a foreign exchange market which, moreover, claims to be free of all responsibility as to the international operation of the gold standard."

VI. Particular issues

1) Considerations on the inflationary or deflationary effect of financial deficits

"Aperçu de la situation monétaire" [Overview of the monetary situation], published on the eve of the French devaluation by the Finance and Economic Committee of the League of Nations, raises a very important question: Why has the effect of budget deficits been deflationary in France but inflationary in the United States? The terms deflation and inflation are taken primarily in their monetary sense inasmuch as the "Aperçu" gives as evidence figures showing the contraction of the money market in France. These show a decrease in the gold reserve and on-demand commitments of the B. F., a decrease in commercial bank deposits and loans, a rise in short- and long-term interest rates, and the exact opposite movements in the United States. Posed in this way, the question raises a whole series of problems in monetary theory, only a few aspects of which we shall examine here.

The deflationary effect of a deficit is produced when it can be covered immediately by vigorous compression of spending. If on the contrary the government proves itself incapable of such an effort or if it is obliged to let the deficit persist due to national necessity, or indeed if it voluntarily increases it, the matter becomes more complicated.[9] To deal with surplus revenue needs, the state has two means: issuing bonds or turning to the issuing bank. This second option is inflation pure and simple and was employed particularly in the immediate aftermath of the war. Setting aside direct deflation and inflation, we can limit the question from the "Aperçu" in the following way: Why did the issuance of bonds to cover budget deficits cause—or rather why did it coincide with—deflation in France and inflation in the United States?

The direct and immediate effect of state borrowing is to take disposable assets away from savings and the money market, assets that are then spent by

9 As Prof. Ohlin in his report on *Reconstruction économique internationale* to the International Chamber of Commerce, *op. cit.*, p. 56, rightly observes, "when one speaks of financial deficits in times of crisis, one must clearly establish the distinction between two species of deficit. From the business point of view there is a very sharp difference between a deficit that is produced in a deflationary country *in spite* of a reduction in public expenditures and a deficit that is the *consequence* of public works undertaken by the state and other public expenditures. In the latter case the deficit is the instrument for stimulating the expansion of overall demand, whereas in the former it is the result of the contraction of demand."

the state. Borrowing will therefore have an inflationary or deflationary effect, 1) according to whether the turnaround of the borrowed sums is more or less perfect—that is, according to whether or not they flow back into savings and the money market, and 2) according to whether international capital movements are favorable or unfavorable to the country in question in offsetting or accentuating the effects of the state's demand for money.

Regarding the turnaround of the borrowed sums, the "Aperçu" notes not only that private hoarding hindered it in France, but especially that the money market had not contributed to the loans, which were mainly underwritten by savings. In the United States, on the other hand, the banks largely financed the needs of the Treasury, so that thanks to the state's productive expenditures the borrowed sums immediately found their way back into circulation in the form of deposits. It is true that in France there is a tradition of hostility to the expansion of credit by means of public subscriptions, both on the part of the Central Bank (open market policy) and of private banks with their concerns about not immobilizing their assets. But even in this area doctrine has gradually had to give way to the facts, and the banks have clearly done everything possible to help the state, which, in turn, has arranged the "*mise en pension*" at the B. F.—the rediscounting of its securities so that the liquidity concerns responsible for the banks' hostility have all but disappeared. There are unfortunately no precise figures on this since the banks combine their negotiable instruments and the state assets they hold under a single heading. Mr. Dieterlen has estimated the state assets of the four big credit banks at 14 billion out of a total portfolio of 19 billion (*Revue d' Économie Politique*—May–June 1935—"Les Banques"). It is clear that this is by no means a negligible proportion. It is also worth remembering the important role held in France by deposits in savings banks (commercial banks complain bitterly about their competition); such funds are concentrated at the "Caisse des Dépôts et Consignation," which invests them exclusively in government securities. And finally, the recent creation of a *soutien* annuity fund and very recent measures to mobilize state funds and securities representing state orders mark an important stage in the reform of the Paris money market.

We therefore believe that the coincidence of deficits and inflation in the United States, and deficits and deflation in France must be explained mainly by the importation of capital into the United States and its export from France. In fact, without capital exports we would certainly have witnessed a substantial expansion of monetary holdings given that their contraction was far from being proportional to gold losses. Mr. Dieterlen, a reliable chronicler of the annual situation of French banks in the *Revue d'Économie Politique*, writes: "One may well ask how it happens that the exportation of capital, having brought about the contraction of bank resources to the noted amounts, has not been stronger." And the most important point in his view is that "the cash withdrawn from the French market was returned to it almost automatically through the credit inflationary procedures that the government and B. F. were forced to resort to. It is clear that if the contraction, in conformity with orthodoxy—which they boasted of— had been allowed to take place, the decrease incurred by deposits would have been more noticeable. It would perhaps have got some of the banks into trouble. It is not an unsurprising aspect of the present situation that the needs of the Treasury are at once a threat to the banking system and the reason for its apparent soundness."

But if the export of capital could not completely counteract the "reflationist" influence of state loans, the indirect or direct inflation engineered by the state since 1936 was also incapable of averting the depressing effects of capital exports. In fact, the overall total of 30 billion that the B. F. has advanced so far to the state has not come back in an increased circulation of banknotes and deposits, in the way the reduction of the gold reserve saw them diminish before direct inflation.

Certainly, the ease with which the 8 billion national defense loan last March was underwritten shows the sense of relief that inflation has exerted on the treasuries of banks and individuals. But in general, the money market remains contracted and interest rates are still three times or more what they are in London or New York.

One of the main arguments for devaluation, and the best supported by the experience of other countries, was that once the monetary operation has been carried out and the insurance premium against devaluation through incorporation into the interest rate eliminated, capital would flood back—causing a reduction of the interest rate, with all its attendant favorable consequences. But far from coming back, capital continued to emigrate, for the reasons we have seen. Now the interest rate problem can only be satisfactorily solved by a return of capital. Inflation will lead to further monetary depreciation, the prospect of which chases even more capital away, so that its easing effect is quickly nullified. And partial measures, such as the recently introduced interest rate subsidies for certain industrial activities (new constructions), will not be able to change the fundamental trend of the money market.

More than any other consideration, the hope of being able to bring exported capital back to France has kept and will keep the government on the path of monetary liberalism since foreign exchange controls would permanently extinguish this hope. If the franc proves to have found a certain level of equilibrium following the devaluation, capital repatriation will quickly be able to solve the monetary situation. If instead the outflow continues, the government will, in spite of everything, finally be obliged to make France a "trap" for capital, but it will be a trap without mice.

2) Backwardations on franc futures after 1935 and their effects

A study of recent monetary events in France would be incomplete without at least a brief mention of a phenomenon which for the past two years has elicited much comment—backwardations on franc futures. A recent book by Dr. Einzig, *The Theory of Forward Exchange*, brilliantly illustrates the technical and theoretical aspects of the currency futures market. Along with numerous newspaper and journal articles, the League of Nations publication and Prof. Cabiati's book, both cited above, also deal with this issue and emphasize its importance.

Beginning in May 1935, abnormally high backwardations were quoted on the franc, corresponding to interest rates that sometimes rose to 30% or 40% or more, and rarely fell below 10% per annum for one- and three-month franc futures. The reason was evidently the market's lack of confidence in the future of the franc, the hope of futures sellers to be able to supply devalued francs at maturity and the futures buyers' fear of having to take them.

We may note at the outset that some backwardation on franc futures against the pound and the dollar was justified by the fact that short-term interest rates were higher in Paris than in London and New York. But, in fact, the backwardations expressed in yearly interest rates were far greater than the differences between interest rates—which Dr. Einzig calls the "undervaluation of the franc future in relation to its interest parity," not to be confused with the "simultaneous overvaluation of the spot franc in relation to its purchasing power parity."

The effects of this are:

1. The partial ineffectiveness of the B. F.'s discount rate policy. By raising its discount rate the B. F. seeks to defend the franc in two ways. Making credit more expensive in France tends on the one hand to lower prices—whose relative elevation is at the root of the economic imbalance. And, at the same time, it makes it comparatively profitable

to transfer short-term capital to France.[10] This second function is essential because the first function can only be exercised over the long term and cannot make itself felt because of the backwardation on the franc. In fact, when funds are transferred into France to take advantage of the high interest rate—that is, when someone buys spot francs—the same value of spot francs is sold as a hedge against the exchange-rate risk. Now from the moment that the backwardation on franc futures expressed as an annual percentage exceeds the interest-rate difference that the expected return was based on, the cost of the hedging operation will exceed the benefit on the interest arbitrage.

2. In addition, not only does backwardation make the B. F.'s discount policy ineffective, it actually leads to the exact opposite of what the policy was intended to do. Not only is it no longer creditworthy to transfer money from London to Paris, it becomes profitable to sell spot francs and to buy them back as futures because the profit on such a transaction (swap) outweighs the loss of interest. The interest arbitrage of available capital, instead of offsetting the effects of capital exports from France, tends on the contrary to work in the same direction. Swaps (i.e., the spot purchase of pounds and dollars against resale at term) that yield substantial profit through franc backwardizations lead to an increase in the spot supply of francs and contribute to gold outflows with real exports of capital.
3. The third effect of backwardization on franc futures is the influence it has on the money market. Dr. Einzig cites especially the example of France when he discusses the possible effect of currency futures on interest rates (generally it is the reverse effect that is discussed). At first, in fact, in part due to swap transactions, gold outflows contract the market. Then these highly remunerative transactions provide banks with an alternative use of their assets, and bank customers must pay higher interest rates to withstand competition from this "rival market." For their part, and for the same reason, banks must raise interest rates on their fixed-term deposits. Finally, in order to generally reduce

10 In his latest book, *L' Équilibre dans les Relations Économique Internationales*, Prof. Aftalion correctly notes, pp. 121–122, that these two functions of discount rate policy, domestic and international, are in conflict with one another. Therefore, the rise in the discount rate could not be predicted, the inflow of foreign capital being able to offset and even outstrip the effects of domestic credit restriction.

> the pool of funds available for currency transactions, the issuing bank is forced to raise its discount rate again.

We thus arrive at the paradox of money moving from the marketplace where it is expensive to the marketplace where it is cheap, reinforcing the high price of the one and the low price of the other—typical of the unstable equilibrium which according to Prof. Cabiati is characteristic of "bad money."

Even with all this, the effect and importance of backwardizations should not be exaggerated. Recall that as of June 1935, there was almost no foreign capital in Paris and that the only institutions that could have handled a significant volume of swaps on the futures market, the big banks, refrained from doing so at the request of the state. Hence the scale of transactions was restricted, also explaining the abnormal rates which, especially in 1936, were often only nominal. As such they formed an excellent barometer for the market's opinion of the franc's prospects.

The question was raised whether the B. F. should not have resumed its interventions in the currency futures market to bring down backwardations, whose high rates sowed distrust. In this regard, the bank's orthodoxy was appropriate because its intervention would perhaps have prolonged the franc's futile resistance. All the bank did was to advise banks against currency fixed-term transactions and to extend credit only after being satisfied that it would serve only commercial purposes. But as noted above, the effect of these measures was instead to increase the strain of the backwardations.

After September 1936, the Stabilization Fund intervened on several occasions to regularize the rate of franc futures. Thus, we read again recently in the *Temps Financier* of August 2: "It is possible that the action of the Stabilization Fund, which apparently has rather slowed down the decline of spot currencies in recent days, has on the contrary favored the retreat of the hedging operations (on the pound and the dollar) which presents an obvious interest for the domestic money market."

oOo

Part Three
The Franc from an Economic Viewpoint (1931–1937)

I. The overvaluation of the franc from 1931 to 1936

Up to now we have considered the franc from a purely monetary standpoint—that is, we have mainly examined its surface phenomena. A chapter was dedicated to public finance since developments here were generally the immediate point of departure for monetary change. But it should not be forgotten that the situation of public finance and the decrease in revenue are themselves merely effects—whose causes are to be found in the economic crisis.

There is now a consensus that the prolongation of the depression in France (and the other gold-bloc countries) from 1933 on was caused by its resistance to the world currency devaluation, the "overvaluation" of the franc (just as, for that matter, the delay of the crisis in France was probably due to the franc's "undervaluation" in 1929/1930).

What we mean by an overvalued franc in relation to the pound or an undervalued pound in relation to the franc is that the general gold-price level is higher in France than in England—in other words, that the buying power of the franc is higher in England than in France. When we speak only of an overvalued franc, this is meant to indicate that the price level in France has gone above the world level and that it is therefore incumbent on France to make the necessary adjustments. We can easily appreciate the unfavorable effects that an overvalued currency exerts on a country's economic and monetary situation:

1. First the industries working for visible and invisible export will suffer severely under the handicap of high production costs, and an important part of the country's economy will thus be stifled.
2. If under these conditions the country wants to stick to the gold standard and at the same time maintain the gold value of its currency, it will have to try to reduce its prices and production costs in domestic currency. Yet now the prospect of falling domestic prices will slow down the entire economy and worsen the crisis.
3. Finally, we may note the unfavorable psychological influence that overvaluation exerts on money and capital markets—both indirectly through the deterioration of public finance, and directly through the belief that

deflation cannot be carried through and that devaluation will be imposed sooner or later.

Discussing overvaluation, we therefore arrive at the basis of the problem of the franc. In this chapter we will observe it in the disparity between French and foreign prices, the development of foreign trade and the balance of payments in order to examine its evolution and causes. Investigating the consequences of the first devaluation of the franc for the imbalance of the French economy will be the subject of a second chapter.

1) The comparative movement of prices in France and abroad

a) The statistical and economic difficulties of comparisons

In order to analyze overvaluation, we first need a clear definition of it. Saying that there is overvaluation when prices in one country are higher than in others does not tell us much because we need to know *which prices* we want to compare. The difficulties here are well known.

Wholesale price indexes are largely related to raw materials, most of which are quoted on the international market and are conveyed in national currencies at this marketplace's exchange rate. Since for these "international commodities" a disparity between two countries would thus never occur, wholesale price indexes, which are largely composed of them, therefore tend to cancel out or at least greatly diminish the differences between domestic price levels.[11] It has therefore been rightly noted that this is a measurement that changes with what it is supposed to be measuring. The same is observed for price indexes of export goods, where the tendency for international equalization under the effect of international competition is extremely strong.

For this reason, comparisons of prices in different countries increasingly rely on indices of retail prices, living costs, and especially nominal wages as a more important element of the cost of production. But the difficulties are still considerable; especially from a statistical standpoint the comparability of different indices is often doubtful, and a base year has to be chosen in which an initial equilibrium is arbitrarily assumed.

An interesting attempt to dispose of these two difficulties has been undertaken by the "Institut Scientifique de Recherches Économique et Sociales" directed by Rist, in the volume *Écarts de prix France—Étranger* published in September 1936. The institute surveyed department stores in different

11 See among others Aftalion, *L'Équilibre* etc. *op. cit.*, p. 389.

countries to directly compare retail prices. The findings were what might have been expected. At the exchange rates applied in June 1936, most French prices were higher than in all other countries except perhaps Switzerland. But short of setting out once again to construct indices, in which case the difficulties that were meant to be avoided would show up anew, this method can obviously provide nothing but snapshots, while it is mainly the comparative trend that matters for determining the problem.

Indeed, we know from Ricardo that the notion of buying-power parity and international price equilibrium does not imply the necessity of internationally *identical* price levels, and consequently the finding that at a certain time prices in one country are higher than in another does not at all mean that there is an imbalance between the prices and economies of the two countries.[12] There have always been situations where life is more expensive in some countries than in others (the Netherlands, the United States before the war) without these countries feeling the slightest need to adjust their prices or their currency. The higher price and income structures in these countries was by no means seen as an evil that needed to be ended as soon as possible, but rather as a sign of wealth and prosperity. This is because the long-term relative price rises or continuously higher prices in these countries result from changes in basic circumstances or from a different economic structure, things that are certainly favorable to the countries in question.

Assuming an initial price equilibrium between France and England, an equilibrium that can indeed exist despite important actual disparities, we can say that the franc is overvalued relative to the pound when French prices rise relative to English prices without any change in the economic structure in either France or England that might justify such a shift. And it is clear that in this case the relative price rise in France will cause the unfavorable economic consequences that we have seen.

Because we can eliminate the hypothesis of a relative change in economic structure in the space of a few years, especially for countries such as France and England, with economic structures that are comparable, we can examine the overvaluation of the franc through the relative movements of French and English prices, taking the latter as indicators of the world level. We have plotted the curves of wholesale prices (foodstuffs, industrial materials and general index) for the two countries, as well as retail prices (containing mainly foodstuffs), the cost of living, and wages, from 1929 to 1937. For Great Britain the

12 See Cabiati, *op. cit.*, pp. 54 and 72; Aftalion, *op. cit.*, p. 380.

curves bifurcate in October 1931, one expressing the index in national currency, the other the gold index, and likewise for France in October 1936. For all these curves the base year is 1913. In addition, we have plotted the price curves of the export goods of the two countries, but for statistical reasons we could not take 1913 as the base year. We have therefore assumed—arbitrarily—that in 1929 English prices were 10% higher than French prices. What is even more important for these indices than for the others is the relative movement of the curves rather than their absolute positions (see Appendix II for detailed explanations of the sources and construction of the indices).

b) The facts according to the statistical study

What emerges from the graphic representation (see graphs below) can be summarized as follows (here we examine the trend only up to September 1936): that the general trend of all the curves is the same. For all price categories as well as for salaries the French indexes move more or less below the British ones. The latter move closer to the French indices up until 1931. Then, after the British devaluation the French indexes soon find themselves more or less above the English gold indexes and make more or less successful efforts to draw close to them again. They are all below the British sterling indices, which remain very stable with an upward trend starting in 1934.

For two sets of indices, it is apparent that the disparity was never very severe, and that French price deflation almost succeeded in offsetting the 40% devaluation of the pound. These are the price curves of industrial materials and export products, two cases we have already given the reasons for. The wholesale prices of industrial materials are for the most part precisely the prices set by an international market (London in general) and which translate through the exchange rates into the various national currencies. They generally enter industrial countries duty-free or nearly so, and their gold prices therefore cannot fluctuate much. The adjustment of French export-goods prices is also easily explained. Under the pressure of international competition, French exports had to try to make up through lower prices what England had gained through devaluation. This adaptation, which, moreover, remains imperfect, by no means exemplifies that of the export industry in general. We will indicate below the viewpoint from which exports must be seen to reach a conclusion regarding overvaluation.

The most notable and in my opinion fundamental dissimilarity is between the French wholesale food price index and the wholesale industrial commodity price index. While the French curve in the latter case always remains fairly close to the British gold-index, the two gold-price curves for foodstuffs reveal considerable disparities.

The main lines of movement of the French food index are shared by the indexes of retail prices, cost of living, and wages. In fact, the retail price index shows a consistent parallel with the wholesale food price index,[13] while the cost-of-living index strongly resembles the retail price index. Finally, the wage index is quite comparable to the cost-of-living index. In the order of their enumeration, it is only the *amplitude* of the movements that increasingly diminishes, for reasons that are easily understood. The basic difference is between the wholesale prices of industrial materials, reflected in world prices, and all the other indices—which represent domestic prices that are largely independent of the world standard.

If we now examine the development of the disparities between the French and English curves, we can divide the overall period in question into four distinct phases for all the curves except for that of industrial materials.

1. From 1929 to September 1931 we have an undervaluation of the franc (overvaluation of the pound) that is very uneven across the different indices. French wholesale prices in 1929 are only 10% to 15% below English prices (relative to 1913), retail prices are 20% below them, cost of living 32%, and wages 41% (in October 1928). By 1931 all these disparities have greatly diminished or have indeed shifted into disparities in the opposite direction, due to the combined effect of the French upturn and the British downturn. Thus, it is safe to say that the prewar balance between English and French prices was on the verge of being restored when the devaluation of the pound created a new imbalance in the opposite direction from the previous one.
2. From September 1931 to the beginning of 1934 the overvaluation of the franc reached its highest point. Wholesale prices of foodstuffs were 54% higher than English prices, retail prices 40% higher, the cost of living 25%, and wages (in October) 23%.
3. From the beginning of 1934 to the middle of 1935 French deflation brought prices down sharply, while English prices remained stationary or increased slightly. In this way the disparities were reduced—in July

13 Prof. Aftalion demonstrated already in 1931 in his book *L'or et sa distribution mondiale* that the so-called disparity between wholesale and retail prices in France mainly comes down to the disparity in wholesale prices for industrial materials and foodstuffs.

of 1935 the difference was only 13% for wholesale foodstuff prices and retail prices, 10% for cost of living, and 18% for salaries (October).

4. From July 1935 to September 1936 French prices rose much more steeply than British prices, and disparities thus increased. In July 1936 the difference for foodstuffs was 58%, and for living costs 15%, while disparities in industrial commodity prices had also risen to 25%.

c) Lessons of the French experience: the economic limits of deflation

This analysis of the facts points to several conclusions. It was the rise in French domestic prices in 1930–1931 and their continued resistance to decline that led to the overvaluation of the franc up to its peak in 1934. The rise in 1930–1931 can be explained by bad harvests, agricultural protection during these years, and the general increase in purchasing power that persisted until the end of 1930, along with the inflows of gold. The continuing resistance to decline was due to economic and social factors independent of the will of the government (a decline in retail prices, living costs, and wages that was less steep than that of wholesale prices), but was largely due to the effectiveness of the policy of quotas and the protection of the agricultural market.

The period of deflation in 1934–1935 was due to the persistence of the crisis in France and especially to the collapse of agricultural prices—that is, the failure of the agrarian policy pursued by successive governments, which was brought about by the bountiful harvests of 1933 and 1934. In this way, what was on the one hand celebrated in the B. F.'s 1934 and 1935 annual reports as a great success—the adaptation of French prices to international prices—was the cause of serious concern not only for farmers but also for the Minister of Agriculture and the government. This "adaptation" had barely begun making headway when all the political parties, far from celebrating it, published programs to "re-evaluate the prices of products of the earth"—programs, that is, that would make the adaptation impossible. And in the second half of 1935 when agricultural prices rose again, there was general rejoicing at the recovery of the agricultural market. There was no concern that this would contribute to the overvaluation of the franc in general and to the rise in the cost of living in particular, a rise that would be fatally followed by demands for higher wages, which in turn would increase export difficulties.

It would of course be senseless to blame agriculture alone for the non-adaptation of French prices. What it gives us is a particularly clear example of the resistance and the contradictions inherent in deflation beyond a certain limit. But the reason for the strength of such resistance was clearly in the cost of living in the countryside, agricultural wages and the cost of industrial products used by the farmers, which did not fall in the same proportion as selling prices. It is therefore the rigidity of the whole economic system (the incompressibility of fixed commercial expenditures, the organized resistance of workers to the downturn, the isolation of a domestic world price market due to the quantitative limitation of imports), which doomed deflation. As Cabiati, *op. cit.*, p. 609, writes: "The example of England in 1925–1931 and the gold blockage of 1932–1936, suggest that under current social conditions the attempt to reduce costs in currency is doomed to fail unless the reduction is very small." And further on, p. 613: "The deflation process, when that point is passed, triggers a series of government measures aimed at paralyzing the effects of deflation itself—that is, making the effects prevent the cause from operating. The consequence is that the domestic economy and the redistribution of wealth are successively displaced I. by deflation, and II. by the remedies taken to paralyze deflation. This series of blows falls on the most diverse classes of the population, and the undeserved gains of some do not compensate for the equally undeserved losses of others. It is a redistribution of wealth that is produced at random and therefore in the most arbitrary forms and with the most unpredictable consequences."

Let us turn to an important argument from the opponents of devaluation. The disparity between French and foreign prices, it is frequently argued, can be reduced not only by a decline in French prices, but also by a 'deus ex machina' in the form of a rise in world prices, which actually took place from 1935 onward. But the preceding analysis leaves this proposition no hope because the world prices of raw materials have little to do with the fundamental disparity. When they go down, the corresponding prices in France follow, and when they go up French prices are dragged along as well. But this rise leaves the ratio of French and foreign domestic prices relatively unchanged, and consequently the overvaluation of the franc as well.

Table 4.5. *French and British Comparative Indices in 1935 Annual Average (1929 = 100)*

	France	England	Difference
	(1)	(2)	[(1): (2)] × (100)
Export prod. prices	56	47	119
Industrial materials	60	47	128
Wholesale prices gen. ind.	58	42	138
Foodstuffs	56	40	140
Retail prices	72	49	147
Cost of living	86	52	165
Wages (October 1935)	98	58	170
Long-term interest rate	106	71	–
Industrial prod.	67	97	–

As an illustration of the difference in the adjustment of French prices to English gold prices from 1929 to the typical deflation year 1935, the following table shows the averages of the different 1935 indices in relation to 1929 in France and England and the quotients of the French indices through the English gold indices—i.e., the disparities in prices relative to 1929 (recall that at that time the franc was undervalued and the pound overvalued). The different prices follow one another in the order of their adjustment. Long-term interest rate indices (capitalization rate of fixed income values) and industrial production indices have been added as benchmarks for comparison with the general economic situation.

d) From hidden contradiction to open contradiction

We have already seen how, in the monetary and financial sphere, deflation caused its exact opposite in 1936—inflation. We will now observe the same phenomenon in the economic sphere.

Up until 1936 it was at least recognized that the alternative of either deflation or devaluation was well founded. A decision was made at the time in favor of deflation but without the ability or willingness to undertake it seriously. The formula proclaimed by the Blum government was "neither deflation nor devaluation," an unworkable formula unless it leads to exchange controls and the division of the currency into two types for external and internal use. The contradictions that had been latent and hidden until then became open and obvious with the social laws passed as a result of the June 1936 strikes. The Matignon agreement of June 7, 1936, between the General

Confederation of Labor and the General Confederation of French Businesses provided for wage increases of 12% on average (the actual increases were often much higher), two weeks of paid leave per year, and a 40-hour week, with no decrease in wages. The hourly wage increase resulting from these measures thus amounted to 35%–40%. As Dr. Einzig correctly writes (*World Finance, 1935–1937*, p. 182): "What took place in France after the advent of the Blum government represented nothing less than an attempt to square the circle. It is possible within certain limits for a government to defend an overvalued currency through drastic deflationary measures. It is also possible to take various measures that cause a drastic increase in the cost of production. What is completely impossible is trying to combine the two purposes—defending the franc while at the same time intentionally increasing its overvaluation."

The government was in fact aware of this impossibility. As early as July it began negotiations with the British and American governments for the now inevitable realignment, and, in the Chamber, it declared itself particularly opposed to "unilateral devaluation," which suggested that it would not oppose a devaluation coordinated with the Anglo-Saxon monetary authorities. It is more than doubtful, however, whether the government gained through inter-party agreements what it lost by putting off the inevitable devaluation for three long months.

2) Exports and the balance of payments

The most immediate negative effects of devaluing a currency should be a reduction in its exports, an increase in its imports, and a consequent disequilibrium in the balance of payments and in gold losses. These losses should then be the agent of "re-balancing" through the price deflation they cause or the devaluation that they trigger. Rather than noting overvaluation directly with regard to price inequality as before, it will now be interesting to seek it in its effects on foreign trade and the balance of payments.

In an article in *Economica*,[14] Prof. Whale has argued that this is the only method of ascertaining overvaluation with certainty because of the previously mentioned statistical and economic difficulties inherent in international price comparisons. According to him, only an "undue" deterioration in the balance of payments, a disproportionate decline in exports relative to imports and to other countries' exports, will give a sure indication of a currency's overvaluation. The difficulty obviously lies in distinguishing what is undue, and distinguishing what is caused by price differences and production costs alone

14 "International trade in the absence of an international standard," February 1936.

from what could be caused by a change in the basic circumstances of international trade—e.g., countries' moving towards autonomy, customs barriers, the reduced buying power of importing countries. But it would seem that these changes ought to affect two countries exporting mainly manufactured goods to the same extent. The French export industry has proved to be particularly exposed to a decline in purchasing power, as this leads to a more than proportional contraction in purchases of luxury items which hold an important place in French exports. The influence of this factor should not be overstated, however, since the share of luxury goods exports (including silk fabric exports) in total French exports is only about 15%, and this share has decreased significantly during the crisis.

a) Comparison of French and British exports from 1929 to 1936

Therefore, a comparison showing the relative variation of French and British exports will illustrate their respective monetary positions. We will omit the import comparison because, largely thanks to quotas, price differences in France have been prevented from exerting their natural influence on imports. In making export comparisons, consideration of export *values* alone is insufficient and can sometimes lead to completely erroneous conclusions (for the following observations see the table of English and French export indices). It has been possible to show that the French share in world exports rose from 1929 to 1934 from 5,95% to 6,15%, while the British share fell from 10,75% to 10,47%. Analyzing these figures, somewhat surprising at first glance, we find however that there was decline in the British share only from 1929 to 1931 and that after that there was a continuous rise, and that on the other hand the French share has been falling since 1931.

At the same time, taking 1929 as a base, the gold-values of British and French exports in 1934 were still 33,5% and 36,0%, respectively, and only in 1935 did the French figure fall a bit below the British one (31,4 vs. 31,9). Again, in this case it may be noted that the British decrease happened before 1931, and the French mostly after that year. One might see it as perfectly correct that the decline in French exports should catch up with the British exports that had previously outdistanced them. Going by the figures quoted, the imbalance that had developed between French and British exports up to 1931 seems to disappear in the years that follow, and—until 1936 at least—there appears to be no new imbalance, nor any serious overvaluation of the franc (this conclusion comes from the *Revue du Commerce Mondial* of 1933 and 1934). Is this really the case or should we consider a comparison based on export values alone to be insufficient?

The value of exports is the product of volume and price. If the value goes down, the cause may be a greater reduction in prices than in volume or vice versa, or else a decline of equal proportion in volume and prices. The same relative change in the export value of two countries can therefore hide profound differences in the relative changes in prices and volumes.

Table 4.6. *Comparative Movement of French and British Exports (1929–1936)*

Volume (1929 = 100)		
	France	England
1930	89,1	81,9
1931	76,9	62,4
1932	58,7	62,9
1933	59,7	64,4
1934	62,1	69,1
1935	53,7	74,8
1936	50,7	76,2

Price (1929 = 100)				
	France		**England**	
	Gold	**Francs**	**Gold**	**Pounds**
1930	96,4	–	95,5	–
1931	80,4	–	80,0	85,5
1932	67,6	–	57,4	79,5
1933	62,6	–	53,3	78,3
1934	60,4	–	48,5	78,6
1935	58,5	–	46,7	78,1
1936	55,9	61,6	47,9	79,2

Value						
	1929=100				**in % of global exports**	
	France		**England**		**France**	**England**
	Gold	**Francs**	**Gold**	**Pounds**		
1929	100,0	100,0	100,0	100,0	6,0	10,8
1930	86,0	–	78,2	–	6,3	10,5
1931	61,1	–	49,9	53,4	6,3	9,4
1932	39,7	–	36,1	50,1	6,0	9,4
1933	37,4	–	34,3	50,4	6,2	10,4
1934	36,0	–	33,5	54,3	6,2	10,5
1935	31,4	–	34,9	58,4	5,3	10,8
1936	28,3	31,2	36,5	60,4	4,5	10,6

These figures come from the *Revue du Commerce Mondial*, published annually by the League of Nations. World export percentages are skewed for 1935 and 1936 by an absence of statistics due first to sanctions against Italy and then to the Spanish Civil War.

This is especially true for the period and the two countries under consideration, since the British devaluation did not cause an increase in domestic prices and because the volume of British exports increased sharply after 1931. In a country that adheres to the gold standard the reduction in export goods prices will seek to compensate for the devaluation in foreign currencies, but will fully succeed only when 1) the deflation of prices and production costs is extremely severe, or if 2) the exporting industries sell at a loss, making up for it through premiums or by selling the other portion of their products on the domestic market at elevated prices. This is most likely what happened in Italy where the price of exports remained below the gold prices of British exports until 1934. Italy was able in this way to maintain a relatively very high volume of exports. But it is clear that only a country where state intervention in the economy is of great importance could achieve such results.

In France events followed a different course. Exports could not and did not fully adjust their prices to the gold prices of British exports. Under the pressure of competition, this price category adapted more than any other (as we have seen). But for one thing, even the smallest difference between the export prices of two countries exporting similar products will have an immediate effect in the sense of lowering the export volumes of the higher-cost country. And most importantly, there is too often a tendency to look at exports solely from a demand perspective. It is readily asserted that markets "shut out our products," but what likely takes place just as often when we note a decrease in exports is that marginal exporters are neither able nor willing to export at prices which, while bearable to their peers, are out of touch with production costs. Indeed, one could imagine a case where the prices of French export goods adjusted completely to English gold prices, but at a level so low that it could be applied and borne only by a small minority of French exporters, forcing a large part of the French export industry to give up and go out of business.

What actually happened was that relative to 1929 the quantity and price of French exports declined in roughly the same proportion, while for England *the decline in gold prices was greater and the reduction in volume much smaller than in France as early as 1932*, but the effect of this was precisely that the *values* (products of volume and prices) of exports did not incur major relative changes until 1936, and that the reduction in English export value remained greater than the French reduction up until 1935 (again in relation to 1929).

It appears therefore that it is primarily the comparison of volumes of exports that provides us with a sure index of the overvaluation of one currency relative to the other for the case now under review. (I do not want to generalize too much because the above line of reasoning is valid generally only on the hypothesis of a "ceteris paribus" that is always difficult to achieve). For the same reasons, the overvaluation of the pound against the franc in the period before 1931 appears much more conclusive when comparing the trend in export volumes rather than the trend in values.

The fall in exports having also been much greater than the general decline in production, what we witnessed in France after the crisis was the same process of splitting the whole economy into "sheltered" and "unsheltered" sectors that England experienced after the war. This was brought out in a recent statistical study comparing the dividends, benefits and share prices of companies belonging to these two sectors.[15] The conclusion of this study is that for struggling businesses, the issue is not simply one of eliminating crises, and unhealthy, poorly managed establishments, but is rather an organic imbalance between industries working mainly for export and not cartelized on the one hand and industries working mainly for the domestic market and cartelized on the other.

b) The direct and indirect effects of overvaluation on the balance of payments and the balance of trade

The overvaluation of the franc between 1932 and 1935 is thus a result of the movement of French and British price curves and from the comparative volumes of French and British exports. Lastly, we therefore have to look at the development of the balance of payments and the balance of trade in this regard. This is particularly important since a deficit in these balances, according to the theory that has come to be customarily designated as classical, should cause general deflation through gold losses and failing this a devaluation that would make the overvaluation disappear. Now despite the very sharp decline in income from tourism, this regulatory mechanism predicted by theory has not always worked—for several reasons.

15 Dessirier, "Secteur abrité et non-abritè de l'Economie francaise," *Revue d'Économie Politique*, 1935, July–August, continued in the article: "L'Économie française devant la dévaluation," *Revue d'Économie Politique*, 1936, September–October.

1. As shown above, the determining element in gold movements during the crisis was not the balance of trade, income from tourism and other entries in the balance of payments directly subject to the influence of overvaluation, but rather capital movements that often took into account factors totally unrelated to comparative price developments in France and abroad. Thus, the huge gold inflows in 1930/1931, 1932 and 1934 were sharply contrary to the position of the income balance and largely offset its deficits so that they aggravated rather than alleviated the imbalance between French and foreign prices.

Nor were the gold movements in 1933 and especially in 1935 and 1936 driven by the state of the income balance, as gold outflows were much greater than the deficits in this balance. The outflows of gold were once again determined by capital movements, but this time the movements went in the right direction, so that after a struggle of more than a year, the franc "surrendered." This time the "psychological factor" lent valuable support to the economic laws, whose action it had impeded on other occasions.[16] So in the end, overvaluation exerted the influence on the balance of payments that was called for by theory. It did so mainly through the medium of the psychological factor, with distrust of the franc expressing itself through capital exports and backwardization on franc futures. There is no doubt that it was the overvaluation of the franc, as we have noted (see p. 113–4) that directly or indirectly caused these phenomena. In this way, on the strength of the French experience, and perhaps the British as well, one might construct a new theory that Prof. Aftalion would classify (and reject) under the name "theory of re-balancing prices and the balance of payments through the psychological movements of capital."

2. The importance of these movements turns out to be even greater if we note the almost complete absence of any effects of the overvaluation on the elements of the balance of payments that normally ought to be most susceptible to it. The figures for the income balance and its main element, the trade balance, after 1929, were:

16 It is odd that Prof. Aftalion, who in his aforementioned book *L'équilibre dans les relations économiques internationales* gives an almost exhaustive list of the factors of equilibrium, disequilibrium, and the "re-balancing" of prices and the balance of payments, insisting especially on the psychological aspect of these problems, does not note the possibility of the action of psychological movements of capital, which he mentions only in connection with his theory of the balance of payments.

Table 4.7.

	Income balance deficit	Trade balance deficit
1929	– 1.056	– 8.081
1930	– 2.083	– 9.675
1931	– 4.118	– 11.770
1932	– 4.917	– 10.102
1933	– 2.950	– 9.992
1934	– 1.250	– 5.249
1935	– 400	– 5.482
1936	?	– 9.949
(in millions of francs)		

It is comprising the balance of trade, income from tourism and shipping, interest payments and other less important items—i.e., ultimately all the items in the balance of payments except gold and capital movements since the payment of capital debts (depreciation, repairs etc.) is also excluded.

Income and trade balance deficits were cut in half between 1931/1932 and 1934/1935. This lack of an overvaluation effect is easily explained, first and foremost by the quota policy that began in 1932, preventing a reaction of imports to French price levels. The sharp reduction in the deficit should also be attributed in large part to the economic crisis, which brought down French orders for raw industrial materials, a major component of imports. Conversely, the increase in the deficit in 1936 was mainly due to new orders from industry and higher commodity prices.

From a more general point of view, the assets and liabilities of the balances examined decreased during the crisis, and if there was a steeper decline in assets than in liabilities—that is, if the relative deficit increased, this caused a much smaller increase or indeed a decrease in the absolute deficit in the countries with debit balances. An elementary numerical example will illustrate this phenomenon. Suppose a country that exports 100 and imports 200. Its deficit is 100 or $33^1/_3$% of total trade. The country is in economic crisis and its currency is overvalued. As a consequence of the crisis its imports and exports contract, but, because of the overvaluation, exports decrease more than imports, by 75% and 50% respectively. The country will therefore export 25 and import 100. We see that in spite of the proportionally greater decrease in exports, the absolute deficit is reduced from 100 to 75, while the relative deficit expressed as a percentage of total trade has of course risen (from $33^1/_3$% to 60%).

But the theory that posits such a readjustment through gold movements and their consequences clearly takes into consideration only the absolute value of the deficit. We must therefore conclude that its mechanism will work poorly in times of crisis and conversely too well in times of prosperity in countries with an initial debit balance. The reverse is true for countries with a balance initially in credit.[17]

oOo

17 Finally, the discussion of import and export demand elasticity that we will develop concerning the effects of devaluation on the trade balance applies 'mutatis mutandis' to the corresponding effects of the overvaluation.

II. The first devaluation of the franc (September 1936–June 1937) and its economic effects

1) The debates surrounding devaluation

The three economic arguments[18] favoring devaluation were:

1. Devaluation would bring down French gold prices as compared with foreign prices and would in this way revive the export industry.
2. It would at the same time mark the end of the economic contraction and through the influence of rising domestic prices would trigger the expansionist trend that had long been held back.
3. As far as the differential movements of prices, we would see the opposite of what occurred in the deflation—wholesale prices of industrial materials, closely linked to world prices, would rise sharply, while the relative rigidity and isolation of the French economy would keep tight limits on the rise of agricultural prices, retail prices, and production costs.

In this way the viability of businesses would be automatically reconstituted.

This third argument also serves as a response to the opponents of devaluation who imagined a contradiction between the devaluation's two main goals of. In fact, there would be a price rise in France, but for most prices the rise would not be proportional to the shrinking of the franc.

It is often said that devaluation is an indirect, disguised—indeed shameful—way to achieve what could not be or was not achieved directly through deflation. Actually, the words "direct" and "indirect" mean very little if currency is viewed as an ordinary commodity in exchanges between nations, a Ricardian principle that Cambiati appropriately mentioned in his book (see pp. 74 and 473).

When the British-French trade balance was upset by the devaluation of the pound in such a way that the franc acquired a value (expressed in goods) that was higher in England than in France, it is perfectly immaterial whether the difference thus produced was equalized by increasing the purchasing power

18 The monetary argument has already been discussed: capital inflow following the devaluation, see p. . Finally, the financial argument—that is, the improvement of the public finance situation is merely a particularly important corollary of the economic and monetary arguments.

of the franc in France (the principle of deflation) or decreasing it in England (the principle of devaluation).

If we must at all costs talk about direct and indirect adjustment, it seems to me that the *direct* way of achieving a balance upset solely by foreign monetary events is rather a monetary "alignment." Penance is conceivable only if a sin has been previously committed, and it would be absurd to want to condemn the French economy to the "penance" of deflation whenever the British or American authorities decide to decrease the gold weight of the pound or the dollar.

The formula by which devaluation is (or must be in order to succeed) indirect deflation served mainly to combat the sliding wage scale that was at first meant to be attached to the Monetary Law of October 1, 1936. It was then proposed to maintain real wages by increasing them in proportion to the rise in the cost of living, not to the reduction in the value of money as Cabiati, *op. cit.*, p. 549, mistakenly writes. Understood in this way, the formula conveys the idea that devaluation must of necessity cause a decrease in real wages as a result of the rise in the cost of living, and that if it did not, the devaluation would be futile. Now, this is incorrect—the example of England demonstrates this quite clearly. In order for the sliding-scale system to cancel out the benefit of devaluation, the cost of living, dragging wages along with it, would have to rise in the same proportion as devaluation—i.e., by 25%, 43%, 66%, and 100% if devaluation is 20%, 30%, 40%, and 50% respectively, which is extremely unlikely. The drawback of the sliding scale is elsewhere—introducing it means that the authorities anticipate and accept rising prices, that workers will be indifferent to it since they are sure it will not hurt them, and that sellers will feel justified in applying it knowing that demand will not be diminished. In this way the sliding scale becomes an important psychological factor pushing for a rise, which should instead be kept within the natural limits set by the rising prices of imported products. For this reason, it is preferable first to fight speculative price rises, and if a major increase in the cost of living occurs in spite of this there will always be time to adjust salaries. This was finally established with the law of October 1, 1936, which, as in the case of price controls, provided for the establishment of compulsory mediation and arbitration for labor disputes that occurred as a result of rising costs of living.

2) The economic effects of the September devaluation

Although the future course of the second devaluation of the franc on July 1, 1937, cannot yet be predicted, we can in this study give the final results of the first devaluation of about 30%, which lasted nine months.

Let us review the arguments of the devaluationists—in a somewhat reversed order—and see if they have in fact been proven right.

1. The devaluation truly made the economic recovery "take off," and significant figures can be cited supporting the renewal of trade activities. No more could reasonably have been asked, and the halt or even the slowdown in production noted for the past few months is likely due to the precipitous implementation of the 40-hour week and the still abnormally high interest rates.
2. Price developments also confirm the hopes of devaluationists, which is evident from the table below:

Table 4.8.

Prices in June 1937 (August 1936 = 100)	
Wholesale prices, industrial materials	149
Wholesale prices, general index	136
Wholesale prices, foodstuffs	124
Retail prices	124
Cost of living (II. trimester 1937)	120

The same price categories that had proved to be most resistant to decline during the period of deflation (see p. 119–20) thus did better than the others at resisting the rise, which for industrial materials was largely due not only to the devaluation of the franc but also to the rise in world prices.

In this way a certain balance between wholesale and retail prices was reestablished, as was to a lesser extent the balance between production costs and selling prices, whose rise certainly more than offset the increase in hourly wages caused by the 40-hour week.

3. But more interesting to us is the devaluation's effect on overvaluation and foreign trade. Here our conclusions are less positive.

The opponents of the devaluation had argued that the monetary operation would not bring the hoped-for benefits for exports for the following reasons:

a) The increase in the price of imports would drive up domestic prices. While this is unarguable, the price increase due to this factor is certainly less than the reduced exchange rate. Its action can moreover be diminished by reducing the customs tariffs affecting imported products (there was indeed a reduction in certain tariffs in October 1936, but these reductions were removed recently with the new devaluation of the franc). Therefore, in this argument there is nothing the devaluationists should be scared of.

b) A much more obvious danger is the possibility that other currencies (excepting the fatally involved guilder and Swiss franc) could be devalued to cancel the effect of the devaluation of the franc.

c) Or that other countries might, for the same purpose, defend themselves against the cheap French export with higher tariffs, quotas and especially foreign exchange surcharges.

These last two dangers particularly attracted the attention of the French government and, meritoriously, the tripartite agreement eliminated them. But the agreement was concluded with a French quid pro quo—the limitation of the devaluation percentage to a modest figure (30%).

Now although this percentage had been sufficient in 1935 as it was in Belgium, by September 1936 two important circumstances had intervened: an agricultural price rise, and labor laws that had not yet made their full impact on prices at the time of the devaluation. In fact, our curves for French wages and wholesale prices of agricultural products remain higher than the English curves even after the devaluation. This is merely as an indication, since—as noted above—it is the relative movements of the curves that must be taken into account rather than their absolute positions.

Fixing the percentage of the devaluation at too low a level was, along with the gold legislation, the primary error of the September 24 operation. Beyond its not allowing exports expand as much as had been hoped and having a large hand in compromising the return of capital. It is hoped that the new devaluation will restore a true and final balance between French and foreign prices.[19]

It is often stressed that the French devaluation was carried out when world prices were rising, while they were falling at the time of the pound's devaluation. This is certainly of great importance for domestic price movements and as we shall see shortly, for the balance of trade, but since the rise or fall is worldwide, it exerts a specific influence on country-to-country price disparities only to the extent that one country's price level correlates more

19 It is actually possible that at the level reached after the latest decreases, the franc is once again *under*valued.

closely with world prices than the level in another country. Therefore, it is absolutely wrong to say that the worldwide price rise in raw materials up to 1937 stood in the way of French and foreign price adjustments, as shown with great clarity by the graph of the wholesale prices of industrial materials in France and England.[20]

Still left to be examined is the effect of the first franc devaluation on foreign trade.

First of all, we should recall certain theoretical data. The fall in the exchange rate normally produces an almost proportional rise in import prices unless the country in question has a monopoly position as a buyer, in which case the supplier country will be forced to make greater price concessions to avoid too steep a reduction in its sales. This not being true of France, the devaluation's effect would have been almost entirely on import prices. As for export products, their prices will be affected by the increased prices of the imported products that they partly contain, sometimes significant in industrial countries that export skilled labor in the form of goods (textile exports for example). Taking this factor into account, exporters can set themselves two different goals after devaluation: I. increase their sales volume while keeping prices as stable as possible; and II. rebuild profit margins by selling at a higher price in devalued francs. Generally, these two purposes are combined—this is also reflected in price theory—but with the former taking priority. If the price of exports in France went up more than their volume, this was due mainly to the 40% rise in the price of raw materials exports (minerals such as iron, bauxite, etc.), an increase easily explained by the worldwide "boom."

We now need to examine the influence of the rise in franc prices of imported products and the fall in gold prices of exported products on the volume of imports and exports. This influence governs the movement of export and import values and consequently the course of the trade balance.

It is well known that the notion of elasticity of demand is crucial in this matter. When we say that exchange rate depreciation will have a favorable effect on the trade balance, it is generally implied that the two demands for imported and exported products are elastic. In a general sense, international demand for exported products is inelastic if the exporting country occupies a monopolistic position for its exports, while domestic demand for imported products will be inelastic if the importing country mainly imports products

20 A close examination of the differences between the conditions under which the devaluations took place in France and England is beyond the scope of this paper.

that it cannot produce and which its economy at the same time permanently needs. It follows from this that demand in the industrialized countries of western Europe tends to be inelastic in the case of imports, but elastic for exports.

Consider a country in equilibrium. A devaluation may make its balance positive:

I. If the elasticity of demand for imported products is greater than the inelasticity of demand for export products;
II. If the elasticity of demand for export products is greater than the inelasticity of demand for imported products (a requirement for industrial countries);
III. If the demand for imports and exports is elastic in both cases.

Now suppose that the country in question already carries a deficit—say it imports twice what it exports. In this case a devaluation can reduce the deficit only:

I. If the elasticity of demand for import products is *more than double* the inelasticity of demand for export products.
II. If the elasticity of demand for export products is *more than double* the inelasticity of demand for import products (a requirement for industrial countries).
III. If the demand in both cases is elastic.

It is therefore clear that *the more unfavorable the trade balance situation at the time of devaluation, the more difficult it will be to exert a favorable influence.* It follows I. that the more a devaluation is delayed, the weaker will be its favorable effects on the trade balance, and II. that *the mechanism regulating the effect of exchange rate movements on the balance of payments ceases to operate precisely in cases where its action would be most urgent and necessary.*

Developments in French foreign trade since the September devaluation clearly illustrate the above theoretical deductions, but since in reality economic phenomena never occur in a pure state, certain other elements that have also exerted an influence must be included. The following table shows the figures and indexes for import and export volumes and prices. Monthly averages for the eight months following the devaluation have been given alongside the monthly averages for the previous nine months.

Table 4.9. *Monthly Averages of the Value, Volume, and Prices of Imported and Exported Products for the Eight Months from October 1936 to May 1937. (Monthly average, Jan.-Sept. 1936 = 100)*

	Value	Volume	Price
Imports			
food items	143	105	139
materials required by industry	169	109	155
manufactured items	151	122	124
Total	158	110	144
Exports			
food items	151	135	112
materials required by industry	172	123	140
manufactured items	133	115	116
Total	146	119	126

Table 4.10. *Import and Export Values in Absolute Figures*

	Monthly Averages (millions of francs)						
	January–September 1936				October 1936–May 1937		
	Imp.	Exp.	Diff.		Imp.	Exp.	Diff.
Food items	589	180	–409		845	271	– 547
Raw materials	1.050	334	–616		1.774	573	–1.201
Manufactured items	289	668	370		449	887	438
Total	1.937	1.182	–755		3.068	1.731	–1.337

These figures were extracted in part from the monthly bulletins of the *Statistique générale de la France*. Those necessary for the calculation of the volume and price indexes given above were kindly provided to me by Prof. Huber, Director of the *Statistique générale de la France*.

Regarding exports, an increase of 19% should be noted, and the increase in prices is even greater, due mainly to the rise in raw materials exports, as noted above. The increase in export value thus touches the not negligible share of 46%. But imports increase even more, by 58% (in value), and since imports had been much higher than exports before devaluation, the deficit worsened alarmingly from 775 million francs, the monthly average before devaluation, to 1.337 million francs, which was the monthly average from October 1936 to May 1937.

Looking at the increase in imports we immediately notice an abnormality—the increase in the import volume after the devaluation. The theory perfectly explains the increase in the *value* of imports in the case of inelastic demand, since the price increase will be proportionally greater than the reduction in volume, but the theory always assumes the latter reduction in the absence of a demand curve that rises with the increase in price. The increase in import volume is therefore an exceptional phenomenon that can be explained.

1. For imported raw materials by the economic recovery following the devaluation.
2. For manufactured products for which the increase in volume is greater (22%) by increased purchasing power in the French market that was not matched by a proportional increase in domestic production.

In conclusion, a multitude of causes exerted their combined influence in causing the worsening of the budget deficit.

1. The relative inelasticity of import demand.
2. The international boom in raw materials which, not being immediately followed by a corresponding rise in the prices of manufactured items, worsened the terms of exchange in all industrialized countries.
3. Economic recovery in France's causing an increased demand for materials needed by industry without initially provoking corresponding exports.
4. And finally, the 40-hour week and wage increases, which brought about an increase in purchasing power on the one hand and a slowdown in domestic production on the other.

Of these four factors, the last three can only be passengers, and it would therefore be erroneous to conclude from the current figures that the balance of payments imbalance is deep and permanent—imbalance that after all will be largely eliminated by tourism revenues. The government is nevertheless right to worry about it and recent measures sharply increasing tariffs, along with the second devaluation, may exert a favorable influence.

At the conclusion of this study, a question that arises spontaneously is whether or not the devaluation of the franc in September 1936 succeeded. A negative answer is suggested by the fact that a second one had to be carried out just nine months later.

Indeed, in the financial and monetary spheres the devaluation has not had the felicitous consequences that devaluations have generally brought in other countries. And while in the economic domain it caused an initial economic *démarrage*, a better balance between different price categories and an increase in exports, it did not deliver all that could have been hoped for due to intrinsic causes (too small a devaluation) and the extrinsic reasons cited above.

The first devaluation would thus have been primarily a "sanction," a formulation dear to Jenny, the financial ed. of the *Temps*. It remains to be seen whether the second one, carried out in a more favorable environment and coordinated with a fresh economic and financial effort, will be a remedy.

oOo

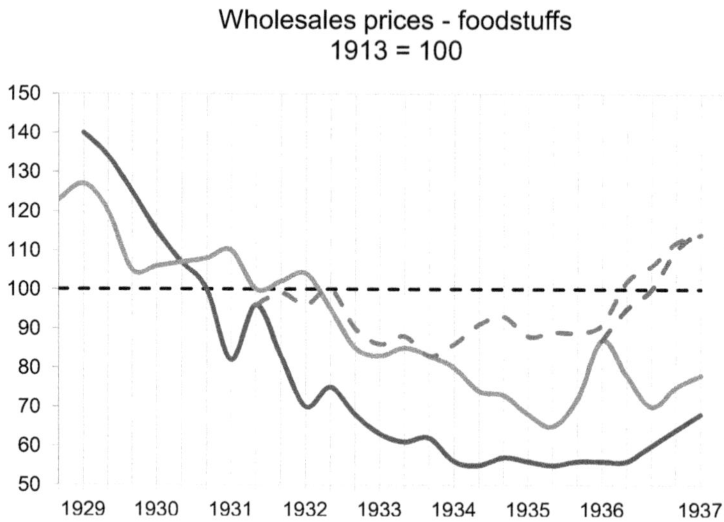

Graph 4.1. *Wholesale Prices—Foodstuffs*

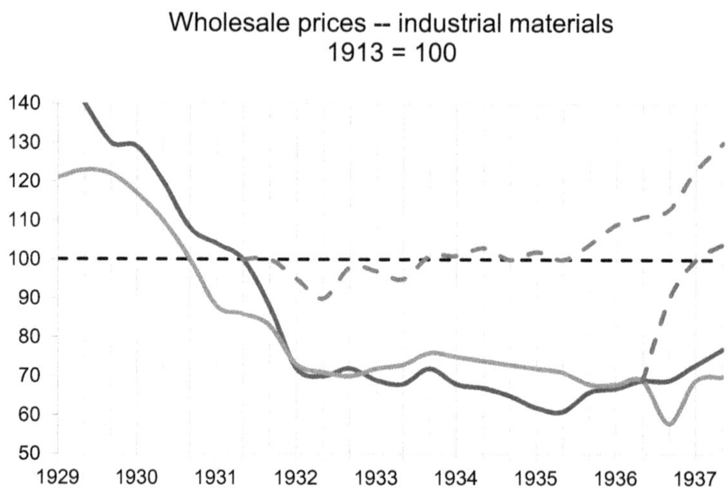

Graph 4.2. *Wholesale Prices—Industrial Materials*

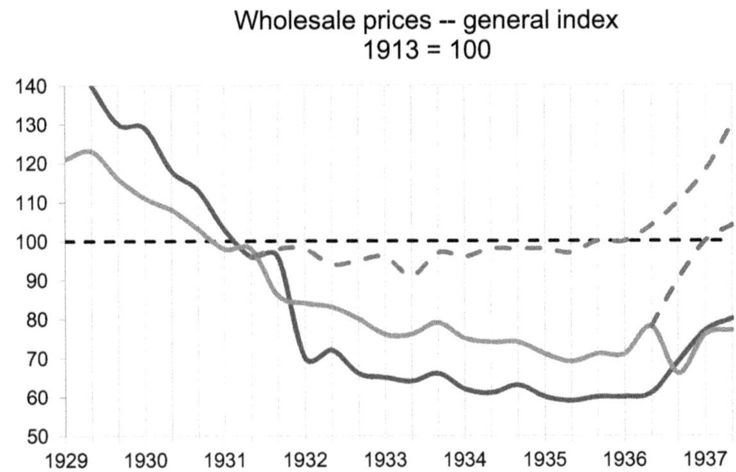

Graph 4.3. *Wholesale Prices—General Index*

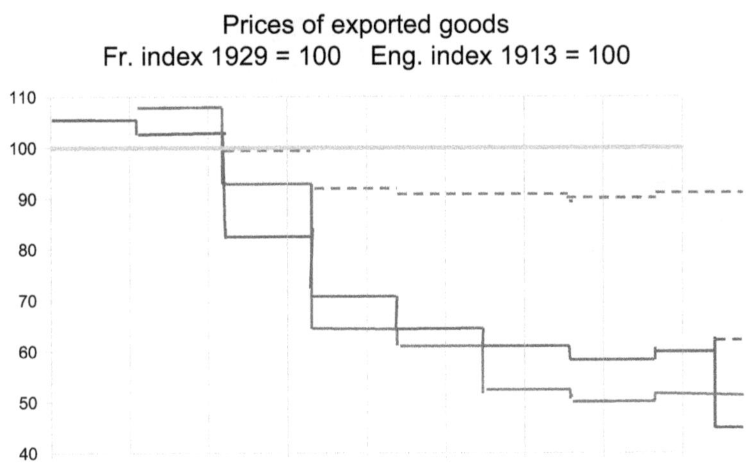

Graph 4.4. *Prices of Exported Goods*

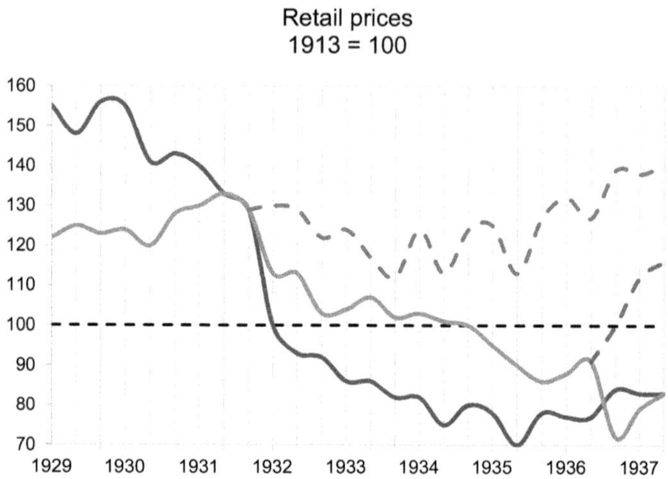

Graph 4.5. *Retail Prices*

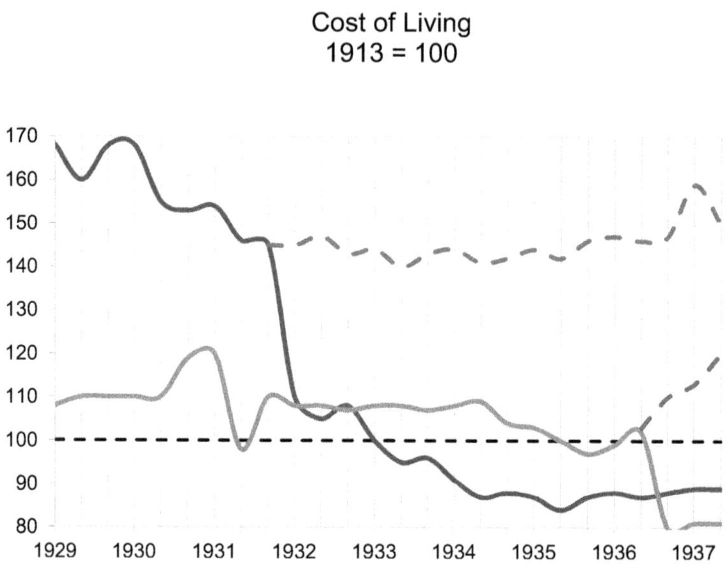

Graph 4.6. *Cost of Living*

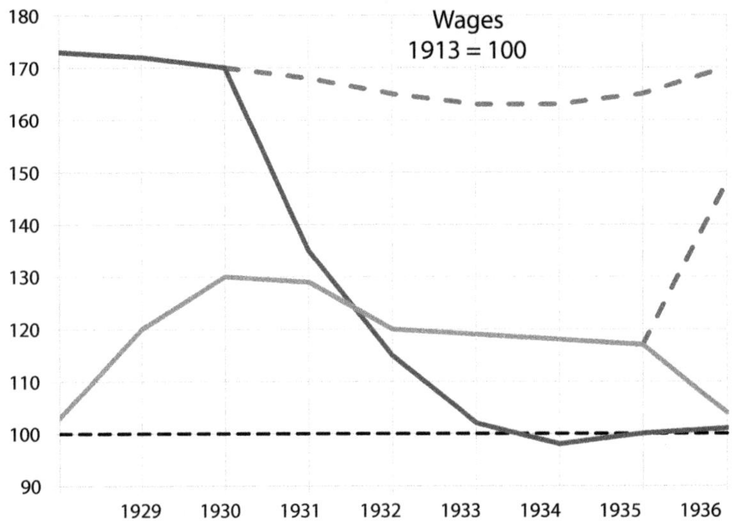

Comparative movement of prices and wages in France and England

French indices British indices
Continuous lines represent gold indices
Dotted lines represent indices in devalued currency

Graph 4.7. *Comparative movement of prices and wages in France and England.*

Appendix I: The Reform of the Charter of the Bank of France (Act of July 24, 1936)

"Against the financial oligarchies," "against the two hundred families," and "make the Bank of France the Bank *for* France" were the slogans that accounted for a good part of the success of the French Popular Front in the May 1936 legislative elections. The reform of the Bank of France, an important point in the joint program of the parties of the left, was a demand that had broad support even outside the usual narrow circle of political organizations. The idea had gradually crystallized in public opinion that the various rulers of France had their headquarters in the "rue du Vieux Colombier," the Napoleonic Institute that—matched only by the codes—had withstood all political upheavals, revolutions and wars. It is therefore no surprise that as soon as the social unrest subsided, the Blum government set to work immediately on the promised reform. After the original draft had undergone some moderating amendments in the Senate, the law on the new charter of the Bank of France was passed by both houses on July 24, 1936.

The Bank, as created by Napoleon in 1803, had the legal status of a corporation, but with important deviations from the general rules in place under the Commercial Code for joint stock companies. The new law left intact the constitution of the Bank as it was—i.e., anonymous; what it re-regulated were precisely the aforementioned deviations from the common law.

One of these irregular stipulations, dictated in its time mainly by practicality, limited the right to attend the general meeting of shareholders to the Bank's 200 strongest French shareholders. (Hence the famous slogan about the "200 families").

The first article of the new law not only eliminated this exception, but created a new one in the opposite direction, stipulating that "The general assembly shall be composed of *all* shareholders of French nationality. All members have the right to vote *whatever the number of shares they possess*."

But this democratization of the shareholders' assembly came hand in hand with a restriction of its powers. Whereas the old assembly elected the *régents* (about whom more below) and the censors in charge of control, the new assembly retained the right only to appoint the latter (Art. 2) along with two advisors to the General Council (Art. 9).

Another extremely important deviation of the Bank's organization from common law was that its governor, who performs the functions of the anonymous corporations' chief executive officer, would be a government appointee, as would the two deputy governors. In this way it was explicitly stated that the management of the central bank must take their cue from national guidelines, the public interest, and that the interests of shareholders should take second place. In reality, however, it was evident that the governor easily fell under the influence of financial groups represented primarily by the "régents" for two reasons. First of all, the governor was required to own personally 100 shares in the Bank, a fortune that generally had to be borrowed from the régents. In their turn, these leading figures of Parisian high finance did not hesitate to dangle before the governor the hope of a handsome bank manager's position upon completion of his tenure.

Thus, the governor—and the same went for his deputies, who each had to own 50 shares—was far from having the necessary independence. To guarantee him this, the new law stipulates in article 3 that "the governor and his two deputy governors shall not be obligated to possess shares in the Bank." Articles 4 and 6 discuss the governor's oath of office, salary and representation allowance. Article 7 prohibits the governor and deputy governors, during the time of performing their duties, from taking any interest in a commercial, industrial or financial enterprise or providing any services or advice. Finally, article 8 aims to protect the governor against attempted bribery, keeping him as far as possible from the influence of promises relating to the time after his term of office. The article in fact states: "The governor or deputy governors who cease to hold office shall continue to receive their salaries for three years, subject to the proviso that during this period they do not engage in any private employment. They are also prohibited during the same period from rendering their services to private businesses and from receiving remunerations for work or advice."

But the most important core of the new law is the organization of the Bank's "General Council," which takes the functions of the "board of régents." Actually, this latter had been the main target of critics of the Bank's administration, and its functions were extremely important. It set the discount rate, determined the terms for discounts, rediscounts and advances, and served as the bank of banks—the supreme regulator of credit.

But the "régents" all belonged to the very tight circle of Parisian "high banking," and here the personal element continued to prevail. Nominally elected at the shareholders' meeting, they were confirmed 'pro forma' and passed on their office to their successors, so that true financial dynasties were created.

The régents were criticized for performing the national task entrusted to them in a way that would suit their own caste interests and for having too narrow and orthodox views on monetary matters. Various political episodes were cited in which the council of régents reportedly would have overthrown the government and subverted its will. The parties on the left regarded it as one of the main strongholds of the famous "*mur d'argent*," and the right admitted that it was an anachronism. In fact, no one—except its members—regretted its disappearance.

The body that replaces the Board of Régents in its powers is the General Council as defined in Articles 9 and 10 of the reform law. It is what in Italy would be called an "organ of corporate structure" in that it is a deliberative body which in addition to government representatives includes representatives of "organized interests." An interesting distinction is made in the law between "economic and social interests" and the "collective interests of the Nation."

Article 9 says: "The bank shall be administered by 20 counselors and supervised by three censors. The governor, deputy governors, counselors and censors form the General Council, in which the censors have an advisory vote."

Two counselors are selected from among the shareholders, 9 represent economic and social interests, and 9 represent the collective interests of the Nation

I. Two are elected by the general assembly from among manufacturers, producers or merchants, excepting those persons who render services through labor or advice or as directors of a banking establishment.

II. One is designated by the National Economic Council from among its vice presidents
One by the high commission of Savings Banks from among its members
One is elected by secret ballot by the staff of the Bank from among the staff members
Six are chosen by the Minister of Finance from lists of three names presented by each of the following organizations:
General Federation of Consumer Cooperatives; General Confederation of French Handicrafts; Association of Presidents of the Chambers of Commerce of France; General Confederation of Labor; Permanent Association of Presidents of Chambers of Agriculture; Commercial professional sections of the National Economic Council

III. Three represent the Minister of Finance, the National Economy and the Colonies, six are 'ex officio' members:
President of the Finance section of the Council of State
Director of the general movements of funds
General Director of the Deposit and Loan Bank

The attorney of Land Credit
Director of National Credit
Director of the National Agricultural Credit Bank
No parliamentarian may serve on the General Council

Article 10. Councilors elected or chosen by a minister upon presentation by interested parties may not serve on the Council for more than three consecutive years. One-third of these members shall be replaced each year. Outgoing councilors may not be reappointed less than three years after leaving the council.

Anticipating that this college is too large or too loosely integrated for continuous administration, Article 11 says: "The General Council of the Bank may delegate all or part of its powers to a permanent committee consisting of the governor, the deputy governors, and four counselors, one of whom shall be chosen by the Minister of Finance from among 'ex officio' members and three designated by the General Council."

This concludes the commentary on the law.*

Democratization of the shareholders' meeting, strengthening of the governor's position and independence, and replacement of the regency Council with a General Council—these are the three cornerstones of the reform of the old Napoleonic Institution.

The Bank of France has not been nationalized. The reform does not involve the transfer of ownership of even a single one of the Bank's shares into the hands of the state. But its management has been placed under the strict and unhindered control of "collective interests." Thus, the character of the bank is transforming itself. It can certainly be said that the elements that are public in nature now clearly prevail over those that are private. And it would be logical to recognize this state of affairs legally, by raising the Central Bank, as in Italy, to the status of an institution under public law.

oOo

* Of the articles, only Article 13 on mandatory rediscounting of floating debt securities, which we have already commented on in its proper place, is of interest.

We should recall, for the sake of completeness, that the management of the Stabilization Fund had been entrusted to a committee of experts last March. But with their elimination in June, the Stabilization Fund again came under the direct administration of the Bank.

The newly created sales *soutien* fund was placed under the administration of the Autonomous Depreciation Fund.

Appendix II: Statistical sources for the graphs

Wholesale prices came from the international index calculated by the London and Cambridge Economic Service specifically for comparing international wholesale prices. The same standards were used to establish the indices for eleven countries with comparable economic structures. The same items are included for each, and their weighting is uniform. The general index is divided into *foodstuffs and industrial materials*. It is calculated based on 1925, but the January, April, July and October indexes are based on 1913. The latter figures were collected, which is why the other indices for these four months also had to be calculated instead of taking quarterly averages.

Retail prices were taken from the British index of 600 cities, and those in Paris from 43 articles, published in both cases by the *Statistique Générale de la France*. The quarterly index for Paris and the British index published by *Statistique Générale* were used for the *cost of living*. The values from the British index were used for the four months cited above because we wanted to compare not only each pair of indices in isolation, but especially the relationships between the different pairs. For this reason, there seems to be less of a disadvantage in combining these two indices than would result from comparing quarterly averages for the cost of living with other indices determined for only one month of each quarter. I have therefore assumed that the indexes for Paris are not quarterly averages but represent the values for the four months cited above.

Comparing *salaries* was more difficult. Taking salaries as an element of production costs—which the present work does—should require an hourly wage rate index. Now the only existing general index in Britain is the Ministry of Labour index for weekly wages. For France, the index of the daily wages of workers in the Paris region was calculated by the *Statistique Générale* according to the annual surveys of the *Conseils des Prud'hommes*. These two indexes actually show workers' earnings and cease to be indices of wages as an element of the cost of production when there are changes in labor time. This is what has now happened in France with the introduction of paid vacations and especially the 40-hour week, and why the increase in the French index in October 1936 does not represent the full increase that the cost of production has undergone as a result of the labor laws. It should be noted, however, that the 40-hour week was not generally applied in French industry until after October 1936, the date when our graph terminates.

The two indexes should be aligned with the 1913/1914 base. The French index is set with 1911 as a base, and it was assumed, following Denuc ("Les fluctuations des salaires et du chômage dans quelques pays," *Bulletin de la Stat Gen*, April-June, 1930), that from 1911 to 1913/1914 French wages increased by about 3%. The English index has the month of December 1924 as a base, so the index calculated by Prof. Bowley has been replaced by the present index. At the time it was shown (*London and Cambridge Econ. Ser. Special Memorandum* N. 28, Bowley, "A new Index Number of wages") that wage rates in 1924 were at 175 in relation to 1914, while actual earnings were at 195. This difference would be due mainly to the displacement of workers into higher-wage industries and to labor relief when piecework wages remained stable. But since it is likely that similar changes occurred in France that the *Statistique Générale* index does not take into account, the English index must be recalculated on the basis of 175 in 1924. Since the French index is compiled in October of each year, it was compared to the value of the English index—which is monthly—only in October of each year.

The *prices of exported products* are from the indexes of the Board of Trade and that of the *Statistique Générale de la France*, indexes also reproduced in the League of Nations publications on world trade. The comparison is annual. Despite differences in calculation the indexes are comparable for short periods.

oOo

Bibliography

I. Periodicals

Revue d'Économie Politique, May–June issues: "La France Économique" (in particular the articles on public finance, the money market and the banks).
Revue de Science et de Législation Financières (quarterly), "Chronique financière française".
Revue Politique et Parlementaire (monthly), "Chronique financière" (F. Jenny).
L'Activité Économique (monthly publication of the "Institut de recherches économique et sociales" directed by C. Rist).
Le Temps Financier, weekly supplement of *Temps*.
L'information Économique et Financière.
Bulletin Quotidien (and its annual supplements on the French economy, banking and foreign trade).
Statistique Générale de la France (annual, quarterly and monthly bulletins).
League of Nations. *Revue du Commerce Mondial* (annual), *Monnaies et Banques* (annual).
Revue de Législation et de Statistique Comparée, Text of budget laws and other finance laws.
Banque de France. *Annual reports.*
The Economist.

II. General works

Cabiati. (1937). *Fisiologia e Patologia Economica negli scambi della ricchezza fra gli Stati.* Torino.
Aftalion. (1937). *L'équilibre dans les relatons économiques internationales.* Paris.
Ohlin. (1935). *Interregional and International Trade*, Cambridge University Press.
Whale. (1934). *International trade.* London.
Whale. (1936, February). International Trade in the absence of an International Standard. *Economica.*
Nogaro. (1935). *La monnaie et les phénomènes monétaires contemporains.* Paris.
Einzig. (1937). *The theory of forward exchange.* London.
Einzig. (1937). *World Finance 1935–1937.* London.
Royal Institute of International Affairs. (1934). *The future of monetary policy.* London.
Chambre de Commerce Internationale. (1936). *Reconstruction Économique Internationale* (Reports by Profs. Ohlin and Gregory). Paris.
Lhomme. (1936). *Le taux de l'intérêt et l'évolution économique 1919–1935.* Paris.
Alberti. (1937). *La sconfitta dell'oro.* Milano.

III. Works referring exclusively to the French monetary, financial and economic situation

Pirou. (1936). *La monnaie française depuis la guerre 1914–1936.* Paris.
Sapiens. (1936). *Une Hypothèse: La dévaluation française en 1936.* Paris.

Nogaro. (1935, January). Le problème de la dévaluation en France. *Revue Économique Internationale.*
Duchemin. (1934). *Yaurait-t-il intérêt a dévaluer le franc?* Paris.
Reynaud, P. (1934, September 12). Discours à la Chambre des députés. *Information.*
Europe Nouvelle, Special issue on devaluation, January 1936.
Bordar and Schwob. (1936). L'inflation et la dévaluation. *Annales du droit et des Sciences Sociales.*
Dessirier. (1935, June–August). Secteur abrité et non abrité dans le déséquilibre actuel de l'économie française. *Revue d'Économie Politique.*
Dessirier. (1936, September–October). L'Économie Française devant la Dévaluation. *Revue d'Économie Politique.*
Jéramec. (1935, October–December). La Fonction Exportatrice dans l'Économie Françaises. *Bulletin de la Statistique Générale de la France.*
Institut Scientifique de Recherches Économiques et Sociales. (1936). *Écarts de prix France-Étranger*. Paris.
Strohl. (1935, December). La circulation des billets de 1.000 et de 500 francs depuis la stabilisation du franc. *Revue Politique et Parlementaire.*
Einzig. (1934). *France's Crisis*. London.
Lachapelle. (1936). *Les finances de la Troisième République*. Paris.
Germain-Martin. (1936). *Le problème financier. 1930–1936*. Paris.
Dufour. (1936). *Le problème de l'équilibre budgétaire en France depuis la guerre*. Paris.
Damougeot-Perron. (1936). *L'économie française et les décrets-lois*. Paris.
Desmyttère. (1935). *Le problème de la réduction du taux de l'intérêt en France*. Paris.
Sir Robert Cahill. (1934). *Economic Conditions in France* (consular report). London.

IV. Special bibliography for Part One

Aftalion, A. (1932). *L'or et sa distribution mondiale*. Paris.
Coste. (1932). *Les grands marchés financiers*. Paris.
Einzig. (1931). *The fight for financial supremacy*. London.
Einzig. (1931). *Behind the scenes of international Finance*. London.
Einzig. (1932). *Finance and politics*. London.
Hawtrey. (1932). French monetary policy. In *The art of central banking*. London.
Rist, Ch. (n.d.). Le problème de l'or.
Rist, Ch. (n.d.). Le mécanisme de l'—étalon—or a-t-il été faussé?
Rist, Ch. (1933). La mauvaise répartition de l'or dans le monde. Articles republished in *Essais sur quelques problèmes économiques monetaires*, Paris.
Schwob. (1935, August). French monetary policy and its critics. *Economica.*
Hawtrey & Schwob. (1936, February). French monetary policy. *Economica.*
League of Nations. (1930). *Selected documents submitted to the Gold Delegation of the Financial Commmittee* (in particular the articles by Sir Henry Strakosh and M. Aftelion). Geneve.
Royal Institute of International Affairs. (1931). *The international gold problem*. London.

oOo

CONTENT

· 5 ·

HISTOIRE DE LA LIRE DE LA REVALORISATION AU CONTRÔLE DES CHANGES*

Introduction

Pendant la guerre et dans l'immédiat après-guerre l'évolution monétaire italienne était une image quelque peu retouchée de l'évolution bien connue de la monnaie française. La lire et le franc, liés avant 1914 par l'Union Monétaire Latine et définis par un poids d'or égal, se déprécièrent, lentement d'abord grâce aux crédits interalliés, rapidement dès la cessation de ces crédite après la fin de la guerre. Toutefois il n'y eut pas de synchronisme rigoureux: de 1915 à 1921, la chute de la monnaie italienne distança le franc de sorte qu'en 1921 il fallut donner en moyenne 175 lires pour 100 francs. Le mouvement comparé se renversa dans la suite et la parité s'était rétablie on Novembre 1925 quand les deux monnaies cotaient 122 par rapport à la livre.

En Italie, les premières années d'après-guerre avaient provoqué une chute particulièrement vive, soit à cause des troublés sociaux, soit parce que la crise de 1920 avec sa menace de faillite pour le système bancaire et l'industrie lourde avait entraîné une inflation considérable même pour le compte de l'industrie

* Pas publié, 1938.

et du commerce. De 1922 à 1924, la lire ne se déprécia que modérément tandis que le franc s'affaiblit pour des raisons que nous n'avons pas à évoquer ici.

Mais, d'une façon générale, les causes, extérieures d'abord (déficit de la balance commerciale), intérieures ensuite (déficit du budget) agirent de la même façon et entraînèrent les mêmes effets dans les deux pays et trouvèrent même souvant une expression technique identique. Ainsi le principal problème qui se posait aux Trésoreries Italienne et Française était celui du renouvellement et de la consolidation de la dette flottante.

Après une forte attaque de la spéculation à la baisse, le Trésor Italien contracta, dans la deuxième moitié de 1925, successivement deux prêts de 50 et de 100 millions de dollars auprès de la Banque Morgan et pensa assurer à l'aide des devises ainsi obtenues, la stabilité de la lire au niveau de 122 par rapport à la livre. En effet ce cours pu être maintenu pendant 8 mois; de Septembre 1925 jusqu'en Avril 1926. Mais alors se produisit, en relation avec la grève de mineurs en Angleterre et la faiblesse du franc, une deuxième attaque spéculative qui porta en Août la lire à 150 par rapport à la livre.

Quand la lire était au plus bas M. Mussolini prononça à Pesaro son fameux discours où il énonça la volonté inébranlable du Gouvernement de défendre la lire et de la révaloriser. Après être sorti victorieux d'une crise politique d'une extrême gravité (la crise Matteotti) le fascisme engagea sa première bataille économique, la bataille de la lire.

I. La révalorisation de la lire

Ce qui caractérisait la décision prise par le Gouvernement, ce fut la volonté de relever la lire du niveau très bas où elle était tombée pendant une attaque de la spéculation, non seulement jusqu'aux environs du cours qui était sa moyenne pendant les dernières années (120 par rapport à la livre), *mais bien plus haut*. On s'est beaucoup ingénié à donner la raison de cette politique qui allait provoquer une crise économique intérieure, amoindrir les possibilités de l'exportation et du tourisme, enfin rendre plus lourde—en termes réels—les charges budgétaires, celles au titre de la dette en particulier.

Par son discours de Pesaro, M. Mussolini avait fait d'une question de technique monétaire un symbole de prestige national. Il est possible que lui personnellement ne se rendait pas très bien compte des conséquences économiques de la révalorisation qu'il annonça, mais on ne peut le supposer de la part de ses conseillers qui étaient des techniciens avertis. Ceux-ci ont dû penser que le gain de prestige, la réparation des injustices sociales commises précédemment par l'inflation,[1] l'encouragement donné à l'épargne, compenseraient les dégâts qui seraient causées par la déflation. La rigueur même de l'opération a probablement tenté le gouvernement fasciste. M. Mussolini s'était fait à plusieurs reprises le défenseur d'une doctrine de "finances sévères;" tout ce qui était difficile, impliquait des sacrifices, lui apparaissait par la même comme le chemin à suivre.

Enfin on a supposé que le fascisme ait délibérément plongé les banques et l'industrie dans le marasme pour qu'elles aient à demander le secours de l'État qui se trouverait être ainsi l'arbitre de leurs destinées. Mais tout en admettant que les choses se sont passées en partie de cette façon nous ne croyons pas qu'il y ait eu là une action préméditée.

La révalorisation débuta avec le décret-loi du 7 septembre 1926 qui réalisa en premier lieu une importante réforme monétaire. En Italie il y avait jusque-là trois Instituts d'Émission: la Banque d'Italie, le Banco di Napoli, et le Banco di Sicilia. Quant aux réserves en or et en devises elles étaient distribuées entre ces trois banques, l'Institut pour les changes avec l'étranger et le Trésor. Le décret-loi réalisa d'abord l'unité de direction dans la bataille monétaire qui allait commencer. La Banque d'Italie reçut les réserves des deux Banques méridionales, le monopole de l'émission et le Trésor lui céda les devises provenant des prêts Morgan en défalcation de sa dette envers la Banque. L'Institut pour les changes fut réorganisé comme "émanation de la Banque d'Italie au début de 1927."

Le décret-loi cité stipula en autre qu'une somme annuelle de 500 millions de lires serait affectée pendant huit années consécutives à l'amortissement de la dette du Trésor envers la Banque d'Italie. Cette mesure prouve qu'on escompta une revalorisation lente et d'une ampleur considérable; car autrement la prévision du bénéfice de la réévaluation des réserves de la Banque l'aurait rendue sans objet.

D'une importance capitale fut la restriction rigoureuse de crédit mise en œuvre par la Banque d'Italie désormais maîtresse du système monétaire et bancaire, au moyen d'une élévation du taux d'escompte, d'une aggravation des conditions d'escompte et d'un relèvement de l'écart séparant la valeur des titres présentés pour l'obtention d'avances et le montant de l'avance. La gêne croissante des Trésoreries des entreprises et des banques entraîna alors

1 On sait que cette réparation au profit des receveurs de revenu fixe est très douteuse surtout si l'inflation a déjà duré longtemps, car si ce sont des catégories opposées qui gagnent et perdent lors de l'inflation ou de la revalorisation, il n'est pas sûr du tout que ces catégories soient composées des mêmes individus lors des mouvements contraires de la monnaie.

le non-renouvellement des bons du Trésor venant à échéance. Déjà dans la période de baisse violente de la lire les bons du Trésor avaient été délaissés pour les valeurs dites réelles ou des devises étrangères; la déflation aurait dû favoriser les bons mais le contraire arriva à cause des changements trop brusques opérés dans les conditions de crédit. La situation devint alarmante car le Trésor ne pouvait rembourser les bons que grâce à une nouvelle inflation: ainsi tout le programme du Gouvernement semblait remis en question quand intervint en novembre 1926 une consolidation forcée de toute la dette flottante y compris les bons quinquennaux et septennaux par un emprunt perpétuel 5% appelé Littorio. Au lieu d'être remboursés à 100 les porteurs de bons recevaient des titres qui allaient valoir 80 sur le marché et qui étaient difficilement réalisables.

Cet épisode est instructif car il montre comment une politique déflationniste a failli mener à un renforcement de l'inflation et comment une politique destinée a favorisé les épargnants aboutit à une violation pure et simple des contrats que l'État avait passés avec l'Epargne.

La raréfaction du crédit et la consolidation forcée de la dette flottante contraignaient beaucoup d'entreprises à déposer leur bilan. En 1927/1928 nous comptons 986 faillites par mois contre 628 en 1925/1926: l'augmentation est de 50%. Mais les collectivités publiques et la grande industrie trouvaient pour s'en sortir le moyen des emprunts étrangère qui pendant toute la période de hausse de la lire (d'août 1926 jusqu'à juin 1927) prirent une extension considérable arrivant à un total d'environ 4 milliards de lires. Ces emprunts non seulement délivraient les entreprises qui les contractaient de tout souci de trésorerie mais encore il leur sembla particulièrement avantageux de recevoir des dollars qui rapportaient au moment de la conclusion de l'emprunt 25 lires et qui allaient valoir beaucoup moins au moment du paiement des intérêts et du remboursement.

Mais comme le non-renouvellement des bons ces emprunts risquèrent de menacer le programme déflationniste du Gouvernement. La circulation des billets ne diminua pas car la réduction des opérations actives de la Banque d'Italie se trouva compensée à l'actif par l'augmentation des réserves en or et en devises. C'est pour cela que les emprunts furent sévèrement rationnés dès 1927 par le Ministre des Finances dont l'autorisation était requise et la matière fut définitivement réglée par une législation restrictive an début de 1928. Si les emprunts étrangers contrecarraient sans doute la politique de déflation économique, ils devaient seconder au contraire le programme purement monétaire du Gouvernement par la constitution de réserves puissantes et la création d'un courant continu d'offres de devises contre lires.

En juin 1927 la lira était ainsi descendue au cours 87 pour la livre et de 17.9 pour le dollar. Emu par la crise industrielle, la multiplication des faillites et les doléances des exportateurs, le Gouvernement se décida de s'arrêter là. Après un léger affaiblissement, la lire fut stabilisée par le décret-loi du 21 décembre 1927 complété par deux décrets datant du 26 février 1928. La lire état définie par un poids d'or fin de 79.19 g. La Banque d'Italie était dans l'obligation de convertir les billets présentés à son choix, en barres d'or d'un poids minimum de 5 kg. ou en devises convertibles en or. Elle devait en outre maintenir une réserve en or et devises par rapport à ses engagements à vue d'au moins 40%. La loi monétaire introduisit donc, on Italie le gold or change standard dans sa forme la plus pure.

Le produit de la réévaluation fut affecté à l'extinction de la dette du Trésor envers la Banque et au dédommagement de la Banque pour les pertes qu'elle subissait du fait qu'elle avait acquis antérieurement de l'or et des devises du Trésor et des banques d'émission méridionales à des prix supérieurs aux prix résultant de la stabilisation. Pour bien marquer sa volonté de ne plus laisser toucher à la lire le Gouvernement fixa par décret des points d'or très étroits. La lire devait se tenir entre le cours de 18.90 et 19.10 par rapport au dollar.

Toutefois certains décrets de la période antérieure qui stipulaient en substance que des devises ne pouvaient être obtenues que pour des besoins du commerce et du tourisme restaient encore en vigueur et ce ne fut qu'en début de 1930 que la liberté inconditionnelle du commerce des devises fut officiellement rétablie; le contrôle avait d'ailleurs été très libéral pendant les années antérieures.

La stabilisation de la lire à un niveau relativement élevé eut comme conséquence que l'Italie ne participa que dans une mesure très réduite à la prospérité des années 1928/1929. L'industrie est soumise à un effort pénible de réajustement. Au point de vue intérieur, la baisse des coûts de production n'égale pas la baisse des prix de vente. Au point de vue extérieur, la balance commerciale accuse des déficits importants. Pour soutenir certaines exportations de matières premières (marbre et chanvre) on organisa des comptoirs obligatoires de vente. Cependant on peut considérer que le processus de réadaptation était accompli vers la fin de 1928.

Dans un important secteur les valeurs ne s'étaient pas réajustées au nouveau mètre monétaire: celui des finances publiques. Les dépenses restèrent au niveau pré-déflationniste de 20 milliards de lire soit à cause de l'incompressibilité des paiements au titre de la dette, soit à cause de l'agrandissement de l'appareil de l'État et de la politique des travaux publics. La lire ancienne valait 3,66 fois la lire de 1927 mais les chiffres du budget avaient plus que septuplés. La pression fiscale c'est-à-dire la part des dépenses publiques dans le revenu national était passée suivant des calculs du Professeur Mortara de 13% en 1913/1914 à 25% en 1928/1929. Toutefois pendant toute cette période le budget était en léger excédent.

Une autre conséquence de la déflation fut l'immobilisation croissante de l'actif des grands établissements de crédit. En raison de l'absence d'un marché pour des obligations industrielles, le système bancaire italien avait toujours ressemblé plutôt au système allemand de la banque mixte qui pratique à la fois le crédit de roulement et le financement à long terme. Or, dans les années de déflation, les banques avaient absorbé une large quantité de titres des firmes auxquelles elles étalent déjà liées, pour éviter des baisses trop brutales. Ainsi les grandes banques devenaient de véritables holdings financiers ce qui allait créer une situation intenable dès une secousse plus sérieuse.

II. Le système bancaire, la politique monétaire et les mouvements de capitaux pendant la dépression mondiale

La crise économique mondiale qui se fit sentir très vite en Italie, suivit de si près la crise de déflation entraînée par la revalorisation de la lire, qu'il y eut une discussion parmi les économistes italiens sur le point de savoir s'il s'agissait de la continuation de l'ancienne maladie ou de l'apparition de troubles nouveaux. On dut se convaincre bientôt qu'on avait affaire à une crise sui generis ne fût-ce qu'à cause de son intensité. Nous allons traiter d'abord des répercussions au point de vue monétaire et bancaire intérieur. L'évolution de la lire sur le marché international nous fera comprendre ensuite les raisons qui ont mené à l'établissement du contrôle des changes.

La situation bancaire devint vite critique en raison de la baisse du marché financier et des retraits de fonds de l'année 1931. Il y eut un bon nombre de faillites de petites banques, mais cette solution était impraticable pour les trois grands établissements de crédit italiens, la Banca Commerciale Italiana, le Credito Italiano, et le Banco di Roma, tous trois fortement ébranlée en raison de leurs immobilisations excessives. A partir de 1930/1931, il y eut [. . .] ininterrompue d'opérations de "démobilisation," d'autant plus compliquées que leur principe et leur but étaient toujours le même: obtenir l'assistance de l'Institut d'Émission pour soutenir la trésorerie des banques en péril. Nous ne pouvons pas donner ici les détails des fusions, scissions, cessions de portefeuilles, etc... Généralement les banques cédèrent de leurs titres, leur participation et la partie immobilisée de leurs créances en compte courant à des consortiums financiers contre des sommes liquides que le consortium s'était procuré près de l'Institut d'Émission par des avancées en en présentant à l'escompte du papier financier. Tôt ou tard la pléthore de consortiums se dissolvait dans deux grands instituts qui furent fondés avec l'assistance de l'État en 1931 et 1933 avec le but précis d'exercer le crédit industriel à moyen et à long terme: l'Institut Mobilier Italien (I.M.I.) et l'Institut de Reconstruction Industrielle (I.R.I.).

La caractéristique de ces deux Instituts de droit public est qu'ils ne peuvent pas recevoir des dépôts ni entretenir des comptes courants débiteurs. Leurs moyens, outre que du capital initial souscrit par l'État et les Caisses d'Epargne, des subventions régulières de l'État (285 millions de lires par an pour l'I.R.I.) proviennent uniquement de l'émission d'obligations jouissant de privilèges divers. En outre ils ont eu recours à l'Institut d'émission. L'I.M.I. fut destiné surtout à concéder des crédits à moyen terme (10 années). Récemment encore il a été autorisé à émettre une série spéciale d'obligations dont le produit doit servir au financement de l'autarcie surtout dans la moyenne industrie.

Bien plus importantes sont les fonctions et l'œuvre de l'I.R.I.; c'est chez lui qu'après de multiples péripéties sont venue s'échouer les paquets d'actions et les participations des grandes banques avec la majorité des actions de ces banques mêmes; c'est lui qui opéra en outre les plus importants sauvetages industriels de la crise (dans l'industrie électrique notamment). L'I.R.I. se divise en la section de démobilisation et la section de financement. La première est chargée de gérer les participations industrielles et bancaires provenant des sauvetages et de replacer dans le public les titres dont la conservation n'intéresse pas l'État. La section de financement doit concéder des prêts industriels à long terme et elle a procédé pendant les dernières années à des réorganisations de branches entières de l'économie italienne, telle la Marine Marchande et la Sidérurgie, en s'assurant bien entendu le contrôle financier de ces industries.

Par le décret-loi du 24 juin 1937 l'I.R.I. a été promu organe permanent pour la gestion des participations intéressant l'État et en lui a confié la fonction d'assister le financement de l'autarcie et la mise en valeur de l'Ethiopie dans les limites d'un fonds de dotation de 7 milliards de lires. L'I.R.I. devient ainsi de plus en plus un immense holding de l'État.

Les opérations de démobilisation et l'émission d'obligations permirent de réduire la dette de l'I.R.I. et des banques qu'il contrôla envers l'Institut d'émission du chiffre énorme de 7.353 millions de lires au début de 1933 à 4 milliards 708 millions à la fin de 1936. Ce chiffre reste toujours considérable par rapport à la circulation totale de 16 milliards et demi à la même date.

[. . .]la dette de l'I.R.I. doit être réalisée d'après un [. . .] de 35 années.

Ainsi l'allégement de la position des banques commerciales n'a été obtenu que par une immobilisation d'une partie importante de l'actif de la Banque d'Italie. C'était là le résidu du passé, le reflet d'une industrialisation qui avait été poussée au deçà des facultés de l'épargne individuelle. Quant à l'avenir, la séparation du crédit commercial et du crédit de financement fut consacrée par la *réforme bancaire* qui, quoique définitive seulement en 1937, doit être évoquée ici puisqu'elle est l'aboutissement des vicissitudes que nous venons de voir.

La réforme procéda d'abord à une classification des établissements de crédit en instituts recevant de l'épargne à moyen et à long terme et en instituts recevant de l'épargne à court terme. Parmi ces derniers on donna une discipline particulière aux groupes des instituts de crédit de droit public, tels que les Banques de Sicile et de Naples; ensuite aux banques d'intérêt national (les trois grands établissements de crédit nommés ci-dessus), dont les actions doivent être nominatives et dont les assemblées n'admettent pas les porteurs étrangers.

La pièce principale de la réforme est la création de l'"Inspection pour l'exercice du crédit et la défense de l'épargne" mise elle-même à la dépendance d'un comité de ministres dont fait partie le Gouverneur de la Banque d'Italie qui est en même temps Chef de l'Inspection. Celle-ci contrôle tous les instituts exerçant le crédit à moyen et à long terme à l'exception de l'I.R.I. qui dépend directement du Ministère des Finances. L'action de l'Inspection est particulièrement importante dans le secteur des banques recevant l'épargne et exerçant le crédit à court terme puisque c'est elle qui détermine les taux auxquels s'exécutent les opérations actives et passives; elle fixe en outre les diverses proportions à maintenir entre les différents postes du bilan des banques et même la répartition des escomptes et avances entre les diverses branches de l'économie nationale.

La Banque d'Italie fut elle aussi réorganisée. Ses actions furent remboursées au porteur et replacées par des quotes-parts souscrites uniquement par les caisses d'épargne, les grandes banques et les compagnies d'assurances. En lui défendant, sauf dans quelques cas exceptionnels, l'escompte direct on a voulu lui assigner clairement son rôle de banque des banques.

La réforme devait définitivement garantir le système bancaire contre le retour des difficultés qui l'avaient si fortement ébranlée dans la crise. Et cependant à peine fut-elle devenue loi que les investissements énormes nécessités par la mise en valeur de l'Ethiopie et la politique autarcique remirent en question son principe même: la séparation du crédit à court terme du crédit à moyen et à long terme. Un premier avertissement fut donné en 1937 par le Ministre des Finances qui déclara qu'il faut éviter de retomber dans les erreurs qui ont rendu nécessaire "l'assainissement bancaire qui, de 1919 à 1337, a coûté à l'État plus que la guerre éthiopienne." Tout récemment la discussion sur le financement de l'autarcie a donné lieu à des déclarations officielles semblables. Toutefois en même temps on a engagé les banques à souscrire largement aux titres émis par l'I.M.I. en contrepartie de financements autarciques et c'est bien là une nouvelle immobilisation ne fut-elle qu'indirecte.

La tendance continue vers l'investissement à long terme des dépôts bancaires constitue à notre avis une caractéristique essentielle de l'économie italienne et s'explique par l'insuffisance, par rapport au développement industriel, de la formation de l'épargne prête à s'investir directement à long terme. Aucune réforme technique ne pourra arrêter cette tendance; si on la juge malsaine il faudra s'attaquer à la véritable cause qui consiste dans le forcement des investissements.

Au point de vue de la monnaie les sauvetages industriels et bancaires de la crise devaient naturellement empêcher les sorties d'or et le marasme des affaires d'avoir leur plein effet sur la circulation des billets. La déflation était bien toujours la doctrine financière et économique officielle du Gouvernement. Les traitements des fonctionnaires et, à leur suite, les salaires furent réduits à deux reprise, en 1930 de 12% et en 1934 de 6% à 12%. Mais en fait le renforcement de la protection douanière (augmentation des droits sur le blé et surtaxe générale ad valorem de 15% après la dévaluation anglaise) et les sauvetages démontrèrent que la déflation ne put être poursuivie jusqu'au bout. D'autre part le Gouvernement contrecarra directement la déflation par sa politique de travaux publics et la revalorisation des produits agricoles. Ainsi un début de reprise interne provoqua une demande accrue de matières premières d'importation étrangère tandis que l'inachèvement de la déflation fit obstacle aux exportations. Nous voyons là l'explication de la brusque aggravation du déficit commerciale en 1934 qui a une large responsabilité dans l'instauration du contrôle des changes.

Il est vrai que la résistance de la lire était déjà fort affaiblie en raison des mouvements de capitaux des années antérieures et de l'année 1934 elle-même. En 1931, 1932 et 1933 la lire fut cotée en moyenne à 1,2%, 2,9% et 1,2% au-dessous de sa parité légale ce qui était en contradiction formelle avec la loi de 1926 qui avait fixé les points d'or à une distance de 0,5% environ de la parité. (Pour ne pas faire apparaître cette contradiction la fixation officielle du prix de l'or fut suspendue en 1932). La crise internationale de crédit en 1931 avait naturellement entraîné pour l'Italie aussi des retraits des capitaux étrangers. Pourtant elle n'était point aussi exposée à cet égard que l'Allemagne ou les pays d'Europe Centrale; son endettement étranger à court terme était peu important car les emprunts contractés pendant la revalorisation de la lire étaient tous à moyen ou à long terme. L'initiative des mouvements de capitaux qui causèrent la faiblesse de la lire pendant les années 1931/1934 et firent adopter finalement le contrôle des changes ne venait point ne l'extérieur mais des Italiens eux-mêmes.

Suivant les publications de la Banque d'Italie et du spécialiste italien en matière de balance des paiements, le professeur Borgatta, la balance des revenus était en équilibre de 1931 à 1935 les partes d'or de 2 milliards et demi de lire de l'Institut d'émission pendant cette époque correspondraient à une "amélioration de la situation patrimoniale de l'Italie par rapport à l'étranger." Est-ce là uniquement une désignation euphémistique de ce qu'on appelle généralement "fuite de capitaux"? Nous ne le pensons pas car il s'agit en grande partie d'exédents de remboursements sur la stipulation d'emprunts nouveaux et de rachats de titres italiens émis et circulant à l'étranger. Avant la guerre une telle nationalisation de la dette publique et privée avait été saluée comme la preuve de la force accrue de l'économie italienne. Mais la différence avec la situation d'avant-guerre était que les revenus du tourisme et les remises des émigrants suffisaient à peine à équilibrer le déficit commercial et que par conséquent les mouvements de capitaux en question entraînèrent une diminution des réserves de la Banque d'Italie.

Au début de 1934, la stabilisation du dollar et la conversion du 5% perpétuel en 3,5% amortissable accélérait les achats de valeurs américaines et italiennes émises aux Etats-Unis. En même temps, le déficit commercial augmenta brusquement à cause des contradictions de la politique économique du Gouvernement comme nous l'avons expliqué plus haut. La faiblesse de la lire et la diminution des réserves entrainèrent alors des exportations de billets et un mouvement spéculatif. On fut alors que le Gouvernement se refusant d'envisager une dévaluation et ne voulant pas non plus briser la reprise économique qui s'amorçait par une nouvelle déflation, décréta les premières mesures de contrôle des changes.

III. Le contrôle des changes

1) La législation afférant au contrôle

Examinons d'abord rapidement la législation complexe qui a été créé à partir de 1934 pour règlementer toutes les opérations donnant lieu à des paiements entre l'Italie et l'étranger.

Les décrets-lois du 26 mai 1934 stipulèrent d'une façon générique qu'aucune opération de charge ne pouvait être exécutée si elle ne répondait pas à "de réelles nécessités de l'industrie et du commerce ou à des besoins de ceux qui voyagent à l'étranger." L'achat de titres étrangers et italiens émis à l'étranger est interdit et les titres de cette espèce circulant en Italie doivent être estampillés. L'exportation de billets de banque est limitée a la somme de 5.000 lires pour les touristes; cette somme sera graduellement réduite à 350 lires auxquelles peuvent s'ajouter des devises que le touriste italien doit acquérir en Italie même. La réimportation de billets sortis sera interdite elle aussi.

Pour rétrécir le plus possible le marché extérieur de la lire on défend d'une façon générale toute opérations qui apparaisse comme moyen de se procurer à l'étranger des disponibilités de lires: telle la concession de crédit en lires par escompte ou avance à des personnel résident à l'étranger.

Mais ces mesures ne suffirent pas à arrêter les sorties d'or. Une réglementation plus stricte et sur laquelle repose encore le régime actuel fut instituée par les décrets de 2 décembre 1934. Le monopole de toutes les opérations de change fut confié à l'Institut Nationale pour les changes avec l'étranger (Istcambi). La Banque d'Italie fut chargée du service de caisse de l'Institut et elle délégua à son tour certaines opérations aux grandes banques tenues a une comptabilité spéciale.

Les exportateurs vers les pays avec lesquels l'Italie n'est pas en rapport de clearing, doivent s'obliger avant de faire partir leurs marchandises à l'étranger, de céder les devises qu'ils obtiendront à l'Istcambi. Tous les crédits étrangers possédés par les banques et les sociétés lui doivent être cédés et les titres émis à l'étranger doivent être déclarés.

Les premiers mois de 1935 définissent le régime des importations et en général la nouvelle politique commerciale. Le 18 février, on décrète le contingentement général des importations admises désormais dans des pourcentages fixés par rapport aux importations de 1934. En même temps on essaie de conclure des accords de clearing avec le plus grand nombre de pays possible. Les compensations privées sont organisées pour permettre des importations extra-contingents en contrepartie d'exportation d'articles peu vendus jusque-là à l'étranger ou dirigés vers des marchés nouveaux.

A l'approche de la guerre abyssine le contrôle s'avère comme un rouage très utile pour la préparation économique de la guerre. Il est renforcé considérablement. En mai un organe est créé pour surveiller toutes les opérations de change: c'est la Surintendance aux Echanges et aux Devises qui sera transformée ultérieurement en Sous-Secrétariat (décembre 1935) et an Ministère (novembre 1937). Son organe est l'Istcambi.

La régime des importations est aggravé: pour le charbon et plusieurs autres produits de base des monopoles d'importation sont institués. La plupart des autres marchandises passent du régime de l'admission au prorata de l'importation de 1934 au régime de la licence ministérielle.

La mesure la plus radicale est une réquisition générale des titres étrangers ou italiens émis à l'étranger et la cession contre paiement en lires de tous les crédits étrangers (décret-loi du 28 aout 1935). Les titres sont échangés à leur cours de bourse lors de la date du décret-loi et au change officiel contre des bons du trésor 5% à 9 ans. Ultérieurement cette législation a été étendue à tous les crédits et titres qui seraient entrés après le premier décret ou qui entreraient pour n'importe quelle raison dans le patrimoine des Italiens.

On aura noté qu'à l'encontre de ce qui s'est passé dans presque tous les autres pays au contrôle des changes, les premières mesures italiennes ne comprenaient pas des restrictions au transfert de ses dettes financières ni le blocage des crédits à court terme. L'intérêt se concentra plutôt sur la réquisition des crédits et titres étrangers détenus par les Italiens. Cela confirme ce que nous avons dit à propos des causes de l'établissement du contrôle; elles ne résidaient pas dans un endettement excessif et un retrait de capitaux étrangers, mais dans une exportation de capitaux, un désendettement et une nationalisation de la dette extérieure trop rapides par rapport à l'état de la balance des comptes.

Ce ne fut qu'au moment des sanctions que l'Italie bloqua toutes les créances commerciales et financières des pays sanctionnistes. Après la fin des sanctions elle conclut avec ces pays des accords de clearing qui prévoyaient de dégel progressif des créances bloquées grâce à une balance commerciale favorable à l'Italie. Quant aux avoirs étrangers en Italie ceux qui étaient antérieurs aux sanctions étaient soumis à un régime assez sévère puisque même leur utilisation à l'intérieur du royaume subissait des restrictions tandis que les sommes transmises après le début des sanctions étaient simplement déclarées intransférables. Vers la fin de 1936 on institua des comptes libres formés par des cessions nouvelles de devises de la part d'étrangers ou italiens résident à l'étranger et dont les mouvements ne subissaient aucune sorte de restriction.

2) Le contrôle et la lire

On a souvent posé l'alternative: contrôle des changes ou dévaluation, mais en réalité, on a voulu opposer liberté ou règlementation des opérations de change. Au point de vue de la valeur de la monnaie la véritable alternative se pose entre déflation d'une part et dévaluation et contrôle des changes de l'autre, car le contrôle rejoint toujours par des chemins plus ou moins longs le résultat atteint directement par la dévaluation.

En Italie en particulier les deux opérations monétaires ont été confondues dès le début. En mai 1934, la lire était déjà descendue à 3% au-dessous de sa parité et cette dépréciation de fait du cours officiel augmenta progressivement pour atteindre 12% à la veille de l'"Alignement" d'octobre 1936. Le cours des billets de banque circulant à l'étranger était beaucoup plus déprécié encore. Un autre indice était le prix de 15,50 lires que l'Istcambi offrait vers la fin de 1935 pour le gramme d'or fin qui, suivant la loi de 1927, valait 12,60 lires seulement. Cette offre constituait une reconnaissance officielle d'une dépréciation de la lire par rapport à l'or de 18,5%. D'ailleurs la loi monétaire de 1927 avait déjà reçu un premier coup formel le 21 juillet 1935 par l'abolition de la limite de 40% qu'elle avait assignée à la proportion entre réserves et engagements à vue de la Banque d'Italie.

Mais les symptômes les plus significatifs de l'affaiblissement de la lire sous le contrôle des changes sont ceux qui reflètent la disparité croissante entre prix italiens et étrangers, c'est-à-dire la diminution de la valeur réelle de la lire par rapport aux autres monnaies. Lors de l'institution du contrôle, la lire était déjà surévalués et on a vu que cela a été un des facteurs de l'établissement du contrôle même. Ensuite, par un effet en retour, le contrôle des importations accéléra la hausse des prix qui fut stimulée surtout par l'augmentation de l'activité économique intérieurs entrainée par la guerre abyssine. Mais de cette façon, les exportations et le tourisme versaient dans des conditions de plus en plus difficiles. Au début de 1936 on créa la lire touristique dont le rabais par rapport a la lire officielle—elle aussi dépréciée—fut d'environ 23,5%. Quant aux exportations on les assista soit par des primes directes appelées "facilitations," soit par des compensations privées qui donnaient lieu à des primes importantes payées par l'importateur à l'exportateur. En août 1936, ce système fut transporté dans les clearings et on obligea les importateurs à acquitter 20% en plus du prix facturé tandis que les exportateurs recevaient une prime de 15% sur les sommes qui leur étaient dues. Il est évident que ces mesures équivalaient exactement a une dévaluation et c'est pourquoi le Gouvernement italien saisit l'occasion qui s'offrit avec la dévaluation des monnaies du bloc-or de procéder a une simplification de ses rapports monétaires avec l'étranger.

Le décret-loi du 5 octobre 1936 s'apparenta étroitement a la stabilisation du dollar de février 1934 puisqu'il diminua la valeur or de la lire de 40,94% et laissa au Gouvernement la possibilité de porter cette dévaluation jusqu'à 50% par simple décret. Par rapport au cours officiel de la lire en septembre 1936, la dévaluation d'octobre ressort à environ 33%. Depuis lors la lire officielle n'a pas été touchée et a été maintenue invariablement au cours de 19 par rapport au dollar.

La dévaluation fit cesser la disparité entre prix italiens et étrangers. En conséquence on put abolir toutes les primes à l'exportation sous toutes leurs formes (facilitations, compensations privées, primes en clearing): la lire touristique fut maintenue mais son cours se rapprocha, comme d'ailleurs celui des billets circulant à l'étranger, du cours officiel. L'écart ne fut plus que de 6,5%.

Vers la fin de 1936 on peut même constater une tendance vers l'atténuation du contrôle. Ainsi la permission de tenir des comptes en devises étrangères fut étendue des Compagnies d'Assurances et de Navigations a toutes les Sociétés dont l'action s'explique surtout à l'étrangers. Quelques exonérations furent accordées quant à la cession obligatoire des crédits et titres étrangers.

Ces velléités, cependant, n'allaient pas loin. Le déficit commercial particulièrement élevé (5,7 milliards de lires) de 1937 rendit plus que jamais nécessaire le monopole des opérations de change; mais nous voulons surtout insister ici sur l'évolution comparée des prix italiens ou étrangers qui fit bientôt réapparaitre une certaine disparité affaiblissant de nouveau la lire.

Par rapport au franc et dernièrement aussi par rapport à la livre cela est dû en partie aux dépréciations de ces monnaies. Mais même en comparant les prix italiens avec les prix de pays dont la monnaie est liée à une parité or déterminée, comme la Belgique ou les États-Unis, on trouve qu'il y eut disparité en faveur de l'Italie vers la fin de 1936 tandis qu'aujourd'hui les indices italiens sont sensiblement supérieurs aux indices belges et américains. L'explication réside dans la hausse particulièrement forte des prix italiens en 1937 et dans leur résistance à toute baisse dans la suite.

Cette évolution est d'autant plus remarquable que, lors de la dévaluation, on prit diverses mesures pour maintenir la hausse dans des limites étroites: les droits de douane sur plusieurs produits alimentaires furent réduits, la taxe ad valorem de 15% fut abolie et les prix des loyers, du gaz, de l'électricité, et des services publics, "furent bloqués." Un contrôle rigoureux de tous les prix fut organisé sous les auspices du parti fasciste d'abord et des organes corporatifs ensuite. La hausse des prix italiens traduit donc une tendance fondamentale et tient à plusieurs faits qui caractérisent la phase actuelle de l'économie fasciste.

D'abord, comme le remarque le rapport de la Banque d'Italie pour 1937, il y a la moindre disponibilité de biens de consommation. Ensuite les besoins financiers de l'État dépassent depuis plusieurs années de très loin ses recettes; de 1935/1936 à 1937/1938 les dépenses non couvertes pas des recettes s'élèvent à 41 milliards de lires, c'est-à-dire à environ 40% des dépenses totales. Les financiers fascistes ont essayé de contenir le plus possible l'inflation par une série de mesures frappant le capital (1935: reconversion de la rente amortissable 3,5% en 5% perpétuel par versement à fonds perdu de 15 lires par 100 lires de capital. 1936: emprunt forcé immobilier et taxe immobilière destinée à payer les intérêts de l'emprunt. 1937: impôt de 10% sur le capital et les réserves des sociétés par actions. 1938: impôt de 7,5% sur le capital des sociétés de personnes et les entreprises individuelles). Néanmoins le recours à l'inflation n'a pu être totalement évité. Il a été évalué à 25% des dépenses non couvertes normalement.

Une cause plus profonde encore de l'évolution des prix est la politique autarcique qui a conduit à un renchérissement soit par l'exploitation plus intensive et par conséquent a coûts croissants des ressources nationales, soit par la substitution de produits nationaux plus couteux aux produits d'importation étrangers.

L'affaiblissement de la lire en raison de l'évolution des prix a trouvé les mêmes expressions qu'avant la dévaluation d'octobre 1936: écart croissant entre le cours des billets et de la lire touristique d'une part et le cours officiel de l'autre, réapparition des primes à l'exportation. Il paraît même qu'on va créer une lire spéciale pour les remises des émigrants.

La leçon de l'évolution des deux dernières années est donc que, pour rétablir le contact entre une monnaie contrôlée et les monnaies libres, une dévaluation consacrant l'état de fait est nécessaire mais non suffisante; encore faut-il qu'il y ait un certain alignement de la politique économique puisque sans cela la tendance autonome du système des prix risque de provoquer de nouveaux déséquilibres. Et puisque rien n'indique que l'Italie soit prête à renoncer à l'autarcie on ne peut pas s'attendre non plus à une atténuation prochaine du contrôle des changes dont les rouages sont au contraire constamment perfectionnés.

L'histoire récente de la monnaie italienne a été fort accidentée depuis que le fascisme en a pris le sort entre ses mains. L'interventionnisme, contraire au programme économique de la première heure, mais si conforme à l'essence même du fascisme s'est déjà révélé par l'expérience de la revalorisation. A ce moment il a dû encore se couvrir par des mots d'ordre orthodoxes, tels que l'abandon du cours forcé, et retour à l'étalon or. Dans la crise l'État fasciste acquiert le contrôle du système bancaire et des industries-clés mais plutôt par nécessité que par initiative propre. Dans la troisième période, le fascisme ayant pleinement pris conscience de sa puissance sur l'économie nationale isole la lire des monnaies librement négociables et en fait un rouage de la direction de toute l'économie vers des buts essentiellement extra-économiques.

Graduellement et souvent en rechignant la lire avait changé de camp, tout comme l'Italie.

· 6 ·

ITALIE*

Conjoncture

En octobre, on peut noter quelques symptômes d'amélioration dans la situation industrielle. L'indice général de la production, en effet, a atteint à 115,9 (1928=100), son niveau le plus élevé de l'année, et n'est ainsi inférieur que de 1,3% à l'indice correspondant de 1937, alors qu'en août la différence négative était encore de 13,2%. Ce relèvement est dû à une augmentation de la production textile, qui reste cependant inférieure de 12% au niveau de l'année précédente, et surtout à une forte reprise du bâtiment dont l'indice s'élève à 107,5 contre 93,9 en octobre 1937. Cela s'explique probablement par le fait que les autorisations de construire, qui avaient été sévèrement limitées depuis 1935, sont maintenant accordées d'une façon plus libérale.

Pas de changement au contraire dans l'activité des échanges intérieurs. Les chargements sur chemins de fer restent inférieurs de 10% environ aux niveaux de 1937 et, d'autre part, le nombre de faillites est en augmentation pour la première fois depuis 1932; de septembre à novembre on en compte

* Institut de statistique de l'Université de Paris et Institut scientifique des recherches économiques et sociales, *L'acivité économique Bulletin trimestriel*, n. 16, 31 janvier 1939.

732 contre 625 pendant la période correspondante de 1937 et le montant des traites protestées s'élève à 39 millions de lires contre 27 millions.

Pour les prix le seul mouvement à noter est la hausse des matières alimentaires d'origine animale,[1] s'élevant de 81,9 en août à 87,7 en novembre. Sous leur influence, l'indice général des prix de gros progressé de 96,0 à 97,2 et l'indice du coût de la vie de 98,6 à 99,5 (1928 = 100).

Commerce extérieur

De nouveaux progrès ont été accomplis vers l'équilibre de la balance commerciale, par suite cette fois de la réduction des importations de toutes catégories. Voici les chiffres pour l'ensemble de l'année, à l'exclusion du commerce avec les colonies:

Tableau 6.1.

	Importations	*Exportations*	*Déficit*
1937	13.592	7.853	5.739
1938	10.918	7.959	2.959

en millions de lires.

Néanmoins l'équilibre de la balance des comptes n'est pas encore assuré, en raison surtout des résultats très médiocres du tourisme. Il est vrai que plus d'un tiers du déficit (962 millions de lires pour les onze premiers mois) provient du commerce avec l'Allemagne[2] et se règle en clearing. Les 31.000 ouvriers agricoles italiens qui ont travaillé en Allemagne pendant la campagne de 1938 ont envoyé 86 millions de lires d'économies à leurs familles. Un nouveau contingent de 32.000 ouvriers agricoles et probablement de 10.000 ouvriers du bâtiment est prévu pour 1939.

Grâce à la réduction des importations le solde débiteur des clearings s'est réduit d'une façon notable. Il s'établit à la fin de décembre à 248 millions contre 330 millions à la fin de 1937 et 545 millions à la fin de juin 1938.

Un décret a créé trois grandes Compagnies pour l'importation du café, dont le siège respectif est à Gênes, Trieste et Naples. Ces Compagnies absorberont toutes les firmes d'importation et se proposeront, outre l'approvisionnement du marché italien, d'organiser une réexportation active.

1 Après une longue chute antérieure, voir *Activité Economique*, n. 14, p. 140 et n. 15, p. 251.
2 Alors que les échanges commerciaux italo-allemands ne représentent que 23% du volume total du commerce extérieur italien.

Finances publiques

On a publié le projet de budget ordinaire pour 1939–1940. Il se présente avec un déficit de 4.755 millions de lires, puisqu'il comporte 29.316 millions de dépenses et 24.561 millions de recettes (contre 25.035 et 25.072 millions pour 1938–1939). L'augmentation des dépenses est due en première ligne aux dépenses militaires, qui comprennent la première tranche (2.476 millions) d'un nouveau programme d'armement de 10 milliards de lires. La légère diminution des recettes s'explique par des évaluations plus prudentes. En soi, le chiffre du déficit est sans grande signification, si l'on n'a aucune indication sur le montant du budget extraordinaire. On peut se demander toutefois pourquoi le Gouvernement a fait apparaître cette année dans le budget ordinaire un déficit considérable alors que l'année dernière il l'avait dissimulé tout entier dans le budget extraordinaire. La raison en est probablement qu'il veut préparer l'opinion à des sacrifices ultérieurs.

Dans le domaine de la fiscalité extraordinaire, il ne reste cependant plus beaucoup à faire depuis qu'un nouvel impôt de 7,5% sur le capital des entreprises autres que les Sociétés anonymes a mis officiellement fin au cycle des mesures frappant le capital (conversion de la rente amortissable 3,5% en 5% perpétuelle par versement à fonds perdu de 15 lires par 100 lires de capital en 1935, emprunt immobilier et taxe relative à cet emprunt en 1936, impôt sur le capital des Sociétés par actions en 1937). Les modalités du nouvel impôt sont très complexes. La base est établie en capitalisant—au taux de 8%—le revenu déclaré, avec des déductions variant suivant le montant du revenu et le genre d'entreprise (les industriels sont plus frappés que les commerçants). Un système d'avances bancaires est institué pour permettre le paiement en bloc avec escompte; autrement le paiement pourra s'échelonner au maximum sur cinq années. Le nouvel impôt équivaudra dans la majorité des cas à un doublement de l'impôt sur les revenus industriels et commerciaux pour toute la durée de son paiement. La différence entre le nouvel impôt et l'impôt sur le capital des Sociétés par actions est que celles-ci pouvaient faire appel à leurs actionnaires pour le paiement tandis que les entreprises individuelles devront subir directement les nouvelles charges. Le produit de l'impôt sera assez modique; on compte sur 1,5 à 2 milliards de lires.

Autre indice des difficultés financières: bien que le Comité corporatif central du 31 mai dernier ait décidé que tous les prix des services publics resteraient bloqués pendant deux années, l'administration ferroviaire a décidé une augmentation de 20% sur les tarifs-voyageurs à partir de 1939.

L'autarcie

Le problème du financement de l'autarcie a retenu tout particulièrement l'attention de la Commission suprême de l'Autarcie qui a siégé en octobre et novembre. La Commission a voulu écarter comme mode de financement des investissements autarciques non seulement l'inflation par les billets, mais encore l'extension du crédit et l'immobilisation des fonds bancaires. Il a été dit et redit que les résultats de la réorganisation bancaire de 1931 à 1936, (qui avait nettement séparé le crédit à court terme et les participations industrielles) ne devaient en aucune façon être remis en question et que les activités autarciques devaient être financées uniquement par "l'épargne effectivement disponible."

Mais peu de temps après, il a été constitué une section spéciale de l'Institut Mobilier Italien qui devra émettre des obligations pour le financement de l'autarcie; une émission de 250 millions a été autorisée jusqu'ici. Les banques sont obligées de réserver une partie de leurs fonds à la souscription de ces obligations—obligées de faire par conséquent ce qu'on leur avait défendu, c'est-à-dire de financer avec leurs dépôts, indirectement il est vrai, des participations industrielles.

Pour créer une unité de direction dans le domaine du crédit, la compétence de l'"Inspection pour la défense de l'épargne et l'exercice du crédit," chargée jusqu'ici du contrôle des banques a été étendue aux Compagnies d'assurances. Enfin, la préparation et le contrôle de toutes les initiatives autarciques—et par là même la direction centrale de toute la vie économique du pays dans la phase actuelle—viennent d'être confiés à un Comité interministériel où siégeront à côté des ministres des départements économiques (finances, corporations, agriculture, transports, commerce extérieur), le directeur de la Banque d'Italie, le chef d'État-major et le commissaire général pour les fabrications de guerre. Avec ces mesures la mise sur pied de guerre de toute l'économie italienne fait de nouveaux progrès.

ITALIE*

Production et activité économique – Grâce au relèvement qui s'est produit au cours des derniers mois de l'année, l'indice de la production industrielle italienne n'a baissé en 1938 que de 1,2% par rapport à 1937. Supérieur encore d'environ 5% pendant le premier trimestre, inférieur de 5% dans les deux trimestres suivants aux chiffres de la période correspondante de 1937, l'indice a retrouvé son niveau de l'année précédente dans les derniers mois de 1938 pour le dépasser de 3,4% en janvier 1939. Nous notons une évolution nettement divergente dans les différentes industries; quatre branches montrent en 1938 des écarts positifs: métallurgie (+6,1%), industries mécaniques (+2,0%), industries productrices d'énergie électrique (+1,6%), industries extractives (+5,5%); quatre autres des écarts négatifs: textiles (-0,8%), industries chimiques (-2,6%), papier (-4,9%), bâtiment (-5,4%). Ainsi en 1938, la situation de faveur faite aux industries militaires et aux industries de biens de production par rapport aux industries civiles et aux industries de biens de consommation se traduit par une évolution en sens opposé des deux catégories d'industries tandis que jusque-là on avait constaté plutôt un rythme différent dans l'accroissement. Cependant il convient de noter que l'industrie du bâtiment est en reprise marquée depuis quelques mois par rapport aux niveaux exceptionnellement déprimés des trois années précédentes.

L'activité économique interne, telle qu'elle est reflétée par le trafic marchandise sur chemins de fer, montre en 1938 une diminution de 7% par rapport à 1937. Toutefois là aussi on note une reprise dans les derniers mois et en janvier-février le nombre de wagons chargés rejoint, à peu de chose près, le chiffre de 1938 qui était lui-même supérieur à celui de 1937.

Tableau 6.2.

	janvier-février 1938	janvier-février 1939
Commerce, avec l'étranger		
Importations	2.060	1.487
Exportations	1.260	1.194
Déficit	800	293

(*suite*)

* Institut de statistique de l'Université de Paris et Institut scientifique des recherches économiques et sociales, *L'activité économique Bulletin trimestriel*, n. 17, 30 avril 1939.

Commerce avec les colonies (chiffres en parenthèses pour l'Éthiopie seulement)		
Importations	45 (35)	35 (18)
Exportations	446 (335)	312 (223)
Excédent	401 (300)	270 (205)

en millions de lires.

Commerce extérieur – Il nous paraît cependant improbable que la reprise actuelle puisse se généraliser et s'amplifier. Le fait nouveau du début de 1939 est, en effet, la contraction violente des importations. Voici les chiffres pour les deux premiers mois de 1938 et de 1939.

Une diminution de 28% d'une année à l'autre des importations en provenance des pays étrangers ne saurait être expliquée par les progrès de l'autarcie ni par la situation agricole (les importations de blé ont même légèrement augmenté), ni, on l'a vu, par l'activité industrielle. Nous sommes donc portés à y voir le reflet d'une situation difficile de l'Institut pour les Changes quant à l'approvisionnement en devises étrangères. Cette impression est renforcée par le fait que les importations en provenance des pays avec lesquels l'Italie est en rapport de clearing ont moins baissé que les importations que l'Italie doit régler en devises. L'indice de la quantité des marchandises importées est en janvier de 45,1 (1929 = 100) contre 65,6 en janvier 1938 et 60,6 en janvier 1936 au moment des sanctions. La réduction des importations par rapport à l'année dernière et souvent même par rapport à l'année des sanctions, où par rétorsion toutes les importations avaient été sévèrement réduites, affecte presque tous les articles à l'exclusion de quelques matières premières de la métallurgie, comme il ressort du tableau suivant:

Tableau 6.3. *Importations en Italie dans les deux premiers mois de chaque année*

		1939	1938	1936
Bovins	n.	1.400	12.500	6.800
Viandes	qx	7.500	76.200	60.600
Poissons	—	90.100	152.200	57.700
Café	—	47.400	55.700	46.700
[3]Huile d'olive	—	2.900	12.100	900
Coton brut	—	193.500	297.700	223.800
Cellulose	—	470.900	698.200	521.300

3 A l'exclusion de l'importation temporaire.

Tableau 6.3. *Suite*

Bois	t.	50.700	118.100	88.000
Engrais azotés	—	12.100	44.100	14,500
Engrais potassiques	—	9.000	12.700	4.900
Houille	—	1.510.900	1.750.000	1.777.400
Coke	—	26.900	69.100	149.200
Minerais de fer	qx	666.700	430.400	176.000
Ferrailles	—	1.114.900	1.021.800	603.200
Cuivre en lingots	—	195.700	159.400	211.600

Tableau 6.4. *Remises des ouvriers travaillant en A.O.I.*

	Nombre	Montant (en millions de lire)
1937	1.821.000	2.449
1938	1.278.000	1.542
Janvier 1938	122.000	139
Janvier 1939	85.000	91

A la lumière de ces chiffres, les paroles de M. Mussolini "faire table rase de toute vie civile" en faveur de la préparation militaire reçoivent une interprétation et un sens très précis. La satisfaction des besoins de la consommation en certains articles essentiels et l'approvisionnement en matières premières de certaines industries ne risque-t-il pas d'être sérieusement compromis si la réduction des importations se maintient à l'échelle actuelle?

L'activité de l'Italie dans ses colonies et en particulier en Ethiopie diminue fortement, comme on a pu le voir d'après les chiffres sur le commerce italo-colonial. On observe (voir aussi le graphique) une corrélation, facilement explicable d'ailleurs, entre le déficit du commerce italien avec les pays étrangers et son excédent avec les colonies. On ne donne plus le nombre des ouvriers travaillant en Afrique orientale italienne, mais le nombre et le montant des remises effectuées par les ouvriers en Italie en fournissent une indication.

Pour la première fois depuis près de deux années, le solde des clearings est devenu créditeur à la fin mars. Le crédit atteint 54 millions, contre un débit de 248 millions à la fin de décembre. Cela tient surtout à l'arriéré important de 271 millions que l'Allemagne a accumulé en l'espace de quelques mois. Étant donné que le commerce italo-allemand est très déficitaire pour l'Italie, la position créditrice italienne s'explique, suivant un communiqué officiel

Tableau 6.5.

	Italie	Grande-Bretagne	Belgique
	(Inst. centr. de Stat.)	(Board of Trade)	(Ministère du travail)
Janvier 1937	57,5	60,8	63,6
Janvier 1939	68,5	55,0	58,9

sur les entretiens commerciaux italo-allemands, par le tourisme et "certaines transactions financières", dont la nature n'a pas été spécifiée. S'agirait-il d'une nouvelle forme de crédits interalliés?

Prix et salaires— Les indices des prix et du coût de la vie sont restés pratiquement stationnaires en 1938 et au début de 1939. La forte hausse de 1937 et la résistance ultérieure à la baisse des prix mondiaux font que les prix-or italiens sont aujourd'hui supérieurs aux prix étrangers alors qu'ils leur étaient inférieurs après l'"alignement" de la lire. Voici une comparaison entre les indices des prix de gros-or en Italie, Grande-Bretagne et Belgique (le belga, comme la lire, étant resté stable depuis 1936) sur la base de 1930:

La situation s'est donc renversée, ce qui n'a pas manqué d'influencer les exportations; celles de produits finis sont en baisse sensible et les systèmes d'aide directe ou indirecte commencent à réapparaître. La nouvelle hausse des salaires de 8 à 10% risque d'accentuer encore ces difficultés. Des ordres très rigoureux contre toute hausse des prix de détail ont été transmis aux organes de surveillance (Conseils provinciaux des Corporations). Mais puisque la quantité d'articles de consommation mise à la disposition des Italiens diminue, ainsi qu'il ressort des chiffres du commerce extérieur, les Conseils sont placés devant une tâche particulièrement difficile, même si l'on fait abstraction de l'incidence de la hausse des salaires sur les prix de revient.

Finances— En relation avec l'augmentation des salaires, les traitements des fonctionnaires et les pensions ont été augmentés de 6 à 8% et le régime des assurances sociales (maladies, vieillesse, maternité) a été élargi. La répercussion sur le budget se chiffre pour les traitements par une augmentation des dépenses de 550 millions.

On ne possède toujours pas de renseignements sur l'exécution du budget de 1938–1939. Aucun emprunt à long terme n'ayant été émis depuis l'emprunt forcé immobilier de fin 1936, les besoins extraordinaires du Trésor ont probablement été couverts principalement par l'émission de Bons du Trésor ou par

Tableau 6.6. *Dépôts et comptes coûtants créditeurs*

	Banques commerciales et coopératives	Instituts de crédit de droit public	Caisses d'épargne ordinaires et postales
Fin 1937	27.107	7.254	44.400
Fin 1938	28.469	9.544	46.188
	+ 1.362	+ 2.290	+ 1.788

en millions de lires.

des avances en comptes-courants auprès de certaines grandes banques et de la Caisse des Dépôts. En 1938, les dépôts ont augmenté d'une façon considérable.

Comme on voit, l'augmentation s'est produite surtout dans les Instituts de crédit en contact étroit avec l'État.

Le rapport de la Banque d'Italie, pour l'année 1938, dont la presse a publié des extraits, contient deux chiffres intéressants: l'un est celui de la circulation-billets, qui était à la fin de 1938 de 18.956 millions de lires contre 17.468 millions à la fin de 1937. Le total des engagements à vue a atteint 20.677 millions contre 18.933 millions. Cette augmentation, qui reste modérée, a sa source dans le développement des opérations actives de la Banque: financement des divers impôts sur le capital, de l'autarcie et des récoltes. Le montant des escomptes et des avances passe en effet de 41.121 millions de lires en 1937 à 57.538 millions en 1938.

L'autre chiffre intéressant est celui de l'encaisse-or et devises de la Banque. Elle montre, par rapport à la fin de 1937 et de 1936, une diminution de 202 millions de lires; elle n'est plus que de 3.826 millions. On sait qu'une réserve en crédits et en titres étrangers, ainsi qu'en titres italiens émis à l'étranger, provenant de la réquisition de l'année 1935 est détenue pour le compte du Trésor par l'Institut pour les Changes avec l'Étranger. En 1937, on n'avait pas touché à la réserve de l'institut d'émission, mais la Banque d'Italie avait signalé qu'au cours de l'année l'Institut pour les Changes avait dû transférer 68% des crédits et 59% des titres réquisitionnés. Le fait que cette fois la réserve de l'institut d'émission a diminué peut indiquer que l'on a préféré, pour faire face au déficit de la balance des comptes, vendre de l'or plutôt que de réaliser des titres rapportant des revenus. Mais vu la diminution impressionnante des importations, nous penchons plutôt-pour l'hypothèse que la réserve de l'Institut pour les Changes est pratiquement épuisée, d'autant plus que le rapport de 1937 avait spécifié que lors des réalisations des titres, on avait commencé par les valeurs les plus appréciées et les plus facilement réalisables.

ITALIE*

La conjoncture – A certains points de vue, la reprise de l'activité économique se confirme en Italie. En avril, l'indice de la production industrielle,[4] quoique légèrement inférieur au chiffre de mars, montre un écart favorable de 10,7% par rapport au mois d'avril 1938, début de la régression industrielle de l'année dernière.[5] Trois facteurs conditionnent cette reprise:

1) le réveil d'industries qui avaient connu un marasme prolongé: ainsi les indices du bâtiment et de la production de matériel ferroviaire sont supérieurs en avril de 57,4% et de 33,5% aux chiffres d'avril 1938;

2) l'industrie des armements fait progresser le secteur métallurgique: la production des fers ou alliages, particulièrement importante pour les fabrications de guerre augmente de 260,8%, la production de fonte de 23,1%, tandis que la production d'acier reste stationnaire;

3) la conjoncture internationale rend possible une augmentation assez importante des exportations italiennes. L'indice des exportations à destination de l'étranger (quantité) montre en avril une augmentation de 20% par rapport au même mois de l'année précédente; la hausse est même de 35% pour la catégorie des matières semi-ouvrées, qui contient des produits importants tels que les filés de coton, les fibres artificielles, la soie grège et le soufre.

On constate toutefois une divergence entre l'indice de la production et celui des heures de travail exécutées dans les établissements industriels. Cet indice, en effet, est en avril 1939 *inférieur* au chiffre d'avril 1938, de 3%. Cela provient probablement du fait que l'industrie textile, qui emploie le plus de main-d'œuvre, n'a pas encore atteint le niveau de l'année dernière.

Le fait que l'orientation de la conjoncture italienne n'est pas encore absolument nette ressort aussi des chiffres du tonnage transporté par chemin de fer qui est à peu près égal, pour les cinq premiers mois de l'année, au tonnage transporté au cours de la même période de l'année précédente; il lui est même

* Institut de statistique de l'Université de Paris et Institut scientifique des recherches économiques et sociales, *L'activité économique*, *Bulletin trimestriel* n. 18, 31 juillet 1939.

4 Le Ministère des Corporations a modifié la pondération de l'indice en diminuant le poids attribué à l'industrie de la soie, poids qui ne correspondait plus à l'importance réelle de l'industrie. Pour établir les pourcentages de variation que nous donnons dans le texte, nous avons recalculé l'indice pour 1938 avec la pondération actuelle; le graphique n'a pas été modifié.

5 Voir *Activité Économique*, 31 juillet 1938, pp. 139–140.

inférieur si l'on déduit du tonnage global, le tonnage en provenance et à destination des ports. Ce dernier est en hausse ainsi que le tonnage maritime. Voici les chiffres intéressants à cet égard:

Tableau 6.7. *Tonnage transporté par chemin de fer*

	Total	En provenance et à destination des ports	Tonnage chargé et déchargé dans les ports
Janvier-mai 1938	21.981	5.444	17.309
Janvier-mai 1939	21.959	5.734	19.100

en milliers de tonnes.

Tandis que le mouvement des prix se maintient dans d'étroites limites, l'indice du coût de la vie qui, pendant une année était resté stable autour de 100, est monté en mai à 102,9. Il s'agit là probablement d'un premier effet des récentes augmentations de salaires.

Commerce extérieur, balance des comptes, contrôle des changes— Le déficit de la balance commerciale avec les pays étrangers a continué à diminuer fortement. Pendant les mois d'avril et de mai, pour la première fois, cette diminution est due dans une plus grande mesure à l'augmentation des exportations (+ 181 millions de lires, par rapport à avril-mai 1938) qu'à la diminution des importations (- 162 millions de lire). Voici les chiffres globaux pour les cinq premiers mois de l'année:

Tableau 6.8.

	Janvier-mai 1938	Janvier-mai 1939
Importations	4.910	4.012
Exportations	3.163	3.291
Déficit	1.747	721

en milliers de tonnes.

Au cours de la discussion du budget, M. Guarneri, ministre des Échanges et Devises, a indiqué que malgré cette réduction importante, le déficit des quatre premiers mois de l'année n'a pas été couvert par les rentrées invisibles, par suite surtout de la diminution du tourisme. La statistique hôtelière nous donne une indication intéressante à cet égard.

Tableau 6.9. *Pourcentages des lits occupés au mois d'avril de chaque année*

	Hôtels de luxe	Tous hôtels
1937	71,4	60,5
1938	65,7	58,5
1939	55,5	50,5

En attendant une amélioration de la situation internationale, les efforts du gouvernement italien se sont portés sur le deuxième poste qui a servi dans le passé à équilibrer la balance des comptes italienne: les remises des émigrants. A l'intention des émigrants et de ceux d'entre eux qui veulent rentrer en Italie, l'Institut pour les Changes a créé une nouvelle lire: *la lire-émigrant* dont le rabais par rapport à la lire officielle sera fixé par l'Institut. Cette lire est mise en quantité limitée à la disposition des émigrants pour les envois à leurs familles. Ceux qui rentrent en Italie peuvent l'obtenir en quantité illimitée.[6]

D'autre part, l'Institut pour les Changes qui, moyennant une provision, accordait des garanties de change pour les opérations s'effectuant à travers la plupart des clearings, a décidé d'en faire autant pour les opérations en *devises libres*. Il assure la contrepartie des *achats et ventes de change à terme* qu'il n'était plus possible de pratiquer depuis l'introduction du contrôle des changes. L'Institut se sert des grandes banques simplement à titre d'intermédiaires et fixe le cours des reports et déports en relation avec les cotations internationales. Cependant il est prévu que l'Institut pourra diminuer le taux d'un déport ou même le changer en report pour avantager les exportateurs. Il s'agirait en somme de dévaluer la lire à terme, qui seule intéresse les exportateurs vendant à crédit, tout en la maintenant stable au comptant.

A côté de ces perfectionnements du contrôle des changes italiens, de nouvelles restrictions apparaissent: le montant maximum de devises par touriste se rendant à l'étranger a été réduit de 2.500 à 1.000 lire; les sanctions contre les exportations de capitaux ont été renforcées.

Finances publiques et étatisme— Les déclarations du ministre des Finances à la Chambre et au Sénat lors du vote du budget ont apporté des précisions sur l'état des finances italiennes. On connaît ainsi les chiffres définitifs du budget

6 Au point de vue économique, les rapatriements équivalent à la liquidation d'un capital placé à l'étranger (dont les intérêts sont représentés par les remises); l'effort du gouvernement en vue d'obtenir le retour des Italiens résidant à l'étranger s'insère ainsi dans la série des mesures qui ont eu pour objet la réquisition et la réalisation des titres étrangers et des titres italiens émis à l'étranger.

1937–1938 et les résultats probables pour 1938–1939; on possède même des indications nouvelles sur les moyens auxquels le Gouvernement a eu recours pour couvrir le déficit. Voici d'abord les chiffres des budgets successifs:

Tableau 6.10.

	1935–1936	1936–1937	1937–1938	1938–1939 (Résultats probables)
Dépenses ordinaires	21.921	23.413	29.615	30.831
Dépenses extraordinaires pour l'Éthiopie	11.136	17.519	9.027	6.500
Dépenses totales	33.057	40.932	38.642	37.331
Recettes	20.371	24.702	27.468	24.581
Déficit	12.686	16.230	11.174	12.750

en milliers de tonnes.

Il ressort de ce tableau que les dépenses pour l'Éthiopie sont en décroissance tandis que les dépenses ordinaires, dans lesquelles sont compris les crédits militaires, augmentent. La diminution des recettes en 1938–1939, qui atteint près de 3 milliards, par rapport à 1937–1938, provient à la fois de ce que l'impôt extraordinaire sur les sociétés par actions avait été acquitté pour la plus grande partie au début de 1938 et de ce que la conjoncture économique de 1937–1938 avait été très favorable.

Les déficits des quatre derniers exercices atteignent 52.840 millions de lires et ont probablement à peine dépassé 49 milliards au 31 mars 1939, date à laquelle se réfèrent les nouveaux renseignements. Quant aux moyens de couverture ces renseignements, complétés par quelques recoupements et évaluations, nous permettent de dresser le tableau suivant:

Tableau 6.11.

Rente amortissable 5% emprunt immobilier	14.182 millions
Réalisation des titres étrangers échangés obligatoirement contre titres d'État	3.500 millions
Bons du Trésor	12.802 millions
Avances en compte-courant de la Caisse des Dépôts	10.702 millions
Avances en compte-courant de la Banque de Naples	2.500 millions
Avances directes de la Banque d'Italie	1.000 millions
Émissions de billets d'État	3.616 millions
Total	48.302 millions

L'émission du 5% amortissable et de l'emprunt immobilier et la réalisation des titres étrangers ont fourni le gros des ressources extraordinaires en 1935–1936 et 1936–1937, tandis qu'on a fait appel aux autres moyens de couverture (augmentation de la dette flottante et inflation) dans les années suivantes.

Le Ministre a prévu que le "budget de l'Italie impériale" se stabiliserait autour du chiffre de 32 milliards; des mesures sont à l'étude pour porter les recettes à ce niveau. A cet effet, on vient d'ordonner une révision générale du cadastre et des bases d'imposition des immeubles urbains. En outre, on prévoit la réduction de certaines dépenses et la limitation des trop nombreuses "zones industrielles."[7] En attendant, les dépenses en relation avec la guerre civile espagnole ont été remplacées aussitôt par des dépenses pour la mise en valeur de l'Albanie: un crédit de deux milliards a déjà été ouvert pour le système routier.[8]

Pour la première fois depuis sa création en 1935 l'Institut pour la Reconstruction Industrielle (I.R.I.) a publié dans son rapport annuel certaines précisions révélant l'importance considérable que ce *holding* de l'État italien a acquise dans l'économie générale du pays. Nous apprenons en effet qu'avec un capital propre d'un milliard, l'Institut gère un montant de 20 milliards de lires, chiffre énorme si on le compare au capital total des sociétés par actions italiennes, qui s'élève à 50 milliards.

Sur les 20 milliards, 9 milliards représentent des intérêts dans les entreprises directement contrôlées (grandes banques, métallurgie, chantiers navals, marine marchande, industries aéronautiques, installations hydro-électriques, cellulose, etc.), 9 milliards des prêts directs ou indirects—à travers les grandes banques—à des industries non contrôlées, et 2 milliards des titres d'État et activités diverses. Tout en assumant de nouvelles participations dans les industries autarciques et dans les industries de défense nationale, l'I.R.I. continue à liquider d'anciens paquets d'actions provenant de divers sauvetages opérés au cours de la crise; c'est même de là qu'à défaut d'émissions d'obligations, il tire ses ressources principales. Cependant l'importance des intérêts gérés ne semble pas avoir conduit à une bureaucratisation excessive: d'après le rapport le nombre d'employés de l'Institut n'atteint pas même la centaine.

7 Créées dans tes banlieues de nombreuses villes (Trieste, Venise, Gênes, Carrare, etc.) ces zones sont de vastes domaines d'exonération fiscale pour toutes les activités économiques qui s'y exercent.

8 Le tarif douanier et les principales lois monétaires italiennes ont été étendus à l'Albanie. Le franc albanais est stabilisé par rapport à la lire à un cours correspondant à la parité existant antérieurement à l'occupation.

Parallèlement à l'élargissement du secteur étatique se poursuit la concentration du secteur privé de l'économie italienne: les deux principales sociétés de fibres artificielles, la Snia-Viscosa et la Cisa-Viscosa viennent de fusionner et le nouvel organisme contrôlera 95% d'une production dont on sait l'importance.

· 7 ·

MÉMOIRE SUR LE CONTRÔLE DES CHANGES EN ITALIE*

Tables Des Matières

* Juin 1939. Institut International de Coopération Intellectuelle, Société des Nations, Paris. Conférence Permanente des Hautes Études Internationales, XIIéme Session, Bergen 1939, Conférence Générale d'Études sur les Politiques Économiques de la Paix.

IV. Commerce extérieur et politique commerciale
  1) Régime des importations
  2) Régime des exportations
  3) Politique contractuelle, clearings, échanges compensés
    a) Généralités
    b) Points particuliers relatives au clearings
      i) Garantie de change
      ii) Opérations bancaires connexes aux clearings
      iii) Le clearing italo-anglais
    c) Les accords de paiements
  4) Les compensations privées
  5) Influence du contrôle sur le commerce extérieur
    a) Dans l'ensemble
    b) Répartition par groupes de pays
    c) Répartition par catégories des produits

V. Monnaie
  1) La lire de 1934 à 1936
  2) L'"alignement" de la lire en octobre 1936
  3) L'évolution des prix après l'alignement et ses répercussions sur la lire
  4) Causes de l'évolution des prix

VI. Économie intérieure
  1) Relations entre le contrôle des changes et le contrôle étatique de l'Économie et de la Politique autarcique
  2) Le Contrôle des Changes et l'approvisionnement en matières première et en articles de consommation
  3) La protection de l'industrie et de l'agriculture

VII. Évolution récente

Tableaux Statistiques

I. Déficit commercial et variations de l'encaisse-or et devises de la Banque d'Italie 1934–1938
II. Situation des clearings 1937–1938
III. Commerce et clearing italo-anglais 1937–1938
IV. Commerce extérieur global 1929–1938
V. Commerce extérieur
VI. Commerce extérieur par groupes de pays 1929–1938
VII. Commerce extérieur par catégories des produits 1929–1938
VIII. Indices-or des prix de gros en Italie, France et Grande-Bretagne
IX. Cours de la lire-billet (grosse coupure sur le marchés officieux de Paris en % du cours officiel—graphique)

I. Origines

1) Les précédents du Contrôle actuel

Avant la guerre mondiale, la monnaie italienne faisait partie de l'Union Monétaire Latine, mais par opposition aux monnaies française et suisse elle était presque constamment au régime du cours forcé; et, cependant, malgré la non-convertibilité des billets de banque en or, la lire se tint très près de sa parité légale, à partir de 1900.

La politique commerciale et monétaire pendant la guerre fut marquée, comme dans tous les pays, par de multiples prohibitions à l'entrée et à la sortie. Parmi ces dernières, il y eut aussi les défenses d'exportation de billets de banque et de titres italiens et étrangers; pour le commerce des changes, on créa en 1917 l'Institut pour les Changes avec l'étranger, qui exerçait le monopole dont il fut investi, à travers les banques d'émission (Banque d'Italie, de Naples et de Sicile) et les principaux établissements de crédit. Ce fut lui qui disposa des crédits interalliés et qui assuma l'initiative de créer des consortiums pour l'importation des produits principaux. En 1918, on institua l'obligation pour les exportateurs de céder le produit en devises de leur exportation à l'Institut.

Une grande partie de cette réglementation qui fut le véritable précurseur de l'organisation actuelle, a été supprimée après la fin de la guerre. Le monopole de l'Institut pour les Changes avec l'Étranger (Istcambi) cessa dès 1919, mais on maintint un certain contrôle sur les opérations de change qui fut renforcé en particulier pendant les époques d'attaque spéculative contre la lire. Ainsi, en juin 1926, des décrets réservaient le commerce des devises aux banques avec au moins 100 millions de lires de capital et toutes les opérations de change devaient avoir un fondement dans des besoins commerciaux ou touristiques qui devaient être vérifiés par les banques autorisées. L'exportation de billets de banque et de toutes espèces de titres de crédit payables en Italie et libellés en lires fut interdite. Enfin, les banques étaient tenues de rendre compte de leurs opérations de change au Trésor.

Cette législation resta en vigueur même après la stabilisation. de la lire par le décret-loi du 21 décembre 1927 qui avait proclamé la convertibilité en or ou en devises—au choix de la Banque d'Italie—des billets de banque; elle ne fut abolie que par le décret du 12 mars 1930 qui rétablit l'entière liberté du commerce des devises. D'ailleurs, l'atténuation du contrôle par voie administrative avait été progressive pendant les années antérieures et même au temps de son application la plus stricte une pièce essentielle manquait à l'efficacité de la réglementation: ce fut l'obligation de céder aux banques les devises provenant des exportations. C'est par cette voie principalement que s'opéraient, dans l'après-guerre, toutes les évasions de capitaux.

2) Causes de l'établissement du Contrôle en 1934

L'établissement du Contrôle des Changes italien tel qu'il fonctionne aujourd'hui date de l'année 1934. Le décret-loi du 26 mai 1934 en posait le principe et contenait, en même temps, le début des mesures d'exécution et les décrets-lois du 8 et du 15 décembre 1934 instituaient le monopole des opérations de change avec diverses autres mesures que nous examinerons, en détail, dans la suite.

Le Contrôle des Changes italien est donc apparu assez tardivement. On sait, en effet, que les contrôles, soit en Allemagne ou dans les pays d'Europe centrale et balkaniques, ont été introduits généralement à la suite de la crise internationale de crédit de 1931. La cause immédiate en fut, dans la plupart des pays, des retraits massifs de capitaux étrangers qui s'ajoutaient à une détérioration de la balance générale des paiements provoqués par la crise.

En 1931, les monnaies européennes se divisaient en trois groupes: les pays nouvellement créés après la guerre et ceux qui avaient vu tomber leur monnaie à zéro dans l'après-guerre adoptaient généralement le contrôle des changes, les pays dont les monnaies avaient subi précédemment une forte amputation constituaient avec la Suisse et la Hollande le bloc-or; enfin, les pays dévaluateurs constituèrent le bloc-sterling.

La lire avait, d'une façon générale, partagé les destinées de la monnaie française pendant et après la guerre et aux yeux du public elle restait solidaire du franc plutôt que de la livre. D'autre part, l'économie italienne ne présenta point les faiblesses qui avaient entraîné, soit la chute de la livre, soit l'établissement des contrôles des changes en Europe centrale. L'endettement extérieur à court terme avait été maintenu dans des limites étroites car par suite d'une crise de déflation particulièrement violente—entraînée par une stabilisation à un niveau trop élevé—l'industrie ne participa que d'une façon très fragmentaire au boom de 1928–1929.

Ainsi des raisons multiples firent se ranger l'Italie dans le bloc-or après qu'elle eût pris des mesures de défense contre les dévaluations monétaires et la baisse des prix mondiaux: un décret-loi du 24 septembre 1931 imposa une surtaxe *ad valorem* de 15% sur tous les produits importés; cette surtaxe agissait fortement dans les sens d'une contraction des importations et surtout des produits fabriqués.

A la même époque, un décret du 29 septembre 1931 autorisa le Ministre des Finances à règlementer par décret le commerce des devises, mais ce ne fut que près de 3 années plus tard que le Ministre usa, pour la première fois, de la faculté qui lui était ainsi ouverte. Cependant, un contrôle officieux du marché des changes fut institué par les Banques sur les instructions de la Confédération du Crédit et de l'Assurance italienne qui est l'organisation syndicale des Banquiers et des Assureurs. Ce contrôle fut pratiqué d'une façon très relâchée dès que les retraits de capitaux étrangers eurent diminué d'intensité.

De 1931 à 1934, l'Italie s'en tint aux règles de l'étalon-or et intervint souvent dans les réunions des Directeurs des Banques Centrales des pays du bloc-or pour faire adopter une ligne commune de défense et de collaboration. On sait quel fut le sort de ces tentatives.

Si l'on essaie aujourd'hui d'expliquer les raisons de l'instauration du Contrôle des Changes italien en 1934, on est naturellement tenté d'y voir le début d'une préparation économique à la guerre abyssine, puisque d'après les publications presque officielles, le chef du gouvernement italien aurait préparé son action justement dès 1934. Nous croyons, cependant, qu'une telle interprétation rétrospective serait trop facile et même fausse. En effet, en scrutant uniquement la situation italienne de 1934, nous y découvrons tant d'éléments explicatifs que nous pouvons nous passer très bien d'une hypothèse qui, à notre avis, fait trop de crédit à la faculté de prévision d'un gouvernement quel qu'il soit. Le Contrôle des Changes a été introduit en Italie comme moyen de défense contre les dangers présents et non pas en vue d'une action offensive future qu'il a favorisée dans la suite.

Comme ailleurs, la cause générale est la détérioration de la balance des comptes. D'après les évaluations du spécialiste italien en matière de balance de paiement, le Professeur Borgatta, la balance des revenus, c'est-à-dire les diverses postes de la balance à l'exclusion des mouvements de capitaux et d'or, aurait été en équilibre, approximatif, les dépenses touristiques, les remises des émigrants et les prêts compensant le déficit des échanges commerciaux descendu au chiffre modeste de 1.500 millions de lires. Si, néanmoins, pendant ces trois années les réserves de la Banque d'Italie diminuaient de 2.227 millions de lires, cela serait dû à des mouvements de capitaux, c'est-à-dire à des achats par les Italiens de titres étrangers ou de titres italiens émis à l'étranger, à des diminutions du solde débiteur des comptes bancaires avec l'étranger et aux excédents de l'amortissement d'emprunts étrangers anciens sur la stipulation d'emprunts nouveaux. Il s'agit, là, en grande partie, jusqu'en 1934, de mouvements de capitaux à long terme et il n'est certainement pas injustifié de présenter ce phénomène non pas sous l'appellation péjorative de "fuite de capitaux" mais sous celle—peut-être un peu trop optimiste—d' « amélioration » de la situation patrimoniale par rapport à l'étranger."[1]

C'était, en effet, une saine politique de l'Italie d'avant-guerre de nationaliser progressivement sa dette publique ainsi que son économie industrielle grâce aux excédents laissés par la balance des revenus. Évidemment, la continuation d'une telle politique était moins défendable si sa contrepartie n'était plus ledit excédent, mais les réserves de l'Institut d'Émission. C'est ce que souligne le rapport de la Banque d'Italie pour 1934: "il se produisit, dit-il, le transfert des disponibilités de la réserve possédé par l'Institut d'Émission dans l'intérêt de l'Économie et de la Défense de toute la nation à l'Économie individuelle de quelques milliers d'individus et de collectivités."

Telle était donc la situation déjà critique des années précédant immédiatement l'établissement du Contrôle des Changes. La lire, par suite, de ces mouvements de capitaux, était soumise à une tension constante. En 1934, la situation empira considérablement; dès le début de l'année, les exportations étaient en régression importante et les importations en augmentation par rapport à 1933; en définitive, le déficit fut de 2.617 millions de lires, supérieur d'un milliard à celui des années précédentes. L'équilibre de la balance des revenus était ainsi rompu, d'autant plus que les entrées invisibles du tourisme s'amenuisaient, elles aussi, rapidement, l'Italie étant devenu un "pays cher." Cette brusque aggravation de la balance des revenus pendant les premiers mois de l'année avec ses répercussions inévitables sur les réserves de la Banque d'Italie est certainement le facteur essentiel de l'établissement du Contrôle. On peut l'expliquer à son tour par toute la politique suivie par l'Italie pendant la crise ou, plutôt, par les contradictions de cette politique.

Officiellement, depuis 1927 déjà, la déflation était devenue la mystique économique officielle et on la pratiqua avec une réelle obstination à maints points de vue. Deux fois, en 1930 et au début de 1934, les traitements des

1 Excellente œuvre récente de la Banque d'Italie "*l'Economia italiana nel sessennio 1931–1936*," (Rome 1938, Istituto Poligrafico dello Stato) précise: "Les emprunts contractés à l'Étranger par des firmes ou des collectivités italiennes avec l'autorisation du Ministère des Finances se montaient, au total, à 293,5 millions de Dollars dans les 6 années 1925–1930, à 10 millions en 1931, à 6,7 millions en 1932, à 0,2 millions on 1933 et ils cessèrent à partir de 1934 (1ère partie p. 114)."

fonctionnaires et les salaires à leur suite furent diminués de 12, d'abord, de 6 à 12% ensuite; mais la déflation si elle avait été aussi importante que le demandait 1) la surévaluation originaire de la lire on 1927, 2) la baisse des prix mondiaux, 3) les dévaluations étrangères, aurait probablement arrêté toute la vie économique du pays d'autant plus que la structure financière de l'industrie lourde et des banques n'était pas des plus saines. Le gouvernement s'en aperçut bientôt et par la création de l'Institut Mobilier Italien (I.M.I.) en 1931 et de l'Institut de Reconstruction Industrielle (I.R.I.) en 1933, vint en aide aux industries et aux banques chancelantes. En 1933, la Banque d'Italie avait fait des avances ou des escomptes au profit de l'Institut de Reconstruction Industrielle, pour la somme énorme de 7.353 millions de lires, soit près de 50% de la circulation de billets! Cette somme représentait des aides directes à l'industrie mais surtout l'actif immobilisé des Banques commerciales cédé à l'IRI contre des moyens liquides. Si le gouvernement ne pouvait permettre ainsi à la déflation de se dérouler jusqu'au bout, il fit de l'autre côté une politique de travaux publics, de revalorisation des produits agricoles, qui devait directement contrecarrer les tendances déflationnistes. L'activité industrielle intérieure reprit fortement en 1934, sous l'influence d'un boom du bâtiment et des armements alors que les exportations se contractaient par suite de la surévaluation de la lire.

Ainsi la reflation interne provoqua une demande accrue de matières premières d'importation étrangère tandis que l'inachèvement de la déflation fit obstacle aux exportations.

Mais dans le discours qu'il prononça à la Chambre des Députés le 26 mai 1934, pour justifier les mesures prises, M. Mussolini indiquait que des 700 millions de lires que la Banque d'Italie avait perdus en or ou en devises depuis le début de l'année, 2/3 étaient en relation avec des causes "réelles" tandis qu'un tiers correspondait à des exportations de capitaux sous différentes formes. Plusieurs faits avaient causé, en effet, une accentuation de cette "amélioration de la situation patrimoniale de l'Italie par rapport à l'Étranger" dont nous parlions plus haut: d'abord, après la dévaluation du dollar et sa stabilisation, les cours et les rendements de beaucoup de titres italiens émis à New-York furent considérés comme avantageux par les capitalistes d'autant plus qu'en Italie la conversion simultanée du 5%, consolidé on 3,5% amortissable abaissait le rendement des titres italiens. Ensuite, il faut mentionner un fait qui a exercé une action psychologique indéniable; jusqu'en 1933, la diminution des réserves s'était répercutée uniquement sur les devises détenues par la Banque d'Italie et l'encaisse-or avait même augmenté grâce à la liquidation progressive du "gold exchange standard," ce ne fut qu'à partir de 1934, que la diminution des réserves se traduisit par une diminution du stock or. Alors se vérifiaient, pour la première fois, des fortes exportations de billets qui furent offerts sur les places étrangères et durent être rachetés par la Banque d'Italie ainsi que le déclara M. Mussolini, dans son discours.

3) Premières mesures

Le premier acte vers l'établissement du Contrôle fut le décret ministériel du 26 mai 1934 dont l'art. 1er stipule, d'une façon générique qu'aucune opération de change ou de devises ne pourra être exécutée si elle ne répond pas à de réelles nécessités de l'industrie et du commerce ou aux besoins de ceux qui voyagent à l'étranger.

L'art. 4 défend l'achat de titres étrangers et de titres italiens émis à l'étranger. L'art. 5 défend l'exportation de billets de banque, de chèques et de titres italiens et limite la somme que les touristes peuvent emporter à 5.000 lires par personne. Enfin, l'art. 7 soumet à l'autorisation du Ministre des Finances l'escompte des lettres de change libellées en lires et tirées par un créancier étranger sur un débiteur italien, ainsi que toutes autres opérations qui apparaissent comme un moyen de se procurer à l'étranger des disponibilités en lires. En même temps, un décret-loi soumit à l'estampillage tous les titres italiens et émis à l'étranger circulant en Italie.

Mais ces premières mesures n'eurent pas toute l'efficacité désirée, les évasions de capitaux restèrent faciles et, d'autre part, la balance commerciale continua à être largement déficitaire. Pour toute l'année, la perte des réserves de l'Institut d'Émission fut en définitive de 1.514 millions de lires dont 1.181 millions en or.

La modération des premières mesures ainsi que plusieurs déclarations publiques de Ministres montent clairement que le Gouvernement italien s'est engagé à contre-cœur dans la politique de contrôle. Mais l'unique alternative, à savoir la dévaluation, était une impossibilité psychologique pour le Régime tant que les autres monnaies du bloc-or résistaient. Ainsi, il ne restait comme issue que le resserrement du Contrôle.

Le 8 décembre 1934, la nouvelle législation prit définitivement corps avec un décret-loi et 3 décrets ministériels qui stipulaient:

1) le monopole des opérations de change près l'Institut National pour les changes avec l'étranger. Seules les entreprises de Transports Maritimes et les Compagnies d'assurance peuvent encore tenir des comptes en monnaies étrangères sur autorisation du Ministère des Finances;

2) la cession obligatoire à l'Istcambi de crédit sur l'étranger de la part des banques et des sociétés;
3) la déclaration obligatoire à la Banque d'Italie de titres étrangers ou italiens émis à l'étranger de la part de toutes les personnes (physiques et morales) domiciliées en Italie;
4) l'obligation pour l'exportateur de céder les devises provenant de l'exportation à l'Istcambi;
5) Enfin, un début d'organisation de tout ce système: la Banque d'Italie étant chargée du service de Caisse par l'Istcambi et certaines grandes banques étant déléguées par la Banque d'Italie pour contrôler la cession de devises dérivant de l'exportation.

On perçoit facilement la lacune de l'édifice ainsi érigé: le régime des importations n'est pas encore établi. Cela ne devait pas tarder et un décret ministériel du 18 février 1935 liquida le contingentement général des importations.

Nous reviendrons plus loin sur le détail du système établi par ce décret et par des mesures ultérieures.

4) Grandes lignes de l'évolution du Contrôle

Toujours est-il qu'à l'abri de cette législation de plus en plus complexe, la conjoncture intérieure en relation avec les préparatifs militaires se développe avec vigueur. En particulier, le contingentement des importations permit (et favorisa à son tour) une hausse des prix qui détermina une aggravation et une complication du contrôle.

Dans la suite, le contrôle s'est ressenti essentiellement des mesures de mobilisation économique et financière connexes à la guerre abyssine, de l'imposition des sanctions par les États membres de la Société des Nations et de l'adoption des contre-sanctions par l'Italie. La cession obligatoire des crédits étrangers détenus par les personnes privées, la réquisition des titres étrangers et italiens émis à l'étranger, ainsi que le versement en comptes bloqués de toutes sommes dues aux États sanctionnistes ont assigné de nouvelles tâches à l'Istcambi. Par contre, la levée des sanctions en juillet 1936 et peu après la dévaluation de la lire ont permis certains allégements non seulement au point de vue de la politique commerciale et douanière, mais encore en ce qui concerne le contrôle des changes et la monnaie. Ainsi, les primes à l'exportation purent être supprimées et la lire touristique s'approcha de la lire officielle.

Mais le contact avec l'Économie mondiale, retrouvé momentanément vers la fin de 1936, fut vite perdu à nouveau. La préparation militaire et surtout la politique d'autarcie exigèrent un contrôle de plus en plus strict de toutes les ressources nationales. Le renchérissement inhérent à l'autarcie compromit en grande partie les avantages de la dévaluation et à l'abri de la législation sur les changes, la conjoncture italienne put évoluer avec une dépendance très relâchée de l'économie mondiale.

Les mesures introduites dans le système du Contrôle en 1937 et en 1938 sont principalement l'ouverture de comptes libres pour l'étranger, l'institution de la garantie des changes dans de nombreux clearings, la mobilisation de l'arriéré des clearings au profit des exportateurs par des titres spéciaux et la permission accordée à certaines catégories d'exportateurs de disposer d'une partie des devises provenant de leurs ventes pour des achats de matières premières étrangères nécessaires à leur industrie. A notre avis, ces mesures constituent plutôt qu'une atténuation, un perfectionnement du contrôle, c'est-à-dire, la tentative de parer à ses inconvénients les plus évidents sans porter aucune atteinte à son principe même. Ces mesures ne sont pas une préface à une disparition du contrôle, mais au contraire, tendent à l'asseoir en tant qu'institution définitive.

II. Organisation Administrative

1) Caractère et étendue de la réglementation

La réglementation du Contrôle des Changes a naturellement donné lieu à des textes très nombreux. Au point de vue législatif, on peut considérer que le système était établi dans ses grandes lignes depuis 1935 et c'est ce qui explique la raréfaction relative de textes de lois après cette année. Le recueil de la B.R.I. qui va jusqu'en mai 1938 contient 10 textes pour 1934, 20 pour 1935, 14 pour 1936 et 6 pour 1937. Il s'agit là uniquement de décrets-lois, de décrets royaux et de décrets ministériels. On peut remarquer que les mesures fondamentales du 26 mai 1934 et celles qui les renforçaient le 9 décembre furent édictées par décret ministériel en vertu du pouvoir conféré antérieurement (en 1931) au Ministre des Finances. Mais généralement tous les textes importants, en dehors de ceux ayant trait à l'organisation administrative, sont des décrets-lois.

Cependant, on n'ignore pas l'importance capitale que revêt dans toute cette matière la pratique administrative; ainsi, le régime des importations est réglé par des circulaires ministérielles trimestrielles. Même pour des mesures d'ordre général telles que la cession de crédits à l'étranger ou la réquisition des titres, les textes législatifs prévoient uniquement *l'offre* obligatoire de ces crédits et de ces titres en laissant l'Istcambi libre de décider de l'acquisition ou non de ces crédits et titres.

Généralement, les lois et décrets italiens ne sont applicables qu'à l'intérieur du royaume (en décembre 1938, 4 provinces côtières de Lybie faisant partie du territoire métropolitain ont été constituées). Mais dans la majorité des cas, le contrôle des changes a été étendu avec les adaptations nécessaires, par voie de décrets aux colonies et aux possessions italiennes.

2) Les organes du Contrôle

La législation administrative en matière de contrôle des changes est extrêmement touffue. Dans le recueil de la B.R.I., on peut relever sur un total de 55, 16 décrets qui s'occupent uniquement de l'organisation ou de la réorganisation des différents rouages administratifs. A part cela, il est évident que les textes concernant les différents chapitres du contrôle contiennent presque toujours des dispositions relatives à l'organisation et la compétence.

L'élaboration du système a été très ardue et a donné lieu à beaucoup de tiraillements entre les diverses organisations; l'évolution est dans le sens d'une concentration de plus en plus marquée de tout le mécanisme dans un seul département. L'Italie est même le seul pays, à notre connaissance, qui ait élevé ce département au rang de ministère; nous parlons du *Ministère pour les Échanges et les Devises*, créé en un décret du 20 novembre 1937, qui avait été successivement la Surintendance près la Présidence du Conseil (20 mai 1935) et le Sous-Secrétariat (29 décembre 1934). C'est le Professeur Felice Guarneri qui a présidé, dès le début, ces organismes successifs avec beaucoup d'autorité.

Le Ministère compte 4 directions générales:

1) Questions douanières, les Affaires générales et le personnel;
2) Échanges avec l'étranger (clearing, compensations, traités de commerce, etc.);
3) Devises (lires touristiques, crédits étrangers, titres étrangers, etc.);
4) Service des importations. (Attribution de licences).

Peu à peu, on a centralisé près du Ministère toute l'administration afférente au Commerce extérieur, aux Douanes, et au Commerce des Changes, par des transmissions de compétence et de personnel du Ministère des Corporations et du Ministère des Finances, (Il faut se rappeler qu'en Italie, le Ministère des Corporations avait absorbé les fonctions du Ministère du Commerce).

L'instrument principal du Ministère pour les Échanges et les Devises est l'*Institut National pour les Changes avec l'Étranger* dont nous avons déjà parlé. C'est lui qui, dans la plupart des cas, est chargé de l'exécution matérielle des décisions prises et des accords élaborés par le Ministère. Un décret ministériel du 23 juin 1926, légèrement modifié dans la suite, lui a donné son statut actuel, selon lequel il a pour but:

1) d'acheter et de vendre au comptant et à terne de l'or, des devises étrangères, des billets d'État ou de banque, des titres étrangers et italiens émis à l'étranger;
2) d'exercer aussi longtemps que durera le monopole des changes le commerce des devises et de tout autre moyen qui puisse servir pour paiement à l'étranger dans toutes les formes possibles;
3) d'exécuter pour le compte du Trésor des dispositions relatives à la cession obligatoire des crédits et des titres étrangers et au commerce de l'or;
4) d'effectuer, de discipliner et de contrôler les opérations de compensation de devises et de marchandises;
5) d'exécuter toute autre mesure de caractère cambiste et de façon générale, toutes les opérations—même bancaires telles qu'émission de chèques, remboursements de bons et lettres de crédit émis à sa charge ou pour son compte, à la charge de tiers—en liaison avec des objectifs et susceptibles de régler et de faciliter le commerce de l'Italie avec l'Étranger.

Parmi ces dernières mesures, nous citerons les opérations relatives à la lire touristique et l'émission de certificats de crédit au profit des exportateurs en instance de règlements en clearing.

Le Ministre pour les Échanges et les Devises est, en même temps, directeur de l'Istcambi qui est relié, en particulier, avec la Direction Générale pour les Échanges et avec la Direction Générale pour les Devises.

Le rôle de l'Istcambi est parfois uniquement celui d'un organe d'exécution, comme dans le cas de distribution des devises aux importateurs ou aux Italiens voyageant à l'Étranger. Mais dans d'autres cas, gestion des clearings, des comptes bloqués, etc... sa liberté d'action est très large, puisqu'elle ne rencontre comme limite, que le contrôle et les directives génériques du Ministère.

On voit que le Ministère pour les Échanges et les Devises et l'Istcambi sont les deux pièces centrales du système tandis que dans nombre d'autres pays, nous rencontrons, à leur place, le Ministère de l'Économie ou des Finances et la Banque Centrale.

Comme on l'a dit, le Ministère des Finances s'est vu retirer graduellement la plupart de ses prérogatives en matière de change. Il lui reste l'autorisation de certaines opérations en dehors des affaires journalières telles que le financement de firmes italiennes à l'étranger et la stipulation d'emprunts à l'étranger par des société ou collectivités italiennes, l'achat de navires à l'étranger, etc... C'est lui, d'ailleurs, qui édicte toujours nominalement les décrets réglant toutes les matières et qui attribue les licences d'importation; mais là, il n'agit que comme exécutant du Ministère pour les Échanges et les Devises.

La *Banque d'Italie*, au contraire, joue un rôle très actif en tant qu'organe d'exécution du Ministère pour les Échanges et de l'Istcambi. D'une façon générale, l'Institut d'émission sert de Caissier à l'Istcambi ainsi qu'il est dit à l'art. 10 du décret du 9 décembre 1934: "Le commerce de tout moyen qui puisse servir à des paiements hors d'Italie sera exercé par l'institut National pour les Changes avec l'Étranger au moyen de la Banque d'Italie."

Mais le rôle de la Banque d'Italie n'est pas uniquement passif; à son tour, elle est chargée de contrôler les opérations extérieures *des Banques*; en effet, pour les opérations de périphérie, l'Istcambi, dont le siège se trouve à Rome, a délégué ses fonctions à la Banque d'Italie et aux principaux établissements de crédit du pays.[2]

Ces Banques ont des pouvoirs déterminés en matière d'attribution de devises aux voyageurs, qu'elles partagent d'ailleurs avec certaines banques étrangères et agences de voyage; mais surtout elles sont seules avec la Banque d'Italie à pouvoir donner le "benestare"[3] à l'exportation que l'exportateur obtient par son engagement de céder à la Banque le produit en devises de l'exportation.

Ces opérations spécialement autorisées doivent être comptabilisées à part et sont sujettes au contrôle de la Banque d'Italie ou elles sont, d'ailleurs,

2 Actuellement: Banco di Napoli, Banco di Sicilia, Banca Commerciale Italiana, Credito Italiano, Banco di Roma, Banca Nazionale del Lavoro, Banca d'America e d'Italia, Istituto di San Paolo di Torino, Monte dei Paschi di Siena.

3 Genre de laissez-passer pour la Douane nécessaire aux marchandises concernant les pays avec lesquels l'Italie n'est pas en rapport de clearing.

centralisées. Ainsi, les services compétents de la Banque d'Italie—l'inspection pour les opérations en devises et le service des opérations financières et de change avec l'étranger dirigent et contrôlent toutes les opérations extérieures des banques qui échappent, par conséquent, à la compétence de l'inspection pour la Défense de l'Épargne et la Direction du Crédit que la réforme bancaire de 1936–1937 avait instituée comme organe directeur de l'activité bancaire.

En résumé, la hiérarchie est nettement établie; elle va du Ministère pour les Échanges et Devises à l'Istcambi, de l'Istcambi à la Banque d'Italie, et de celle-ci aux Banques autorisées. L'unité de direction est nettement établie, mais elle n'empêche pas une certaine répartition des principales opérations entre les différents organes et une autonomie relative de ceux-ci.

Un peu à l'écart du système qu'on vient de décrire se trouve *L'Institut Nationale Fasciste pour le Commerce Extérieur* qui a pour tâche principale la prospection des Marchés extérieurs et la Propagande à l'étranger pour les produits italiens ainsi que la propagande à l'intérieur pour une propagande de qualité et une présentation adroite des produits nationaux destinés à l'exportation. Mais on lui a assigné aussi une fonction importante dans le mécanisme du contrôle, celle de surveiller les compensations privées qui, cependant, ne jouent plus un grand rôle aujourd'hui. L'Institut est, lui aussi, sous la dépendance directe du Ministère pour les Échanges et Devises.

Dans ses parties essentielles, le Contrôle des Changes nous apparaît ainsi comme un édifice purement administratif; cela peut surprendre si on se rappelle que 1934 ne fut pas seulement l'année du Contrôle des Changes, mais aussi celle des Corporations.

Mais dans un ordre du jour du début de 1936, le Grand Conseil Fasciste et M. Mussolini dans son discours devant l'Assemblée des Corporations du 26 mars 1936 ont nettement défini les échanges avec l'étranger comme une fonction d'intérêt général donc, fonction d'État qui demande, par conséquent, une réglementation directe. Ce n'est qu'en descendant du général au particulier que les administrations font appel à la collaboration d'organes constitués de façon corporative, c'est-à-dire comprenant des membres des catégories intéressées; ainsi, les propositions relatives à la répartition des contingents d'importation sont formulées par *10 juntes, pour les principaux produits*.[4] Les Membres

4 Junte pour les matières grasses animales et végétales et pour les engrain, junte pour les fibres végétales sauf le coton, junte pour les minerais, débris et métaux ferreux, junte pour les minerais, débris et métaux non-ferreux, junte pour les machines et appareils, junte pour le charbon (plus tard monopole), junte pour les peaux, junte pour le caoutchouc, junte pour

de ces juntes qui font partie du Ministère pour les Échanges sont nommés par le Ministère des Corporations sur désignation des associations syndicales, patronales et ouvrières. A côté d'elles, on trouve, pour certains produits, des organismes qui avaient déjà fait leur preuve en tant que Comptoir d'achat et qui ont été simplement mis sous les ordres du Ministère des Échanges. Ce sont: l'institut Cotonnier, la Junte des Laines, et la Junte pour les Graines Oléagineuses.

III. Mécanisme des paiements

1) Règlementation des opérations

Le Contrôle des Changes Italien tel qu'il existe aujourd'hui est, peut-être, le plus complet après le Contrôle allemand. Il s'étend à toutes les opérations de change que leur origine soit commerciale, financière, touristique ou autres. Il s'étend, par ailleurs, à tous les moyens de paiements puisque les textes concernent, d'une façon générale, "le commerce de tout moyen qui puisse servir à des paiements à l'étranger."

L'expression "Contrôle des Changes" est peu exacte puisque le système qu'elle indique comprend la *défense* de certaines opérations aussi bien que le *contrôle* de celles qui sont autorisées, en principe, on peut aujourd'hui classer les opérations qui nous intéressent sous trois chefs:

1) les opérations qui sont défendues aux particuliers d'une façon absolue et qui, d'ailleurs, comme par exemple, les opérations sur change à terme sont souvent rendues impossibles par l'institution du monopole des changes;
2) les opérations que les particuliers peuvent faire seulement à travers l'Istcambi qui détient le monopole des changes;
3) les opérations que certains particuliers peuvent faire en dehors de l'Istcambi, mais sous son contrôle ou celui de la Banque d'Italie.

la cellulose, junte pour les produits divers (alimentaires, bois et produits du sol, produits chimiques, drogues et produits coloniaux, autres produits).

Dans deux sections ultérieures, nous traiterons des opérations intérieures affectées par le contrôle des opérations extérieures et du rôle qui incombe aux banques dans le système tout entier.

a) Opérations défendues—La première mesure du contrôle italien, le décret-loi déjà cité du 26 mai 1934, a défendu toutes les opérations en changes et devises qui ne correspondent pas à de réelles nécessités de l'industrie et du commerce ou à des besoins de ceux qui voyagent à l'étranger. D'ailleurs, des prescriptions officieuses dans ce sens avaient été édictées dès septembre 1931 par la Confédération du Crédit et de l'Assurance, mais peu à peu ces prescriptions étaient tombées en désuétude.

La loi précitée spécifiait, d'ailleurs, un certain nombre d'opérations défendues: *la première est l'achat* de titres étrangers et de titres italiens émis à l'étranger. Nous avons vu, en effet, le rôle important joué par l'achat de ces titres dans l'amenuisement progressif des réserves de l'Institut d'émission; il fallait arrêter le processus trop rapide de nationalisation de la dette extérieure italienne à laquelle s'étalent ajoutés *en 1934*, des arbitrages et des spéculations sur titres étrangers. On sait que le mouvement fut successivement renversé par la cession obligatoire des titres au Trésor qui les liquida en grande partie par l'entremise de l'Istcambi.

La défense des autres opérations correspondait au double souci du gouvernement d'empêcher toute exportation des capitaux et de restreindre le plus possible le marché extérieur de la lire.

A ce dernier effet, il fut interdit, en principe, de consentir, en règlement d'importations, à des tirages libellés en lires, et l'escompte de traites de firmes étrangères sur firmes italiennes fut soumise à l'autorisation du Ministère des Finances (aujourd'hui du Ministère pour les Échanges); de même, l'ouverture de crédit en lires au profit de banques ou de firmes étrangères fut subordonnée à cette autorisation.

Le paiement des exportations doit être convenu en principe, on monnaies étrangères que l'exportateur s'oblige à céder à l'Istcambi. Il ne peut se faire en lires que si l'exportateur a un compte lires en Italie et encore faut-il pour cela une autorisation spéciale du Ministre des Échanges. Le règlement par billets de banque italiens est totalement exclu.

L'exportation et l'importation de billets de banque, de chèques et de tous titres libellés en lires ont été diversement réglées. Le décret-loi du 26 mai 1934 défendit l'exportation, d'une façon générale. Toutefois, la somme de 5.000 lires était autorisée pour les personnes se rendant à l'étranger, mais fut successivement réduite (15 décembre 1934) à 2.000 lires, à exporter au moyen de billets à coupures non supérieures à 100 lires. Un décret ministériel du 3 octobre 1935 défendit l'importation de billets de banque admettant seulement la réintroduction des sommes précédemment exportées. Le décret ministériel du 16 novembre 1935 permit, dans un délai de 10 jours, la réintroduction dans le Royaume des billets dont l'exportation avait été interdite, c'est-à-dire des coupures de 500 et de 1.000 lires; les sommes envoyées en Italie furent accréditées aux ayants-droits dans des comptes bloqués spéciaux sans intérêt. Pour pouvoir les utiliser pour d'achats à l'intérieur du Royaume, il faut l'autorisation du Ministère de Finances sur la proposition du Surintendant aux Échanges, (aujourd'hui Ministre). Cette mesure édictée au moment de la guerre abyssine avait un caractère d'amnistie partielle qui fut, d'ailleurs, répétée quelques mois après. On n'a jamais fourni de précisions sur le montant des billets revenus dans le Royaume de cette façon,

Enfin, la réglementation finale de cette matière a été donnée par un décret interministériel du 25 mai 1936 qui limita la somme maxima à emporter et à réintroduire à 350 lires par personne. En outre, l'Italien ou l'étranger domicilié en Italie peut emporter généralement 2.150 lires, mais cette somme lui est donnée en Italie même sous la forme de billets ou de chèques en monnaie étrangère. D'ailleurs, cette somme peut être diminuée si elle apparaît exagérée par rapport aux voyages entrepris et pour certains pays avec lesquels existent des accords spéciaux de tourisme (Suisse, Allemagne), elle peut être supérieure.

Une défense absolue d'exportation frappe les titres italiens de toutes sortes. Les titres se trouvant à l'étranger peuvent être réintroduits en Italie uniquement par la poste et ils doivent être adressés par leur titulaire à la Banque d'Italie ou à une des banques déléguées. Celle-ci les constitue en dossiers et tout mouvement est subordonné à l'autorisation de l'Istcambi.

Inutile de dire que l'exportation de l'or est sévèrement réprimée.

b) Opérations à faire à travers l'Istcambi—C'est là la majeure partie des opérations qui définissent les relations commerciales et financières de l'Italie avec l'étranger. L'obtention de devises pour l'importation et la cession de devises provenant de l'exportation (pour les pays avec lesquels ne fonctionnent pas des accords de clearing) ont, comme point de départ et d'arrivée, l'Istcambi. De même, l'Istcambi détermine l'attribution de devises pour les besoins touristiques des Italiens et reçoit les devises provenant de la Banque de lires touristiques, bons d'hôtels, etc. C'est enfin par l'entremise de l'Istcambi et ses organes d'exécution qu'est liquidé, soit l'envoi de remises des émigrants en Italie, soit l'envoi à l'étranger des intérêts de la dette extérieure publique ou privée. Pour les pays avec lesquels l'Italie est en rapport de clearing, toutes les opérations du côté italien se font en lires près de l'Istcambi qui assure la gestion de tous les clearings.

c) *Opérations contrôlées*—Au moment de la cession obligatoire des crédits étrangers et de l'institution du monopole des changes, on a laissé à deux catégories d'entreprises: aux Compagnies d'assurances et aux Compagnies de navigation, l'autorisation de conserver les comptes en devises étrangères, ceux-ci sont soumis à une surveillance très stricte de la Banque d'Italie à laquelle les entreprises ci-dessus doivent adresser périodiquement l'état de leurs créances et leurs dettes envers l'étranger, tout en indiquant la "mesure qu'elles considèrent strictement nécessaire pour l'exercice normal de leur activité" (Art. 2, décret ministériel du 8 décembre 1934). En outre, elles doivent transmettre trimestriellement à la Banque d'Italie de larges extraits de leur comptabilité par rapport à leur activité avec l'étranger.

Un décret-loi du 28 décembre 1936 a étendu la faculté de maintenir des comptes en monnaie étrangère à des sociétés et collectivités industrielles et commerciales dont l'activité principale se déroule à l'étranger. Mais il leur faut une autorisation spéciale du Ministère pour les Échanges, et elles doivent tenir leurs comptes en devises près la Banque d'Italie ou les Banques autorisées.

C'est là l'unique entorse au monopole des devises de l'Istcambi.

Nous pouvons noter ici encore certaines exceptions qui ont été concédées lors de la réquisition générale des titres étrangers et italiens émis à l'étranger en faveur de personnes physiques ou morales dans le cas où

i) ces titres représentent le capital de sociétés filiales ou des participations financières à l'étranger;
ii) ou ces titres représentent la couverture d'engagements assumés crédits consentis à l'étranger (cas des banques);
iii) ces titres représentent la couverture de risques assumés à l'étranger (cas des Compagnies d'Assurances).

Généralement, les sociétés autorisées à tenir des comptes en devises étrangères et les sociétés libérées de l'obligation de la cession de titres à l'étranger sont les mêmes et on a permis pour ce cas que les intérêts et dividendes de titres à l'étranger maintenus en portefeuille puissent être versés dans les comptes en devises existants.

A la fin de 1936, on a créé les soi-disant "comptes loro libres" alimentés par des cessions de devises. Les mouvements de ces comptes qui doivent être constitués auprès des banques autorisées ne sont soumis à aucune restriction, soit en Italie même, soit pour la reconversion en devises étrangères.

Enfin, un décret-loi du 6 décembre 1937, a voulu favoriser l'investissement des capitaux étrangers en Italie. Dans la situation difficile où la balance des comptes s'était trouvée en 1937, on voulut attirer des capitaux, par des privilèges fiscaux importants: exemption de tous droits d'enregistrement et de transcription hypothécaire et de droits du cadastre pour les investissements immobiliers; exemption de l'impôt annuel de 10% et de l'impôt extraordinaire progressif sur les dividendes pour les investissements en actions et obligations italienne d'autres faveurs pour les emprunts contractés directement à l'étranger par les Italiens et pour les obligations placées à l'étranger. Dans des cas déterminés, ces investissements étaient, en outre, libres de tous droits de succession.

Mais on se rendit bien compte que ce n'était là pas assez pour attirer les capitaux étrangers; il fallait leur garantir de pouvoir rentrer dans leurs pays d'origine et de pouvoir y transférer les intérêts et dividendes perçus. Ce transfert était libre 1) pour les intérêts jusqu'à concurrence de 5% du capital investi s'il s'agissait d'investissements immobiliers et d'emprunts; sans limitation pour les dividendes et intérêts effectivement perçus sur les actions et obligations italiennes. 2) pour le capital jusqu'à concurrence du montant en devises primitivement importées, pour la liquidation d'investissements immobiliers et d'emprunts, sans limitation pour les liquidations d'actions et d'obligations.

Les capitaux étrangers au sens du décret-loi doivent consister en devises libres à échanger contre lires près de l'Istcambi.

Pour justifier les privilèges fiscaux quelque peu exorbitants accordés aux capitaux étrangers, le gouvernement italien déclara qu'il avait été sollicité par des capitalistes étrangers en quête de placements sûrs et profitables. Mais la stipulation que le retransfert pourrait se faire seulement jusqu'à concurrence de la somme *en devises* importées, si elle garantissait les capitalistes contre une dévaluation ultérieure de la lire, excluait toute importation de capitaux craignant un avilissement de la monnaie dans leurs propres pays, et ne permit point de profiter d'éventuelles plus-values en capital. Quant aux investissements en actions et obligations, ils devaient être peu tentants au moment où les sociétés anonymes italiennes étaient frappées d'un impôt de 10% sur leur capital.

On ne connaît pas le montant des importations de capitaux qui ont pu être effectués grâce au mécanisme établi par le décret-loi que nous avons reproduit dans les grandes lignes.

d) Opérations intérieures affectées par la réglementation des opérations extérieures—La réglementation stricte des paiements entre l'Italie et l'étranger se répercute sur certains paiements intérieurs. C'est le cas pour les compensations privées qui donnent lieu, comme on le sait, à un règlement direct outre l'exportateur et l'importateur italien. Pour prévenir certaines fraudes et exercer un contrôle effectif, il a été décidé que toutes les opérations relatives aux compensations privées devraient se faire uniquement par l'entremise de banques autorisées.

Un autre cas de règlement d'opérations intérieures entraînées par le Contrôle des Changes est l'utilisation des comptes bloqués dénommés "vieux comptes loro." Dans ces comptes se trouvent bloqués les avoirs étrangers constitués avant le 18 novembre 1935 (date d'imposition des sanctions) et on y ajoute automatiquement les intérêts, dividendes, remboursements qui seraient le fruit des capitaux bloqués.

Les disponibilités de ces comptes peuvent être employées pratiquement à tous les investissements immobiliers; les investissements en titres et les mouvements des titres sont sujets à l'autorisation de l'Istcambi; certaines catégories de marchandises destinées à être exportées; enfin un grand nombre de dépenses en Italie même sont admises pourvu qu'elles se fassent au profit du titulaire du compte ou de membres de sa famille. Comme on le voit, le régime est assez libéral. Il a été, d'ailleurs, étendu aux comptes spéciaux sans intérêts, qui résultent du renvoi en Italie de billets de banque et de chèques qui ont abusivement circulé à l'étranger (Voir ci-dessus p. 200–1).

Par contre, les disponibilités étrangères qui se sont formées après le 18 novembre 1935 par des remises de devises de l'étranger et qui forment les "comptes loro nouveaux" ne sont soumises à aucune restriction quant à leur emploi en Italie. L'unique limitation à laquelle ils sont sujets est qu'ils ne peuvent être retransférés à l'étranger. Cette dernière limitation a été levée pour les "comptes loro libres" formés par des remises après le mois de décembre 1936. (Voir ci-dessus p. 203)

Enfin, un genre spécialement intéressant d'opérations intérieures réglementées est constitué par les paiements entre la métropole et ses colonies. On a déjà dit que les dispositions du Contrôle ont généralement été étendues aux Colonies quant à leurs rapports avec l'étranger.

Lee rapports encre Métropole et Colonies ont été réglés par le décret interministériel déjà cité du 25 mai 1936; la lire est monnaie légale dans toutes les colonies italiennes et aucun obstacle quantitatif ou qualitatif n'est posé contre des transferts entre l'Italie et ses colonies, au moyen de titres bancaires, postaux ou lettres de change. Par contre, la somme à emporter en billets a été limitée à 500 lires pour le Libye et le Dodécanèse et à 1.000 lires pour l'Afrique Orientale Italienne. Cette limitation se comprend très bien en raison des possibilités d'exportation en fraude, qu'offrent les escales étrangères.

e) Le rôle des banques—Le Contrôle des Changes affecte l'activité bancaire à deux points de vue:

1) il limite les opérations extérieures à un certain nombre de banques spécialement autorisées par la Banque d'Italie; ces Banques exécutent, d'ailleurs, ces opérations en tant que mandataires de la Banque d'Italie; leur nombre a été élargi peu à peu. (Voir la liste des banques en note page 197).
2) le Contrôle influe sur les opérations extérieures elles-mêmes, défendant les unes, surveillant les autres et ajoutant des opérations nouvelles à celles pratiquées jusqu'alors.

Il va sans dire que toutes les opérations défendues aux particuliers, telles qu' opérations sur changes et sur matériaux précieux, le sont également aux banques, à moins qu'elles n'agissent sur les ordres et pour le compte de la Banque d'Italie et de l'Istcambi.

Les banques déléguées jouent un rôle capital au point de vue de l'exécution du contrôle. Elles tiennent les divers "comptes loro" et les comptes en devises étrangères des sociétés autorisées à cet effet. C'est à elles ou aux filiales de la Banque d'Italie que les exportateurs doivent céder les devises provenant de l'exportation; elles servent d'intermédiaires pour les opérations de compensation privées; enfin, elles sont autorisées à payer les chèques et lettres de crédit libellés en lires touristiques.

Quant aux opérations commerciales extérieures, il faut distinguer, selon qu'il s'agit de pays avec lesquels l'Italie est en rapport de clearing ou de pays avec lesquels les paiements se font en devises.

Dans ce dernier cas, les opérations habituelles des banques—avances aux exportateurs et crédit d'acceptation aux importateurs—ne subissent pas de changements si l'exportation et l'importation elles-mêmes sont exécutées selon les prescriptions du Contrôle. Par contre, si les échanges commerciaux se font en régime de clearing, les opérations bancaires connexes en sont considérablement altérées; c'est ce que nous verrons plus loin dans le chapitre consacré au Clearing.

2) Les mouvements de capitaux et les problèmes de la balance des comptes italienne

Nous avons indiqué dans la première partie comme raison de l'établissement du Contrôle des Changes Italien, l'appauvrissement progressif des réserves de l'Institut d'émission dû:

1) à un mouvement d'exportation de capitaux se traduisant par un désendettement et par l'achat de titres étrangers et italiens émis à l'étranger;
2) à une brusque aggravation de la balance commerciale en 1934.

Contrairement à ce qui se produit dans d'autres pays à change contrôlé, les dettes bancaires à court terme ne jouent aucun rôle déterminant en Italie. Il semble, au contraire, qu'au moment de l'institution du Contrôle, l'Italie était créditrice de l'étranger en matière de capitaux à court terme. Aucun accord de *Stillhalter* ni aucun accord de même nature n'a été conclu par l'Italie, sauf le blocage des avers étrangers au lendemain des sanctions dans les vieux et nouveaux "comptes loro," mais ceci fut une mesure de défense élémentaire. *Le problème italien n'est pas là.* Il n'est pas non plus (comme beaucoup de républiques sud-américaines, par exemple) dans les paiements d'intérêts au titre de la dette extérieure publique ou privée, paiements qui n'ont jamais été interrompus. La dette extérieure de l'État consiste uniquement dans le prêt de stabilisation Morgan qui, à l'origine, se montait à 100 millions de dollars et dont un tiers a été amorti.

Au contraire, le Contrôle des Changes Italien n'a pas eu pour but la diminution des paiements d'intérêts à l'étranger, mais il a eu pour effet leur augmentation et la diminution des recettes en intérêts et dividendes provenant de titres à l'étranger.

En effet, si dans d'autres pays, la pièce centrale de la réglementation fut le blocage des crédits extérieurs à court terme, et la suspension du service de la dette extérieure, en Italie, l'intérêt se concentra principalement sur la cession des crédits italiens à l'étranger et des titres étrangers et italiens émis à l'étranger. Cette différence tient d'abord à ce que l'Italie n'est pas un pays débiteur au même titre que les autres pays à Contrôle des Changes. Dans nombre de ces pays, le Contrôle des Changes fut introduit parce que l'endettement *réel* extérieur avait été aggravé de façon insupportable par suite de la baisse des prix mondiaux; en Italie, le Contrôle fut établi, au contraire, *pour empêcher un désendettement en capital qui s'était avéré trop rapide par rapport à l'état de la balance des comptes*.

Par suite des besoins extraordinaires des années 1935 et suivants, on dut même faire marche arrière et renverser les mouvements de capitaux. Voici les étapes principales de toute cette évolution:

> 1929–1934: désendettement des banques et achat de titres émis à l'étranger;
> 26 mai 1934: défense d'acheter des titres émis à l'étranger;
> 8 déc. 1934: cession de crédits à l'étranger, à l'Istcambi et déclaration de titres émis à l'étranger;
> 9 mai 1935: constitution on dossiers auprès des banques autorisés des titres étrangers et italiens émis à l'étranger;
> 26 août 1935: réquisition des titres émis à l'étranger contre les bons du Trésor, 5% en 9 ans (échange au cours de bourse et de change au moment du décret);
> août 1935–1939: réalisation partielle des titres réquisitionnés par l'Istcambi pour le compte du Trésor. Il a été indiqué officiellement que jusqu'en avril 1937 le Trésor a retiré de la vente de ses titres 2.207 millions de lires. Les devises provenant de la réalisation ont servi à combler les déficits importants de la balance commerciale pendant ces années.

Il est difficile de savoir jusqu'à quel point la cession des devises et des titres a été réellement exécutée. Nous croyons, cependant, que les fuites ont été peu importantes:

1) à cause des pénalités sévères dont étaient menacés les contrevenants;
2) à cause du mouvement de patriotisme presque unanime de l'année 1935;
3) parce que les devises et les titres émis à l'étranger détenus par les Italiens ne constituaient pas en grande partie, *dans l'esprit même de leurs détenteurs*, des capitaux exportés, mais une utilisation de leurs ressources

dans l'intérêt personnel mais aussi national. (Désendettement et pénétration de capitaux italiens sur le marché national).

Ce n'est que récemment que les exportations clandestines de capitaux ont pris, paraît-il, une certaine importance en raison de la situation internationale et de la politique antisémite. On en trouve une expression dans la chute récente (fin 1938) du cours officieux des billets de banque italiens. (Voir tableau annexe).

Mais le Contrôle des Changes n'eut pas seulement la tâche d'arrêter et de renverser les mouvements de capitaux, mais il devait encore pourvoir à l'équilibre de la balance des revenus dont les postes actifs (remises des émigrants, tourisme, frêts) fléchissaient tandis que le déficit de la balance commerciale s'aggravait.

Malheureusement, il ne nous est pas possible de donner des chiffres même approximatifs des postes invisibles de la balance; la dernière balance des comptes calculée par le Professeur Borgatta date de 1932.

Il est certain que plusieurs tendances fondamentales travaillaient dans un sens contraire à l'équilibre de la balance des comptes italienne:

1) la vague de propagande de tourisme dans tous les pays qui devait forcément affecter les pays traditionnels de tourisme international et les difficultés faites au tourisme par les autres pays à contrôle des changes;
2) surtout la cessation de l'émigration et la "désitalianisation" graduelle des anciens émigrants qui fit perdre à l'Italie à la fois les remises et des produits à l'exportation; en effet, l'émigrant, grand acheteur d'abord de marchandises italiennes, se familiarisa peu à peu avec les produits du pays d'accueil.

Pour recréer un équilibre sur la base de ces nouvelles données, il ne suffisait, certes pas, d'une simple dévaluation. Il fallait réorganiser l'importation aussi bien que l'exportation, c'est-à-dire, diminuer les importations et orienter les exportations vers de nouveaux marchés ou de nouveaux produits et influer ainsi sur la structure productive du pays tout entier. Il est vrai que pour cela, le Contrôle n'était point nécessaire. Des changements dans le sens indiqué ont été le but de la bataille du blé et de l'utilisation des ressources hydrauliques ainsi que de l'action pour l'exportation des produits de qualité, efforts qui ont été tous développés avant l'établissement du contrôle. Mais c'était des efforts qui ne donneraient des résultats qu'à plus ou moins longue échéance, alors qu'en 1934, on se trouva devant une situation qui commandait un barrage immédiat.

Il est extrêmement difficile de dégager les effets du Contrôle des Changes sur la balance des paiements de 1935 à aujourd'hui parce qu'un grand nombre d'autres facteurs ont agi sur celle-ci. Il est certain que la balance n'a pu être équilibrée que par des pertes d'or et la liquidation partielle des réserves en crédits et titres étrangers détenus par l'Istcambi.

Voici les déficits commerciaux et les mouvements encaisse-or à partir de 1934.

Tableau 7.1. *Déficit commercial et variations de l'encaisse-or et devises de la Banque d'Italie 1934–1938*

	Déficit Commercial	Variations de l'encaisse-or et Devises de la Banque	
1934	2.617	-1.514	lires de 1927
1935	3.074	-2.488	
1936	2.053	-1.021	
1937	5.640	7	lires dévaluées de 41%
1938	2.958	-202	lires dévaluées de 41%

Nous expliquerons plus loin l'évolution du commerce extérieur. On voit que jusqu'en 1936, on a soldé le déficit commercial partiellement en or. Le déficit extraordinairement élevé de 1937 n'a point donné lieu à une diminution de l'encaisse-or. Le tourisme a été assez important pendant cette année; mais avec les remises des émigrants, il n'a certainement pu compenser plus de la moitié du déficit de cette année. Il faut tenir compte, en outre, que les sorties de devises pour services ont considérablement augmenté depuis la conquête de l'Éthiopie, à cause des droits de passage du Canal de Suez, les droits du port à Djibouti et les frais de transport sur le chemin de fer franco-éthiopien. Pour ces dépenses, on a cité le chiffre de 500 millions pour 1937 qui nous parait, cependant, exagéré. En 1936–1937, une grande partie du déficit a été réglée par des ventes de titres étrangers réquisitionnés, puis on a laissé se former un important arriéré en clearing et enfin, on a probablement entamé les réserves cachées telles que le produit des "offres d'or à la patrie" qui ont eu lieu vers la fin de 1935 (environ 700 millions de lires).

L'amélioration de la situation patrimoniale de l'Italie par rapport à l'étranger de 1929 à 1934 a donc fait place à une détérioration de cette situation jointe à une diminution des réserves or. Est-ce à dire que le contrôle a échoué? On ne saurait le dire puisque c'est lui-même qui en a décidé ainsi. Posé devant l'alternative de renoncer à telle importation de pétrole ou d'abandonner telle participation à l'étranger, l'Istcambi a sciemment opté pour le deuxième terme. Et il est évident qu'on ne peut pas faire incomber au Contrôle des Changes le fait même que l'alternative se soit posée. Ensuite, il est toujours possible d'arguer que la situation aurait été pire encore sans le contrôle qui a quand même opposé un barrage assez efficace aux sorties des capitaux.

Enfin, le Contrôle conçu d'abord comme moyen de défense immédiat contre des sorties d'or, destiné ensuite à gouverner la balance des paiements dans tous ses postes s'est vu assigner des buts encore plus vastes; il est devenu un chainon important de la direction de toute l'économie, surtout par le contrôle des importations dont dépendent, dans une large mesure, l'activité industrielle et la consommation. Et c'est dans l'accomplissement de cette tâche que l'efficacité du contrôle est certainement le moins contestable.

IV. Commerce extérieur et politique commerciale

On a vu comment les divers postes autres que la balance commerciale ont graduellement perdu de leur importance dans la balance des paiements: 1) la dette extérieure italienne a été largement réduite, 2) le tourisme est en régression, 3) les remises des émigrants ont complètement perdu leur fonction stabilisatrice d'autrefois, 4) on veut empêcher des sorties d'or ultérieures, le stock d'or étant fortement amenuisé et considéré comme trésor de guerre. Tout cela concourt à redonner au problème de la balance commerciale et du commerce extérieur leur importance capitale des temps du mercantilisme. Nous allons traiter dans ce chapitre les divers aspects de ces problèmes.

1) Régime des importations

Au monopole des changes établi au profit de l'Istcambi, le 8 décembre 1934, fit suite le 18 février 1935 le contingentement général des importations. Celui-ci consista dans l'établissement d'une liste où était indiqué pour chaque numéro du tarif douanier le pourcentage de la valeur de l'importation de l'année 1934 qui serait admise en 1935. Les pourcentages variaient entre 15% et 37%. Cette mesure était moins sévère qu'il pouvait sembler puisqu'elle était conçue surtout comme une arme additionnelle dans la lutte pour de nouveaux avantages commerciaux. D'une part, en effet, le pourcentage n'était qu'une sorte de tarif général à remplacer par des pourcentages conventionnels plus élevés dans des accords de clearing, en échange d'une augmentation concédée aux exportations italiennes, d'autre part, un décret ministériel du 1er mars organisait les compensations privées qui devaient permettre des importations en dehors des contingents fixés.

Cependant, à l'approche de la guerre abyssine, le contrôle dut être renforcé et un décret ministériel du 25 juin 1935 institua le système de l'importation sur licence du Ministère des Finances et en juillet on commença à instituer le monopole d'importation pour un certain nombre de matières premières. Depuis lors, les marchandises qui entrent dans le royaume se rangent dans les cinq catégories suivantes:

1) marchandises soumises au régime de la "bolletta" (fiche douanière) que chaque importateur peut faire venir dans des pourcentages déterminés de son importation en 1934.
2) Marchandises soumises au régime de la licence ministérielle dont l'importation est, par conséquent, sujette à une autorisation préventive.
3) Marchandises soumises à des régimes spéciaux,
   a) l'importation de charbon, des agglomérés et du coke, du cuivre, de l'étain et du nickel sous toutes formes est confiée à un monopole géré par l'administration des chemins de fer;
   b) l'importation d'or brut en lingots, débris, etc. a été confiée au monopole géré par l'Istcambi pour le compte du Trésor;
   c) l'importation de colorants organiques synthétiques des produits intermédiaires est soumise à licence du Ministère des Corporations et il en est de même pour l'importation des huiles minérales, brutes, le résidu et dérivés des carburants et lubrifiants;
   d) l'importation de films cinématographiques est confiée à un monopole institué par le décret-loi du 4 septembre 1938.
4) Marchandise de libre importation. Cette catégorie est, comme on l'imagine, extrêmement réduite; elle ne comprend que les journaux et les manuscrits et les monnaies d'or, d'argent et de cuivre;
5) Marchandise importée en régime de compensation privée. Nous en parlerons plus loin dans une section spécialement consacrée aux compensations privées.

Les deux catégories essentielles sont les deux premières et l'évolution la plus intéressante à noter est le passage de plus en plus complet des marchandises de la première à la deuxième catégorie. Limiter les importations à un pourcentage d'une année de base était une première et grossière façon d'aborder le contrôle des importations, façon qui pouvait rendre service pour parer au plus pressé, mais qui comportait de multiples inconvénients surtout si elle devait se prolonger. En effet, le système du pourcentage permet la création de positions privilégiées dans le commerce d'importation dues uniquement au fait accidentel d'une importation en 1934. Ensuite, non seulement il empêchait les initiatives nouvelles, mais il "fossilisa" tout le commerce d'importation sans tenir compte des changements tendanciels dans sa répartition par pays et par article, et en perpétuant l'état de choses de l'année de base. Pour parer à cela, il faudrait changer constamment les pourcentages, mais alors on se rapprocherait de la réglementation directe par licence tout en réunissant les défauts des deux systèmes. Dans la presse économique italienne, une campagne très vive a été menée contre le système de la "bolletta."

L'inconvénient du système de la licence est l'énorme travail administratif que représente la décision à prendre, dans chaque cas d'espèce, chaque demande devant être adressée au Ministère pour les Échanges et Devises. Comme preuve, nous rappelons que le Ministère a dû créer une direction à part pour le service des importations qui n'existait pas encore du temps où il n'était que sous-secrétariat. C'est dans cette direction que travaillent les Juntes corporatives par produits (v. page 198–9) chargées d'examiner un première instance les demandes d'importation.

Sont soumis au régime de la licence, presque tous les produits alimentaires et matières premières ainsi que toutes les importations de machines et d'appareils et ce sont là déjà les chapitres les plus importants des achats italiens à l'étranger.

Les produits encore soumis au régime de la "bolletta" quoique aussi nombreux que ceux soumis au régime de la licence sont presque tous secondaires. D'autre part, il n'y a plus les pourcentages généraux pour tous les pays, mais seulement des pourcentages fixés d'accord avec chacun dans des accords commerciaux. Il s'ensuit que tous les pays—et il s'agit d'un grand nombre de pays non européens—avec lesquels l'Italie n'a pas conclu des accords particuliers à ce sujet, ne peuvent exporter d'aucune façon, les marchandises se trouvant au régime de la "bolletta."

Bien plus, pour nombre d'importants pays, toutes ces marchandises ont été soumises partiellement ou totalement au régime de la licence. L'exclusion totale du régime de "la bolletta" se constate, par exemple, pour le Japon, les pays baltes et scandinaves, l'Espagne, les États-Unis, la Russie et la Pologne. Pour ce qui est du reste, le pourcentage admis est généralement de 50% par rapport à la valeur de l'importation on 1934. L'Allemagne occupe une position absolument privilégiée puisqu'elle peut importer en Italie 100% de la *quantité* importée en 1934.

Comme le constate l'ouvrage déjà cité de la Banque d'Italie,[5] les contingents ouverts par la fixation des pourcentages n'ont souvent pas été tous utilisés et souvent aussi on a dû admettre des importations en deçà des contingents; dernièrement, on a défendu le transfert des facultés d'importation provenant du fait qu'on a importé en 1934. On imagine à quelle affaire fructueuse ce transfert a pu donner lieu, naturellement, aux frais des consommateurs.

Le contrôle des importations se fait donc principalement lors de l'autorisation préalable d'importer. A cette autorisation fait suite l'obtention de devises pour les pays avec lesquels il n'y a pas d'accords de clearing. Pour cela, l'importateur est tenu de présenter à la Banque d'Italie ou à une des banques déléguées l'attestation par la Douane de l'entrée en Italie de la marchandise achetée. C'est là un deuxième contrôle qui avait déjà été établi avant la fixation préalable des importations en quantité et qui reste nécessaire parce que les contingents autorisés ne sont pas toujours entièrement utilisés.

L'obtention de la licence, l'utilisation de la "bolletta" et les pratiques administratives et douanières complexes que demande toute cette organisation nouvelle du commerce extérieur ont favorisé dès 1935 le groupement des importateurs dans des comptoirs, consortiums et compagnies qui se proposaient en outre de faire une politique d'achats rationnels dont les importateurs individuels ne se montraient pas toujours capables.[6]

Le mouvement de cartellisation du commerce d'exportation, après avoir été combattu comme une bureaucratisation excessive, a repris, pendant les derniers mois, une nouvelle vigueur; on a constitué, en décembre 1938, une Compagnie pour l'importation du café où sont réunies toutes les firmes importatrices et on projette la création de telles compagnies pour d'autres produits.

On sait que la politique douanière a perdu son rôle prépondérant comme régulatrice des importations. Les seules mesures importantes en cette matière sont celles qui furent prises lors de la dévaluation de la lire en octobre 1936: abolition de la sur taxe *ad valorem* de 15%; introduite après la dévaluation de la

5 *Op. cit.*, p. 5.

6 C'est là un curieux paradoxe: théoriquement, une diminution de la demande italienne aurait dû faire baisser les prix dans les marchés d'achat, mais puisque l'importateur italien savait que, de toute façon, il trouverait à vendre son produit, à un prix rémunérateur, à cause des conditions du marché italien, il se souciait peu d'acheter aux prix les plus favorables. Nous voyons donc que les effets d'une diminution *imposée* de la demande sur les prix peuvent être for différents des effets d'une diminution naturelle.

livre on 1931, et diminution de droits sur un grand nombre de produits alimentaires pour éviter, autant que possible, l'incidence de la dévaluation sur les prix. Ensuite, en 1938, les droits ont dû être rétablis sur le bétail et la viande par suite de l'effondrement des prix qui était résulté de la crise fourragère.

D'autre part, un droit uniforme de 3% est exigé sur les valeurs des importations en licence.

2) Régime des exportations

Nous distinguons:

a) exportation vers des pays où il n'y a pas d'accords de clearing ou d'échanges compensés;
b) exportation vers les pays avec lesquels de tels accords ont été conclus;
c) exportation en compensation privée.

Nous réservons le traitement des deux dernières catégories aux sections consacrées aux clearings et aux compensations privées. Nous traitons donc ici des exportations qui sont directement productives en devises étrangères.

Généralement, ces devises doivent être cédées à l'Istcambi et les marchandises à exporter ne peuvent pas quitter les confins de l'Italie sans "benestare" d'une banque déléguée près de laquelle l'exportateur a dû s'engager à céder les devises provenant de sa vente.

Mais le contrôle est plus strict encore, car il faut empêcher que l'exportateur, en collusion avec l'importateur étranger, n'indique un prix trop bas pour se constituer à l'étranger des réserves en devises. Pour la surveillance des prix à l'exportation, il a donc été formé des comités provinciaux près de chaque filiale de la Banque d'Italie. Près du Ministère des Finances, fonctionne un Comité Central de révision des prix chargé de coordonner l'action des comités provinciaux.

Il y a, cependant, des conventions spéciales ("*accords de devises*") entre le Ministère des Échanges et Devises et différentes industries exportatrices pour permettre à celles-ci de conserver une partie, au moins, des devises que leur procure l'exportation à condition de les employer à des achats de matières premières. De tels accords ont été stipulés avec les industries textiles grandes exportatrices (coton, laine, rayonne), et avec des industries mécaniques. L'idée est évidemment de faire dépendre l'attribution de devises pour l'importation de matières premières d'une exportation proportionnée de produits manufacturés. Une politique d'échanges compensés par produit s'ajoute ainsi la politique d'échanges compensés par pays, et, comme on dit aux pays étrangers: importez de chez nous pour que je vous achète quelque chose, on dit aux producteurs nationaux d'exporter pour pouvoir importer sa matière première.

Pour le coton, par exemple, l'exportateur peut retenir 50% et dans certains cas, 75% de ses devises, le reste étant cédé à l'Istcambi; d'autre part, dans l'industrie cotonnière, c'est surtout le tissage qui exporte tandis que la filature importe le coton brut. L'industriel du tissage cède donc ses devises contre les filés à l'industriel de la filature.

Comme l'a remarqué une étude du Professeur Demaria[7] il y a dans cette opération trois cours de change: 1) le change officiel auquel Istcambi achète la partie des devises que l'exportateur des tissus doit lui céder; 2) le "change-coton" supérieur au change officiel auquel le filateur achète les devises; 3) le change plus élevé encore que le consommateur aura à payer pour le coton incorporé dans le tissu qu'il achète puisque c'est sur lui que retombe, en définitive, le "change-coton" et que c'est lui encore qui doit supporter les conséquences du dumping de l'exportateur intéressé à obtenir le maximum de devises.

Cependant, autant que cela résulte des mesures publiées, le dumping n'est pas organisé de façon suivie: il y eut bien des primes à l'exportation de 1935 à 1936, époque à laquelle on laissait, d'ailleurs, glisser le cours officiel de la lire jusqu'à 89% de sa parité officielle; les primes appelées "facilitations" furent concédées par l'Istcambi et variaient suivant la marchandise et le pays de destination; elles étaient calculées *ad valorem* ou bien par rapport à une unité de mesure. La procédure était assez laborieuse. Mais ces primes directes ont été abolies avec la dévaluation de la lire et n'ont pas encore fait de réapparition générale officielle.

Une caractéristique à noter de la politique des exportations a été la multiplication des prohibitions à la sortie qui ont frappé, à partir de la guerre abyssine, un grand nombre de produits, considérés essentiels pour la défense nationale et l'alimentation. Ces prohibitions ont été maintenues, en grande partie, quoique les douanes aient la faculté de permettre le passage de certaines marchandises dont la sortie est prohibée en principe, suivant les instructions du Ministère des Finances. Les prohibitions concernent toutes les céréales, quelques autres produits alimentaires, les minerais et les débris de métaux, d'autres matières premières et plusieurs produits chimiques.

7 G. Demaria, "I rapporti di cambio manovrato in regime di autarchia economica corporativa," *Giornale degli Economisti*, janvier 1938.

3) Politique contractuelle, Clearings, Échanges compensés

a) Généralités

A partir de 1932, l'Italie avait conclu des accords de compensation générale avec plusieurs pays à contrôle des changes de l'Europe centrale, mais elle ne s'orienta délibérément vers la conclusion de tels accords qu'au moment où fut décrété le contingentement général des importations. On pensait obtenir lors de la négociation des accords de clearing une augmentation des exportations en contrepartie d'un relèvement des pourcentages généraux assignés aux importations, pourcentages fixés, comme on sait, par rapport aux importations de 1934.

Lors de l'imposition des sanctions, l'Italie prit un certain nombre de mesures auxquelles elle donna le nom de *contre-sanctions*: 1) toutes les conventions spéciales avec les pays sanctionnistes furent considérées comme caduques; 2) la réduction à l'extrême de ces achats dans les pays sanctionnistes, toute importation étant subordonnée à l'obtention d'une licence spéciale; 3) l'autorisation d'exporter seulement si l'importateur du pays sanctionniste avait fourni d'avance les devises ou une ouverture de crédit confirmée en Italie ou si l'exportateur italien avait obtenu un permis spécial de l'Institut national fasciste pour le commerce extérieur (appelé alors Institut pour les Échanges avec l'Étranger); 4) sauf dérogation de la Surintendance aux Échanges et Devises, le montant du prix des marchandises importées des pays sanctionnistes devait être versé à échéance dans des comptes bloqués sans intérêts près de la Banque d'Italie. S'il s'agit d'un pays avec lequel l'Italie avait conclu un accord de clearing, le prix fut payé près de la Caisse de compensation italienne, mais celle-ci ne donna pas notification du paiement à la Caisse étrangère.

Les contre-sanctions assurèrent ainsi à l'Italie une position contractuelle assez favorable au lendemain de la levée des sanctions; les vieux accords n'existaient plus et l'Italie était débitrice des sommes qu'elle avait congelées; d'autre part, les pays sanctionnistes se pressaient de conclure pour reconquérir le marché italien. Et l'Italie put ainsi exploiter la concurrence que se faisaient les anciens sanctionnistes. Ces circonstances atténuèrent grandement le handicap traditionnel qui résulte, pour l'Italie, du fait qu'elle importe des matières premières qui lui sont indispensables tandis qu'elle exporte pour les 2/3 des légumes, des fruits et des produits textiles qui ne sont pas essentiels, pour l'approvisionnement des marchés étrangers. Dans la deuxième partie de l'année 1936 et au début de 1937, l'Italie conclut ainsi des accords avec tous les États sanctionnistes sauf avec l'Union Soviétique avec laquelle les négociations furent rompues; les accords avec les pays européens prévoyaient tous l'institution du Clearing et étaient, en général, guidés par la volonté de réaliser l'équilibre de la balance des comptes sur une base bilatérale. Ainsi, l'Italie obtenait, en échange du dégel progressif de ses dettes commerciales ainsi que pour d'éventuelles dettes financières, des "pointes" de ses exportations réalisant ainsi son mot d'ordre: paiements en marchandises et non en devises; les contingents d'exportation prévus par les accords étaient fixés en valeurs plutôt qu'en quantités.

A partir de la fin de 1936, l'Italie avait ainsi des accords de clearing avec tous les pays européens (parmi lesquels un accord avec l'Espagne nationaliste et avec la Turquie). Seul, le clearing avec la France ne donna pas satisfaction et fut remplacé au début de 1938 par un accord de paiement. Avec l'Union Soviétique, un accord prévoyant le clearing vient d'être signé.

Les accords de clearing se ressemblent généralement beaucoup; quant aux accords commerciaux, ils prévoient souvent un chiffre global des échanges et toujours des contingentements pour les importations italiennes. Ils sont plus ou moins complets quant à l'inclusion des autres paiements. Si le dégel des crédits commerciaux et le règlement des dettes financières est presque toujours prévu, il n'en est pas de même pour les dépenses des touristes, les frêts et remises des émigrants et d'autres postes de la balance. L'accord le plus complet est, sans doute, le clearing italo-allemand qui étend sa compétence sur presque tous les paiements exécutés entre les doux pays et qui est avec le clearing italo-hongrois le seul à comprendre aussi toutes les relations commerciales avec toutes les colonies italiennes. Pour d'autres pays, Turquie, Grèce, le clearing s'étend seulement aux colonies et possessions méditerranéennes, pour d'autres seulement, à certains produits importés aux Colonies (bois pour la Yougoslavie et la Roumanie); enfin, pour un grand nombre (France, Grande-Bretagne, etc.) les relations avec les colonies italiennes ne sont point comprises dans l'accord de compensation générale.

Quelques accords prévoient des "pointes" en devises en faveur de l'une des parties. Nous en verrons un exemple dans le clearing italo-anglais que nous analyserons en détail dans la suite.

En août 1936, étant donné les difficultés grandissantes que l'Italie éprouva pour exporter au cours du change officiel, l'Istcambi imposa des "primes" et des droits de compensation. Les primes dues aux exportateurs étaient de 15% de la somme encaissée au cours officiel et les droits dûs par les importateurs se montaient à 20% de la somme versée en clearing pour le paiement des marchandises importées. Les primes aux exportateurs devaient rétablir la parité de traitements entre les exportateurs en clearing et les exportateurs en compensation privée qui jouissaient depuis longtemps de primes analogues. Quant aux droits dûs par les importateurs, il paraît qu'ils ne furent pas appliqués aux pays qui n'avaient pas participé aux sanctions.

Les primes aussi bien que les droits purent être supprimés trois mois après leur institution grâce à la dévaluation et qui obtint le même effet d'une façon plus simple et plus radicale,

A partir de la fin de 1936, l'Istcambi publie hebdomadairement la situation de caisse des clearings existant entre l'Italie et l'étranger; le tableau II reproduit la situation à la fin de chaque mois pendant les deux dernières années.

Il peut surprendre qu'au début de 1937, l'Italie ait eu dans la plupart des clearings une position créditrice et qu'un solde créditeur total de 340 millions de lires environ existât en sa faveur, alors que nous savons qu'elle eut à régler des arriérés commerciaux importants. Pour expliquer cette contradiction, apparente, rappelons que suivant les accords passés avec l'Italie, les créanciers d'arriérés commerciaux et autres recevaient non pas tout l'excédent des exportations italiennes vers leurs pays, mais un pourcentage fixe de ces exportations. Supposons que ce pourcentage soit 10%, alors le clearing était en équilibre si les importations italiennes se trouvaient par rapport aux exportations dans une proportion de 90 à 100. Si cette proportion était, en réalité, de 80 à 100, les créanciers anciens n'en recevaient pas moins leur 10% seulement, ce qui permettait de libérer en Italie la somme équivalente en lires au profit des exportateurs nationaux, tandis qu'un autre 10% fut accordé aux exportateurs italiens dans le clearing étranger sans pouvoir leur être transféré en Italie. C'est ce qui se passa vers la fin de 1936 quand les exportations italiennes reprirent relativement plus vite que les importations.

D'autre part, l'amortissement des dettes anciennes se poursuivait de façon automatique même si l'excédent d'exportations italien faisait place à un excédent d'importations. C'est là ce qui arriva dans le courant de 1937. Le mécanisme du clearing permit ainsi simultanément avec la liquidation progressive d'un arriéré étranger ancien, la formation d'un arriéré nouveau soit italienne, soit étranger et ces deux éventualités se sont vérifiées successivement.

Tableau 7.2. *Situation des clearings 1937-1938*

	1937			1938		
	Situations crédit.	Situations debitr.	Balance	Situations créditr.	Situations debitr.	Balance
Fin						
Janvier	371	30	341	86	464	-378
Février	332	57	275	95	490	-395
Mars	268	35	233	92	528	-436
Avril	230	33	197	81	621	-540
Mai	162	83	79	78	618[1]	-540
Juin	207	94	113	77	622	-545
Juillet	201	173	28	79	561	-482
Aout	193	177	16	88	596	-508
Septembre	206	197	9	90	523	-433
Octobre	114	292	-178	90	497	-407
Novembre	98	351	-253	110	403	-293
Décembre	83	415	-332	120	381	-261
			1939			
Janvier	238	363	-125			

en millions de lires.

[1] Le Clearing de la France n'est plus compris à partir de mai 1938 dans les chiffres ci-dessus; à la fin avril elle était créditrice do 115 millions.

Vers la fin de 1937, les arriérés anciens étaient en grande partie liquidés et de nouveaux accords furent passés pour décider de l'affectation des quota-parts des exportations italiennes destinées jusqu'alors au dégel des créances anciennes.

Pendant l'année 1937, la situation des clearings se renversa; au solde créditeur italien de 274 millions à la fin de 1936, se substitua un solde débiteur de 332 millions à la fin de 1937. Pendant l'année, l'Italie avait donc laissé s'affaiblir sa position en clearing de 606 millions ce qui l'aida à supporter le déficit exceptionnel de sa balance commerciale (5,7 milliards de lires) de cette année.

L'année 1938 se divise en deux moitiés; la première voit se continuer l'accumulation d'arriérés en faveur d'exportateurs étrangers; en incluant pour la France un crédit de 100 millions on arrive à un solde débiteur total de 645 millions à la fin juin.

Dans la deuxième partie de l'année, grâce à la réduction sensible du déficit commercial, le solde débiteur se réduit rapidement et se monte, à la fin de décembre, à 261 millions seulement de sorte qu'en définitive, l'année 1938 a vu s'améliorer quelque peu la position en clearing de l'Italie.

b) Points particuliers relatifs aux clearings

Nous allons maintenant essayer d'éclaircir certains côtés particuliers du système de clearing en vigueur entre l'Italie et les autres pays européens.

1) La garantie de change,
2) les opérations bancaires connexes au clearing,
3) étude particulière du clearing anglo-italien, choisi comme prototype des accords de clearing conclus pour l'Italie.

1) Garantie de change—En régime de monnaie libre, les importateurs et les exportateurs se couvrent contre les risques de change en opérant sur le marché des changes à terme. Une telle couverture est impossible en régime de contrôle des changes, le marché des changes et, en particulier, celui des changes à terme, étant aboli. L'absence de ce marché et des facilités qu'il offre est un des inconvénients les plus graves du contrôle surtout dans une période d'amples fluctuations monétaires. Les opérations sur le marché des changes à terme ont, pour but d'assurer les risques de change pour la période qui court entre les stipulations du contrat et le moment du paiement. Or, pour le clearing, l'opération commerciale se fait en trois temps au lieu de deux en régime libre; on a la date de la stipulation du contrat, la date du versement de la part de l'importateur et la date de paiement à l'exportateur et en cas d'arriéré un laps de temps considérable peut s'écouler entre les deux derniers moments. Or, si le Contrôle des Changes permet difficilement de se couvrir pour le temps entre la conclusion du contrat et le paiement de l'acheteur, on a trouvé moyen d'écarter le risque du change pour la période pendant laquelle le montant payé ne peut être transféré à l'exportateur.

Les premiers accords de clearing conclus par l'Italie prévoyaient généralement que le débiteur, soit Italien, soit étranger, no serait libéré qu'au moment où le créancier aurait reçu le montant total qui lui était dû suivant le contrat. Le risque de change incombait aussi au créancier si le paiement était stipulé dans la monnaie du débiteur et, au contraire, au débiteur si la somme à payer était convenue en monnaie du créancier. Ce dernier cas est généralement le plus fréquent. Les inconvénients du système se firent pleinement sentir lors de l'alignement de la lire. Les importateurs italiens de produits allemands qui avaient déjà payé leurs factures mais dont les versements n'avaient pu encore être transférés, l'Italie étant à ce moment débitrice en compte de clearing avec l'Allemagne, durent ajouter deux tiers aux prix antérieurement payés pour reconstituer les montants en marks dont ils étaient débiteurs.

D'ailleurs, les versements "intégratifs," c'est-à-dire, les versements destinés à procurer à l'exportateur étranger la somme entière en monnaie de son pays le jour du paiement sont faits à leur tour en clearing, et il se peut qu'avant le transfert, le cours du change ait varié encore une fois, de sorte qu'un nouveau versement devient nécessaire. On voit ainsi les graves inconvénients de ce système. Pour y pallier, l'Istcambi a peu à peu assumé la garantie de change dans la plupart des clearings moyennant le paiement d'une prime de 0,5% sur le montant de chaque opération garantie s'ajoutant à la commission de 0,25% perçue sur toutes les opérations de clearing. Actuellement, l'Italie qui est en rapport avec tous les pays de clearing européens, sauf la France, n'a pas stipulé la garantie de change pour la Bulgarie, la Grèce, l'Islande, la Lituanie et la Hongrie. Avec tous les autres pays, les risques de change sont couverts par l'Istcambi avec les modalités suivantes:

1. dans un premier groupe de pays, l'Istcambi déclare libératoire le versement de l'importateur italien ainsi que celui de l'importateur étranger;
2. dans un deuxième groupe de pays, le versement de l'importateur italien a toujours effet libératoire et l'Istcambi garantit le paiement exact à l'exportateur de ce qui lui est dû en lires. Cependant, l'exportateur doit lui-même agir contre son débiteur étranger pour le compte de l'Istcambi pour d'éventuels versements additionnels car le versement du débiteur étranger n'a pas, pour celui-ci, effet libératoire;
3. enfin, dans un certain nombre de clearings, l'Istacambi garantit aux exportateurs étrangers le paiement de leurs créances au cours du jour du versement de la part de l'importateur italien, uniquement si la dette de l'importateur italien était libellée en monnaie autre que la lire.

Ainsi, le paiement de l'importateur italien a toujours effet libératoire. Et l'Istcambi garantit toujours à l'exportateur italien le paiement de la contrevaleur exacte en lires du versement de l'importateur étranger au cours du jour du versement de celui-ci. Par contre, le paiement de l'importateur étranger n'est pas toujours libératoire et l'Istcambi ne garantit pas, dans tous les cas, le paiement à l'exportateur étranger au cours du jour du versement de l'importateur italien.

2) Opérations bancaires connexes au clearing—Un deuxième problème au moins aussi grave se posait par suite de l'existence des arriérés de clearings; c'était la question de la mobilisation des créances des exportateurs en souffrance jusqu'ici. Un décret-loi du 11 janvier 1937 a introduit en Italie un nouveau titre bancaire qui se propose justement d'effectuer cette mobilisation.

Il est émis par l'Istcambi sous forme de promesse de paiement à date incertaine; à ce certificat est jointe une lettre de change tirée sur l'Istcambi par l'exportateur pour un pourcentage donné de la créance totale. L'échéance maxima de cette traite est de 6 mois. Le bénéficiaire ne peut être qu'une banque autorisée à escompter ses traites. Si, à l'échéance, l'Istcambi n'est pas encore en état de payer le crédit de l'exportateur, cela est annoté sur la traite et tient lieu de protêt; le porteur a alors le droit de se retourner contre l'exportateur. Cette sorte de mobilisation—elle n'est que partielle, comme on l'a vu—est possible seulement en contrepartie d'une opération commerciale et non en contrepartie de paiements anticipés pour marchandises à fournir.

Il semble, cependant, que la facilité offerte ainsi par l'Istcambi n'ait pas été largement utilisée jusqu'ici. Il y a à cela une première cause très simple. Si au moment de l'élaboration et de la parution du décret-loi en question, les crédits en souffrance des exportateurs italiens étaient relativement nombreux, ils se firent très rares dans la suite et c'étaient les exportateurs étrangers qui durent patienter avant d'être payés. Mais même là où les émissions de titres de l'Istcambi auraient été possibles, il semble que les exportateurs ont préféré se faire accorder des crédits directement par les banques, soit par des ouvertures de crédit pures et simples, soit en donnant comme gages le document où est inscrit leurs créances envers l'Istcambi. L'exportateur peut, on outre, se faire financer par une banque, non seulement pour la période où son crédit est payé mais non transféré, mais avant même que l'exportateur étranger ait payé en cédant à la banque son crédit au moyen d'une délégation irrévocable pour l'encaissement auprès de l'Istcambi. L'opération est semblable et remplit la fonction de l'escompte de traites documentaires dans le commerce international sans clearing.

Il a été plus difficile de suppléer à d'autres formes de financement du commerce International. Ainsi, les acceptations de banques destinées à faciliter le commerce d'importation sont devenues impossibles. Mais un effet semblable est atteint par les versements anticipés que les banques italiennes peuvent faire en clearings, dès que la marchandise étrangère est entrée en Italie, par ces versements, le paiement à l'exportateur étranger se trouve, naturellement, avancé d'autant, la Banque italienne peut être en relations uniquement avec l'exportateur étranger et, dans ce cas, celui-ci doit trouver lui-même une banque disposée à lui mobiliser son crédit; mais il se peut que l'opération soit faite d'un commun accord entre la banque italienne et la banque étrangère. Celle-ci s'oblige, dans ce cas, à ouvrir immédiatement un crédit à l'exportateur et la Banque italienne exécute son paiement anticipé on tant que débitrice directe de la Banque étrangère.

3) Étude détaillée du clearing italo-anglais (choisi comme prototype des accords de clearing conclus par l'Italie)—Après des pourparlers assez difficiles, un accord commercial et de clearing fut conclu entre l'Italie et l'Angleterre après la levée des sanctions le 6 novembre 1936. L'accord commercial prévoit que les marchandises italiennes bénéficieraient au Royaume-Uni du traitement de la nation la plus favorisée (en dehors de l'Empire naturellement). Par contre, les importations anglaises en Italie sont minutieusement réglées en contingents, soit directement, soit en pourcentage de la valeur importée en 1934.

L'accord de clearing stipule que les paiements des débiteurs italiens seraient répartis dans les comptes suivants.

1. Dans un "compte nouveau lires" les sommes dues pour marchandises et frêts à partir du 15 juillet 1936 (date de la levée des sanctions).
2. Dans un "compte arriéré lires A" est viré ou versé par les débiteurs italiens le prix des marchandises anglaises importées ou des frêts dus pour la période du 17 mars 1935 (date d'un accord antérieur italo-anglais) au 18 novembre 1935 (date de l'imposition des sanctions).
3. Dans un "compte arriéré lires B" est viré ou versé par les débiteurs italiens le prix des marchandises anglaises importées ou des frêts dûs pour la période avant le 17 mars 1935 et entre le 18 novembre 1935 et le 15 juillet 1936 (période des sanctions).

Les lires déjà versées lors de la conclusion de l'accord en contrepartie de marchandises sont converties en livres sterling en cours d'avant la dévaluation de 64,46 lires pour une livre, c'est-à-dire que les débiteurs italiens ne sont pas obligés dans ce seul cas à des versements additionnels correspondant à la dévaluation de la lire. C'est là une faveur faite par l'Istcambi aux débiteurs italiens qui pouvaient se prévaloir du décret-loi du 20 novembre 1935 sur le blocage crédit des pays sanctionnistes.

4. Dans un "compte arriéré lires C" sont versées les autres dettes de toutes sortes, en particulier, les dettes financières, sauf celles qui sont expressément exclues par l'accord. L'appellation "arriéré" parait ici inexacte,

puisque le compte reçoit également les versements courants à titre d'intérêts, de dividendes, etc.

Du côté britannique, nous avons près de l' "Anglo-Italien Clearing Office" un "compte général livres" alimenté uniquement par les versements des importateurs britanniques en contrepartie des marchandises italiennes. Les livres de ce compte sont donc distribuées aux créanciers britanniques de la façon suivante:

1. 70% aux "comptes nouveaux livres" destinés au transfert des sommes versées en Italie dans le "compte nouveau lires",
2. 18% aux "comptes arriérés livres A",
3. 9% aux "comptes arriérés livres B",
4. 5% aux "comptes arriérés livres C",

destinés au transfert des lires versées à l'Istcambi aux comptes respectifs en lires.

Une clause intéressante de l'accord est celle qui prévoit que les créanciers britanniques, au lieu d'attendre le paiement par le mécanisme des "comptes arriérés livres" A, B et C, peuvent faire transférer leurs crédits des comptes arriérés lires A, B et C aux comptes lires anciens inaliénables et utilisables seulement en Italie pour certains investissements et dépenses, (voir p. 204). On ne sait pas dans quelle mesure les créanciers ont fait usage de cette faculté.

L'accord prévoit, en outre, des transferts entre les différents comptes en livres au cas où la répartition automatique par pourcentage ne correspondrait plus aux proportions existant entre les diverses catégories de créances à satisfaire. Et, en effet, l'Angleterre et l'Italie passaient un autre accord par échange de notes le 24 décembre 1937 ayant pour but d'effectuer un tel transfert. Mais, bientôt un changement radical devint nécessaire ou fait que les créances arriérées inscrites dans les comptes A et B, c'est-à-dire, tous les arriérés datant d'avant la levée des sanctions—car nous avons vu que le compte C ne constitue pas un véritable compte d'arriérés—avaient été presque entièrement réglées. Par l'accord du 18 mars 1938, les livres qui se trouvaient au crédit des comptes A et B, furent, par conséquent, virées au "compte nouveau lires" à l'exception de:

1. L 10.000 comme couverture d'éventuels transferts ultérieurs de versements effectués en Italie;
2. L 30.000 laissées à la libre disposition de l'Istcambi.

Suivant l'accord nouveau, la répartition des versements des importateurs britanniques au "compte général livres" serait dorénavant effectuée comme suit:

- 87% aux exportateurs et armateurs britanniques. Les 87% sont divisés en un "sous-compte livres charbons" qui recueillit 46% et qui sort à payer les exportateurs britanniques de charbons, et un "sous-compte livres D" qui recueillit 41% et sert à payer les autres exportateurs et les armateurs britanniques;
- 6,5% au "compte arriéré livres C" et
- 6,5% seraient laissés en livres à la libre disposition de l'Istcambi,

Cet accord prévoit donc un excédent d'exportation moins important en faveur de l'Italie (13% des exportations totales au lieu de 30% auparavant), mais cette fois la moitié de cet excédent est simplement versée à l'Istcambi en devises. Cependant, comme cela fut déjà le cas pour les versements aux créanciers d'arriérés, le versement de livres à l'Istcambi n'est point lié à la condition qu'il y ait *effectivement* un excédent d'exportations italiennes en Grande-Bretagne, puisque de toute façon, 6½% des versements des importateurs britanniques sont laissés en livres à l'Istcambi, même s'il y a un excédent d'exportations anglaises en Italie. Il se peut ainsi (et ce n'est point là une hypothèse puisque c'est exactement ce qui s'est passé) que, *quoique l'Italie importe de Grande-Bretagne plus qu'elle n'y exporte non seulement elle n'ait pas à fournir de devises pour régler son déficit, mais que c'est la Grande-Bretagne qui continue à lui verser en devises 6,5% des importations italiennes*. Il en résulte, naturellement, une nouvelle accumulation d'arriérés commerciaux qui devront être réglés tôt ou tard.

Dans les clearings qui ne prévoient pas des pointes en devises, les arriérés constituent simplement des délais de paiements ultérieurs accordés obligatoirement par les exportateurs du pays créditeur au pays débiteur. Avec le système de l'accord italo-anglais, ces arriérés sont partiellement l'expression d'une *véritable avance* au pays débiteur faite par l'ensemble des exportateurs du pays créditeur.

De toute évidence, l'accord du 18 mars 1938 conclu parallèlement à l'accord politique général entre l'Italie et la Grande-Bretagne était très favorable à l'Italie. Mais il paraît que l'Italie a usé un peu trop largement des facilités offertes par l'accord. Elle a, en effet, accumulé, en quelques semaines, un arriéré de 100 millions de lires en clearing, de sorte que le Board of Trade se vit forcé de conseiller aux industriels anglais de ralentir leurs exportations, ce qui donna lieu à quelques polémiques de presse du côté italien. Tandis qu'en 1936 et en 1937, le commerce italien avec la Grande-Bretagne avait été excédentaire, il devint déficitaire on 1938 par suite de la politique d'achat de l'Italie—les contingents d'importation avalant d'ailleurs été augmentés par l'accord du 18 mars 1938—et de la moindre capacité d'absorption de l'Angleterre pour les produits italiens. L'évolution du commerce et du clearing italo-anglais ressort du tableau 7.3. On y discerne comment les mouvements du solde commercial se répercutent avec un retard facilement explicable sur la position du solde du clearing. Mais malgré les excédents d'importations italiennes pendant les mois précédents, le brusque renversement de la position du clearing de fin avril à fin mai 1938 est malaisé à définir. Dans les derniers mois de 1938, sauf décembre, nous voyons réapparaître un excédent d'exportations italiennes, ce qui permet de prévoir une réduction prochaine du solde débiteur qui reste actuellement assez élevé.

Nous attirerons encore l'attention sur quelques points particuliers des accords anglo-italiens du 6 décembre 1936 et du 18 mars 1938:

i) *paiements autres que commerciaux*, quelques paiements ont été expressément exclus du clearing, ce sont les dettes relatives aux:
   - primes et indemnités d'assurance et de réassurance, droit de brevets, licences de fabrication et droits d'auteur;
   - frets dus pour transports sur navires italiens;
   - importation de lingots et de monnaie d'argent;
   - frets et assurances relatives aux importations anglaises de charbons.

Les paiements italiens afférents à ces opérations ne pouvant s'effectuer par clearing devront être réglés en devises, ou serviront à constituer des comptes bloqués utilisables en Italie seulement.

Étant donné la nature des opérations énumérées, il s'agira généralement de paiements en devises autorisés ou contrôlés par l'Istcambi, sauf peut-être pour les droits d'auteur.

Il y a aussi d'autres opérations donnant lieu à des paiements entre l'Angleterre et l'Italie qui, n'étant pas mentionnées par l'accord de clearing, en sont

Tableau 7.3. III. *Commerce et clearing italo-anglais 1937–1938*

	Importations Anglaise en Italie	Exportations Italiennes en Grand Bretagne	Balance[1]	Position du Clearing[2]
1937				
Janvier	9,4	53,1	43,7	110,8
Février	18,3	49,5	31,2	105,9
Mars	28,6	43,2	14,6	38,8
Avril	42,5	50,1	7,6	34,5
Mai	41,6	53,5	11,9	30,3
Juin	54,5	58,0	3,5	45,5
Juillet	47,0	48,7	1,7	40,8
Aout	68,3	57,5	-10,6	22,1
Septembre	51,1	55,3	4,2	16,6
Octobre	60,0	67,1	7,1	19,0
Novembre	56,1	57,6	11,5	19,3
Décembre	82,1	44,1	-38,0	16,8
	560,8	639,7	78,9	
1938				
Janvier	61,1	44,4	-16,7	17,3
Février	56,0	44,6	-11,4	22,2
Mars	72,9	49,5	-22,4	18,1
Avril	60,8	43,7	-17,1	5,6
Mai	49,7	40,4	-9,3	-100,3
Juin	69,1	42,7	-26,4	-82,1
Juillet	52,3	36,6	-15,7	-87,2
Aout	49,1	44,9	-4,2	-98,3
Septembre	43,3	49,5	6,2	-101,7
Octobre	41,5	65,0	23,5	-100,1
Novembre	47,8	62,3	14,5	-92,2
Décembre	92,5	56,6	-35,9	-101,5
	703,0	580,2	-122,8	

Chiffre en millions de lires.

[1] Favorable (+) ou défavorable (-) pour l'Italie.

[2] Montant des crédits arriérés des exportateurs italiens (+) ou anglais (-).

exclues automatiquement, comme par exemple, toutes les opérations relatives au tourisme dont l'Italie retire un solde important en devises.

Par ailleurs, le clearing se rapporte uniquement au commerce entre les deux métropoles et non aux échanges entre l'Italie et les Colonies britanniques ou entre la Grande-Bretagne et les Colonies italiennes ni aux rapports intercoloniaux.

ii) *Précédence des paiements*—Le principe général dans cette matière est que les paiements aux créanciers sont faits dans l'ordre chronologique des versements des débiteurs. Ce principe subit deux entorses dans l'accord italo-anglais:
- dans les paiements faits aux créanciers anglais par le "compte arriéré livres C," la priorité est accordée aux paiements représentant un caractère périodique, tels qu'intérêts, dividendes, loyers, etc.
- dans les paiements aux créanciers anglais par le "compte nouveau livres" ou par le "sous-compte livres D" dans le nouvel accord, la priorité est accordée aux paiements de frêts.

iii) On a déjà pu remarquer que tandis que les paiements anglais pour frêts dûs pour transport sur navires italiens se règlent en devises, les paiements italiens pour frêts dûs pour transport sur navires anglais se règlent en clearing. De ce fait, l'excèdent réel d'exportation nécessaire à l'équilibre du clearing, en faveur de l'Italie, est plus important qu'il n'apparait des proportions 100:70 (premier accord) et 100:87 (deuxième accord). En outre, il est évident que ce traitement inégal des paiements de frêt avantage grandement la marine marchande italienne, en particulier, quand l'Italie est débitrice en compte de clearing.

c) Les accords de paiement

L'Italie est en rapport de clearing avec tous les pays européens, sauf depuis 1938, avec la France. Avec cette dernière, et un certain nombre de pays d'Outre-mer (Brésil, Argentine, Colombie, Uruguay, Indes Néerlandaises, Japon et Mandchoukoo) elle a conclu des accords tendant à assurer l'équilibre des échanges et dénommés génériquement "accords de paiements." En réalité, ces accords n'ont pas de caractère aussi bien défini que les accords de clearing et leurs modalités sont assez variées. On a généralement présenté les accords de paiement comme une atténuation du régime des clearings, mais ceci n'est exact que très partiellement. Les importations italiennes sont toujours étroitement contingentées dans ces accords et le régime de la "bolletta," c'est-à-dire de l'importation au prorata de l'importation de 1934 est, dans ces accords, intégralement remplacé par le régime de la licence. Bien plus, les importations du pays étranger sont, elles aussi, généralement distribuées en contingent alors que cela n'est pas forcément le cas pour le pays avec lequel l'Italie est en rapport de clearing (voir clearing anglo-italien).

Ce contrôle renforcé du côté marchandises s'explique par une liberté plus grande laissée du côté paiements. Le principal avantage des accords de paiement est, en effet, qu'ils évitent les arriérés dûs aux exportateurs de l'un ou l'autre pays. Mais alors que dans les clearings, il intervient après un certain temps une rectification quasi automatique dans le sens de l'équilibre, due au ralentissement des ventes des exportateurs, qui prévoient des délais de paiements trop longs, ce facteur de rééquilibre ne joue pas dans les accords de paiements et il faut, par conséquent, prévoir l'égalité des changes d'une autre façon. Nous distinguons deux classes principales parmi ces accords.

1. La plupart des accords prévoient, outre les contingents d'importation et d'exportation, la surveillance des opérations dans un des pays. L'Istcambi ou l'organe de contrôle dans le pays étranger centralise les devises provenant des exportations et procède à des achats dans la limite des disponibilités en devises ainsi réalisées. Pour les rapports entre l'Italie et les pays sudaméricains, ce sont généralement ces derniers qui assument cette fonction. Pour la France, c'est au contraire, l'Istcambi qui règle les achats en France et les paiements aux créanciers d'arriérés commerciaux et aux créanciers financiers avec le produit en francs des ventes italiennes en France.
2. Dans l'accord que l'Italie a passé avec le Japon et la Mandchourie, on a uniquement fixé les contingents d'importations réciproques. (L'équilibre des échanges est assuré en considèrent pour les contingents, le Japon et la Mandchourie comme un seul territoire). Les paiements se font en devises livres et sont enregistrés en Italie près de l'Istcambi et au Japon près de l'institut correspondant (Yokohama Siokin Ginko). Si, à la fin du semestre, il résulte de ces comptes que l'Italie a versé au Japon et à la Mandchourie plus de devises qu'elle n'en a reçues, elle a le droit, dans le semestre suivant, de diminuer les contingents accordés au Japon et à la Mandchourie du montant exact dont elle se trouve être créditrice. Il en est de même pour le Japon.

Ici, par conséquent, les déséquilibres—provenant de la non-utilisation de certains contingents par les importateurs ou par l'octroi de contingents supplémentaires—peuvent se produire des deux côtés tandis qu'avec le système décrit sous 1), l'excédent ne peut se former qu'en faveur du pays qui centralise les opérations en devises.

4) Les compensations privées

Malgré les complications techniques et les multiples modalités du système, nous ne traiterons que brièvement des compensations privées puisqu'elles ne présentent plus en Italie qu'un intérêt historique.

Elles furent instituées sous la surveillance de l'Institut National Fasciste pour le Commerce Extérieur, le 1er mars 1935, aussitôt après le contingentement général des importations; dans l'intention du législateur, elles devaient servir, en effet, à permettre des importations extra-contingents en contrepartie d'exportations additionnelles qu'on pensait encourager par les primes connexes à la compensation. En réalité, ce ne furent pas des exportations de marchandises nouvelles ou vers de nouveaux marchés qu'on provoqua ainsi mais simplement le passage des exportations anciennes, du régime traditionnel à celui des compensations privées. Ainsi, des importations faites en dehors des compensations privées se trouvaient plus en face d'elles les exportations qu'on avait pensé leur assigner et l'équilibre de la balance commerciale n'était point assuré.

D'autre part, la recherche de contreparties de la part des importateurs donnait lieu à un commerce d'intermédiaires à profits souvent surélevés grâce aux primes payées par les importateurs sûrs de pouvoir revendre à l'intérieur à des prix de monopole.

Ces inconvénients et abus déterminèrent bientôt une réglementation plus sévère et restrictive à partir de juillet 1935.

1. On détermina les marchandises admises au régime de la compensation privée, soit à l'importation, soit à l'exportation. A l'importation, ce furent généralement les matières premières en dehors de celles importées en régime spécial et à l'exportation des produits manufacturés nouveaux ou dont les exportations étaient fortement tombées pendant la crise. En 1936, on décida même que telles marchandises à l'importation ne sauraient s'accoupler qu'avec telles marchandises à l'exportation.
2. Le contrôle de la compensation fut rendu plus efficace, la demande devant être adressée aux organisations syndicales dont l'avis favorable était nécessaire pour obtenir l'autorisation de l'Institut pour le Commerce Extérieur.
3. Enfin, il fut stipulé que l'autorisation une fois obtenue, importateurs et exportateurs devraient s'adresser à des banques spécialement autorisées

pour trouver leur contrepartie respective. Tous les paiements relatifs à la compensation devaient être exécutés par l'intermédiaire d'une de ces banques qui était obligé de tenir une comptabilité spéciale contrôlée par l'I.C.E.

Il fut établi que la prime payée aux exportateurs ne pouvait dépasser 20%. Quant aux compensations effectuées avec des pays avec lesquels l'Italie était en rapport de clearing, les fonctions de l'I.C.E. passaient à l'Istcambi.

Ainsi étroitement réglée et surveillée la compensation privée perdait de plus en plus d'importance. Elle eut, cependant, un regain de faveur pendant les sanctions où on s'efforçait d'organiser des compensations triangulaires. On assure qu'elles furent très utiles à l'Italie pour réaliser son programme contre-sanctionniste: exporter vers les pays sanctionnistes et importer des pays non-sanctionnistes. Les banques déléguées pouvaient autoriser directement ce genre d'opérations.

Après la levée des sanctions, les compensations triangulaires furent abolies et lors du la dévaluation de le lire, les compensations privées, en général, furent défendues sauf si les accords de compensation générale les prévoyaient ou sauf avec certains petits États américains, Mais avec ces pays, elles furent supprimées en 1937 et actuellement, nous ne voyons que le Japon, la Mandchourie et l'Espagne avec lesquels elles soient encore autorisées.

Pour les importateurs, la compensation privée représentait une sorte de survivance conditionnelle de la liberté d'importation (la condition étant de trouver la contrepartie); pour les exportateurs, elle constituait une subvention bienvenue au moment où les prix italiens étaient élevés par rapport aux prix mondiaux. On s'explique ainsi la disparition de la compensation privée dès que l'organisation administrative des importations fut arrivée à un certain degré de perfectionnement et que la dévaluation de la lire eût éliminé la disparité des prix italiens. Toutefois, les "accords de devises" dont nous avons parlé plus haut (p. 214) constituent, en quelque sorte, une variation de la compensation privée avec la différence que l'importateur et l'exportateur ne font qu'une seule personne.[8] Les primes payées en régime de compensation privée de l'importateur à l'exportateur et du consommateur national à l'importateur, sont liquidées dans les accords de devises directement par le consommateur.

8 Ou, tout au moins, appartiennent à la même branche d'industrie, industrielle de la filature, importateur de coton brut, d'une part, et industriel du tissage, exportateur do tissus, de l'autre.

5) Influence du Contrôle sur le Commerce Extérieur

a) Dans l'ensemble

Voici les chiffres du commerce extérieur à l'exclusion du commerce avec les Colonies:

Tableau 7.4. *Commerce extérieur global 1929–1938*

Années	Importations	Exportations	Déficit	Part des exportations dans les importations
1929	21.196	14.573	6.623	68,80%
1934	7.582	4.965	2.617	65,50%
1935	7.662	4.488	3.174	58,50%
1936	5.883	3.829	2.054	65,10%
1937	13.592	7.853	5.739	57,80%
1938	10.918	7.960	2.958	72,90%

en millions de lires.

Les mouvements depuis 1934 sont aisément explicables: en 1935 la préparation militaire et les achats préventifs à cause des sanctions maintiennent les achats à un chiffre élevé tandis que la position de la lire et le début des sanctions nuisent aux exportations. 1936 est l'année où les sanctions se font pleinement sentir dans la première moitié de l'année; en outre, l'Italie réduit ses achats au minimum. En 1937, la dévaluation de la lire donne une forte impulsion aux exportations mais l'avance des importations est beaucoup plus rapide à cause de trois facteurs principaux: 1) réapprovisionnement en matières premières de l'industrie dont las stocks étaient près d'être épuisés; 2) hausse extrêmement vive des prix à l'importation; l'indice des prix à l'importation monte de 43,1 en 1936 à 67,2 (1925=100) tandis que l'indice des prix à l'exportation ne s'élève que de 37,3 à 47,1; 3) besoins exceptionnels en blé et autres produits alimentaires en raison de la très mauvaise récolte de 1936. Les importations de blé à elles seules se montent à 1 milliard de lires.

En 1938, la bonne récolte de 1937, l'addition de maïs à la farine de blé dispense l'Italie d'importation de blé. La crise fourragère rend inutiles les importations de bétail et une certaine stagnation de la production industrielle réduit les besoins en matières premières, Il se peut que les premiers effets de la politique autarcique se soient fait sentir également dans ce sens, mais, d'autre part, l'agencement des industries autarciques a rendu nécessaires des importations exceptionnelles de machines.

La connaissance de ces divers facteurs “réels” sont indispensables pour s’expliquer le mouvement du commerce extérieur. Cela ne veut pas dire que le contrôle des changes n’a joué qu’un rôle d’exécutant; mais la fonction de l’Istcambi et du Ministère pour les Échanges et les Devises n’est jamais que de fixer un *cadre*; toutes les demandes d’importation présentent un certain degré d’urgence et d’intérêt national. Or, à un moment donné, la Ministère vu les ressources dont il pense pouvoir disposer, fixe un degré au-delà duquel les demandes sont agréées et la *quantité* de demandes présentant au moins ce degré peut augmenter ou diminuer, suivant des causes qu’on a énumérées. Évidemment, les critères selon lesquels les demandes sont agréées ou non peuvent changer, mais il n’en reste pas moins que les changements des besoins du commerce, de l’industrie et de la consommation arrivent à se refléter dans les chiffres du commerce extérieur.

Le fait qu’il y a eu, en 1937 et en 1938, des déficits qui ne sont probablement pas couverts par les rentrées invisibles ne signifie pas, dans ces conditions, que l’Istcambi a échoué dans la tâche qui lui a été assignée, mais simplement que le maintien de telle activité productrice ou l’achat de telle denrée alimentaire a été jugée plus importante que la contrepartie abandonnée, soit crédit étranger, soit titres étrangers, soit or.

Le déficit de près de 3 milliards de lires laissé par la balance commerciale en 1938 n’est pas, d’ailleurs, trop inquiétant. Plus de la moitié est réglée en clearing, il reste un milliard et demi de devises à transférer qui devrait rentrer en Italie sans trop de difficultés par les revenus invisibles. Actuellement, cependant, la situation reste tendue et exige un contrôle constant soit à cause des disparités de prix italiens et étrangers qui se sont formés à nouveau, soit parce qu’avec ses réserves d’or réduites et ses réserves de crédit et de titres étrangers presque liquidées, l’Italie est forcée de maintenir un équilibre de tous les instants.

b) Répartition par groupes de pays

Dans le changement de la répartition du commerce extérieur par pays, l’influence du contrôle est tout aussi difficile à isoler que dans le mouvement général du commerce. En premier lieu, on a réparti les pays en deux grands groupes: pays avec clearings, et pays sans clearings. Et on constatera qu’en particulier, si on ne tient pas compte du commerce très déficitaire italo-allemand, le commerce en clearing est mieux compensé que le commerce libre.

Tableau 7.5. *Commerce extérieur*

	Pays avec clearing				Pays sans clearing			
Années	Import.	Export.	Déficit absolu	Déficit relatif (1)	Import.	Export.	Déficit absolu	Déficit relatif (1)
1935	4264	2801	1463	34,30%	3399	1688	1711	50,30%
1936	3323	2299	1024	30,80%	2560	1531	1029	40,20%
1937	6838	4548	2290	33,50%	6754	3308	3446	51,00%
1938	6454	4760	1694	26,20%	4465	3199	1266	28,30%

en millions de lires.

Mais il serait erroné d'en conclure que le clearing crée l'équilibre des échanges.

Nous pensons, plutôt que possibilité d'arriver à un commerce équilibré est une prémisse nécessaire pour l'établissement du clearing pour autant qu'il n'y ait point à effectuer entre les doux pays en question de nombreux paiements autres que commerciaux.

(C'est précisément le cas des relations italo-allemandes: presque tout le tourisme allemand est dirigé en Italie, l'Allemagne a des dettes financières à payer à l'Italie et assure, en outre, le transfert des économies des travailleurs agricoles italiens qui viennent travailler saisonnièrement chez elle). Pour les pays sans clearing, il s'agit surtout de pays d'outre-mer avec lesquels la balance commerciale italienne fut toujours, à quelques exceptions près, (Égypte, Argentine, Uruguay) fortement passive et dont les importations constituées presque uniquement par des matières premières et denrées sont particulièrement sensibles au mouvement de la conjoncture et aux à-coups des récoltes. C'est précisément une des raisons pour lesquelles l'établissement d'un accord de clearing avec ces pays est malaisé.

Le tableau 7.6 montre le commerce extérieur italien avec les principaux groupes de pays, répartition qui nous a semblé plus rationnelle que la répartition par continent. Les chiffres de 1935 sont dominés uniquement par les effets de la guerre abyssine et les sanctions et ne présentent, par conséquent, pas d'intérêt pour notre étude. Par contre, les chiffres de 1937 et 1938 font apparaître les conséquences durables de ces événements et du contrôle des changes sur la répartition du commerce extérieur. (Il faut faire attention surtout aux mouvements intervenus après 1934, dernière année des changes non contrôlés; nous avons, cependant, jugé bon d'ajouter les chiffres de 1929 car il ne faut pas oublier que 1934 fut une année de dépression relative tandis que 1937 et 1939 sont ces années d'activité industrielle assez intenses).

Tableau 7.6. *Commerce extérieur par groupes de pays 1929–1938*

(en millions de lires)								
	Importations				Exportations			
	1929	1934	1937	1938	1929	1934	1937	1938
Allem. Autr.	3.320	1.438	3.121	2.981	2.204	956	1.792	1.983
Europ. Cent. Balkan[1]	1.746	768	1.935	1.598	1.482	635	1.063	1.081
Europ. Sept. & Occ.[2]	5.780	1.981	2.089	2.010	4.468	1.673	2.044	1.947
États-Unis	3.561	957	1.539	1.315	1.718	388	783	775
Arg. Brésil, Uruguay, Chili	2.106	510	1.408	636	1.446	328	584	626
Emp. Brit.[3]	2.616	762	1.370	824	738	222	367	379
Autres pays	2.167	1.166	2.330	1.554	2.517	763	1.220	1.169
TOTAL	21.196	7.582	13.592	10.918	14.573	4.965	7.853	7.960
(en pourcentages)								
Allem. Autr.	15,3	19,1	23,0	27,4	15,1	19,3	22,9	25,0
Europ. Cent. Balkan26	8,2	10,1	14,2	14,6	10,2	12,8	13,5	13,6
Europ. Sept. & Occ.27	27,3	26,1	15,4	18,4	30,6	33,7	26,0	24,4
États-Unis	16,8	12,6	11,3	12,1	11,8	7,8	10,0	9,7
Arg. Brésil, Uruguay, Chili	9,9	6,7	10,4	5,8	9,9	6,6	7,4	7,8
Emp. Brit.28	12,3	10,0	10,1	7,5	5,1	4,5	4,7	4,8
Autres pays	10,2	15,3	15,6	14,2	17,3	15,3	15,5	14,7
TOTAL	100,--	100,--	100,--	100,--	100,--	100,--	100,--	100,--

[1] Albanie, Bulgarie, Tchécoslovaquie, Grèce, Yougoslavie, Pologne, Roumanie, Hongrie, Turquie.

[2] Belgique, Luxembourg, France, Grande-Bretagne, Norvège, Pays-Bas, Portugal, Suède, Suisse.

[3] Australie, Malaisie britannique, Indes, Canada, Afrique du Sud.

Voici les principaux mouvements à dégager des chiffres:

1. l'augmentation de la part revenant à l'Allemagne dans le commerce italien est continue et comme on le voit par la comparaison dus chiffres pour 1929 et 1934, antérieure même au contrôle italien et au rapprochement politique des deux nations. Depuis 1934, en Allemagne le mouvement s'est accéléré et ceci plus pour les importations allemandes que pour les exportations: en 1938, le déficit du commerce italo-allemand a été de 998 millions de lires, c'est-à-dire plus d'un tiers du déficit total alors que les échanges italo-allemands ne constituent que 26% des échanges globaux.

Comment s'expliquer l'augmentation impressionnante du commerce italo-allemand? Il est dû au début au système que l'Allemagne a généralement appliqué en Europe Centrale et en Amérique du Sud, c'est-à-dire des achats massifs qui, en régime de clearing, étaient nécessairement suivis de ventes. En Italie, toutefois, le Reich n'a pas seulement acheté des produits agricoles et certaines matières premières, mais y a déversé également tout son tourisme, à partir des premiers accords de 1934. Pendant les sanctions, l'Allemagne a été le principal fournisseur et l'Italie a un peu appliqué le système allemand contre le Reich. Dans la suite, le rapprochement politique explique l'intensification des échanges. Ainsi, la presque totalité des achats exceptionnels de machines pour l'agencement des industries autarciques a été réservée à l'Allemagne.

2. L'augmentation de la part revenant aux pays de l'Europe Centrale et Balkanique est, elle aussi, importante quoique moindre que pour l'Allemagne et avec tendance à se ralentir: là aussi, l'augmentation est plus forte pour l'importation que pour l'exportation.
3. Une baisse très forte imputable surtout aux échanges avec la France, la Grande-Bretagne, la Belgique ut les Pays-Bas, est survenue dans le commerce de l'Italie avec l'Europe occidentale et septentrionale c'est-à-dire, avec les pays européens à monnaie librement négociable qui ont, cependant, stipulé des accords du clearing ou de paiement avec l'Italie. Cette baisse date uniquement du 1934 et s'explique par le fait:
   a) que l'orientation donnée par l'Italie à son commerce d'importation pendant les sanctions fut partiellement maintenue;
   b) que l'Italie adopta avec ces pays le principe des échanges compensés, comportant avec un certain nombre d'entre eux une pointe d'exportation en sa faveur destinée au paiement de dettes financières et autres. Ainsi, une restriction des importations fut rendue nécessaire en dehors même des tendances politiques et on observe, en effet, que la réduction des importations est plus importante que celle des exportations. Les chiffres absolus pour les années 1937 et 1939 montrent, d'ailleurs, une stabilité et un équilibre entre importations et exportations tout à fait remarquable.

Notons encore lu renversement des positions relatives de l'Allemagne et du Groupe des pays européens à monnaie libre: en 1929, la part de ces derniers était supérieure à la part austro-allemande de 80% pour les importations et de 100% pour les exportations. En 1938, elle lui était inférieure de 33% pour les importations et légèrement inférieure pour les exportations.

4. La réduction des pourcentages des États-Unis et les 4 principaux pays de l'Amérique du Sud dans le commerce italien date d'avant 1934; il

y a eu, après, une stabilisation pour les importations et une légère augmentation pour les exportations.

5. Le commerce avec l'Empire britannique qui, en termes relatifs, est le plus déficitaire des groupes considérés, montre une tendance très nette vers la diminution, surtout quant aux importations.
6. Le groupe des autres pays, constitué en majorité par des pays d'outre-mer, occupe depuis 1934 des parts presque égales dans l'exportation et l'importation. Par rapport à 1939, les chiffres se rapportant à la foule des autres pays permettent de dégager des centralisations des achats et une centralisation des ventes vers les principaux débouchés, c'est-à-dire, vers l'Europe ou dans l'Europe, comme on l'a vu, vers l'Allemagne.

c) Répartition par catégories de produits

La diminution des ventes italiennes dans les pays d'outre-mer et leur augmentation on Allemagne n'a pu manquer d'exercer son influence sur *la composition du commerce extérieur* dont nous donnons, ci-dessous, les changements absolus et relatifs:

Tableau 7.7. *Commerce extérieur par catégories des produits 1929–1938*

Importation									
	Mat. prem.		Mat. semi-ouvr.		Prod. fabriq.		Prod. aliment.		TOTAL
1929	8.029	37,7%	4.415	20,7%	4.224	19,8%	4.635	21,8%	21.303
1934	3.434	45,3%	1.561	20,6%	1.523	20,1%	1.064	14,0%	7.582
1937	5.989	44,1%	2.890	21,3%	1.908	14,0%	2.805	20,6%	13.592
1938	5.202	47,8%	2.375	21,8%	2.013	18,3%	1.317	12,1%	10.918
Exportation									
	Mat. prem.		Mat. semi-ouvr.		Prod. fabriq.		Prod. aliment.		TOTAL
1929	1.614	10,8%	3.253	21,9%	6.431	43,2%	3.585	24,1%	14.884
1934	598	12,0%	1.081	21,8%	1.702	34,3%	1.584	31,9%	4.965
1937	948	12,1%	1.723	21,9%	2.724	34,7%	2.458	31,3%	7.853
1938	807	10,1%	1.580	19,9%	2.864	36,0%	2.708	34,0%	7.959

Chiffres absolus en millions de lires.

Le fait saillant qui se dégage de ce tableau est la diminution des achats et l'augmentation progressive des ventes d'articles alimentaires. La concomitance de ces deux mouvements indique une baisse de la consommation italienne (corroborée, d'ailleurs, par les chiffres directs de la consommation, même en tenant compte de l'amélioration du sol et de l'augmentation de la superficie cultivée). De plus, l'augmentation des ventes d'articles alimentaires signifie un retour en arrière sur l'industrialisation de l'Italie qui, jusqu'en 1929, avait progressivement marqué sa balance commerciale. L'influence du commerce italo-allemand est ici certaine, car l'Allemagne achète à l'Italie principalement des produits maraîchers et fruitiers.[9]

Le diminution des ventes d'articles manufacturés est surtout sensible depuis 1929. En 1938, on en constate une légère reprise ayant pour contrepartie la diminution des exportations de matières premières et semi-ouvrées. Ici, c'est l'autarcie qui explique l'utilisation croissante de certaines matières premières exportables (chanvre, fibre artificielle, marbre, bauxite, pyrite) en Italie même. Du côté des importations, des matières premières et semi-ouvrées se sont substituées aux denrées alimentaires.

Dans l'ensemble, il n'y a aucun doute que le contrôle des changes et les clearings ont déclenché ou accéléré une tendance vers l'équilibre bilatéral des échanges. Ceci se constate, en particulier, avec les pays de l'Europe occidentale et de l'Amérique du Sud. D'une façon générale, les excédents des exportations tendent à se réduire et l'importance relative du déficit dans le commerce avec chaque nation tend à se rapprocher de la valeur relative du déficit total dans le commerce global.

On remarque, en outre, de plus en plus fréquemment, que si le commerce avec tel pays a été excédentaire dans une année, il tend à devenir déficitaire dans l'année suivante, de sorte qu'un équilibre bilatéral s'établit sur une échelle de plusieurs années. Cette évolution est très intéressante, car elle ne laisse rien subsister de la division traditionnelle entre pays avec lesquels le commerce est excédentaire et d'autres avec lesquels il est déficitaire pour des raisons de structure économique; le commerce avec chaque pays est tantôt excédentaire, tantôt déficitaire suivant des nécessités accidentelles de régler telle ou telle position débitrice en clearing.

Dans quelques cas, une bilatéralité d'un degré supérieur se substitue à la bilatéralité des échanges: c'est celle des paiements; l'exemple le plus remarquable en est le clearing italo-allemand équilibré malgré un déficit commercial énorme. Mais à défaut des mouvements de capitaux importants, un tel résultat ne pouvait être atteint qu'entre deux États qui contrôlent non seulement les changes, mais encore les décisions des individus et peuvent disposer l'envoi de touristes dans un pays et de travailleurs agricoles dans l'autre.

9 L'excellente tenue des exportations d'articles alimentaires dans les deux dernières années est due, en outre, à l'éclipse de la concurrence espagnole (pour les oranges, l'huile d'olive, etc.) pendant la guerre civile.

V. Monnaie

1) La lire de 1934 à 1936

La revalorisation de la lire annoncée par M. Mussolini dans son discours de Pesaro, en août 1926, et sa stabilisation en décembre 1927 au niveau élevé de 92 et 19 par rapport à la livre et au dollar respectivement, avait entraîné l'économie italienne dans une première crise de déflation très rigoureuse. Elle dura jusqu'en 1928 et après un répit de quelques mois à peine, la crise mondiale replongea l'Italie dans une deuxième déflation plus sévère encore. Fallait-il soumettre le pays à une troisième épreuve ayant pour but de compenser par un effort intérieur le dévaluation presque universelle des monnaies? Le gouvernement fasciste qui avait fait de la déflation une véritable mystique l'a essayé, mais sans grande conviction et tout en pratiquant une économie politique qui devait avoir des effets reflationnistes. Nous avons vu comment cette situation engendra un déficit commercial, croissant on 1934, cause directe de l'institution du Contrôle des Changes.

A un moment, où la lire étant surévaluée par rapport aux principales monnaies, les prix et la production industrielle étaient en reprise modérée, l'alternative dévaluation ou contrôle—devait se poser comme en France en 1936, à moins qu'on ne brisât la hausse des prix et des affaires par une nouvelle déflation comme la France l'avait fait en 1934–1935. Déflation et dévaluation ayant été exclues, il resta le Contrôle des Changes. Il convient, cependant, d'observer que, au point de vue de la valeur de la monnaie, la véritable alternative se pose entre déflation d'une part, et dévaluation et contrôle de l'autre. Ces deux dernières opérations ont toutes les deux le but de laisser se continuer la reprise économique et la hausse des prix en levant l'obstacle monétaire; la dévaluation y arrive directement tandis que le Contrôle utilise les restrictions à l'importation, les subventions à l'exportation et la multiplication des cours du change pour les divers moyens et catégories de paiements. A maints points de vue, le contrôle aboutit à une dévaluation indirecte, voilée, fractionnée.

En Italie, en particulier, les deux opérations monétaires ont été confondues dès le début. En mai 1934, la lire était déjà descendue à 3% au-dessous de sa parité or, et jusqu'en octobre 1936, cette dépréciation du cours officiel atteint successivement 12%. Il est intéressant de noter qu'elle n'avait aucune base légale. La loi monétaire du 21 décembre 1927 ayant pour titre "Loi pour la cessation du cours forcé et la convertibilité en or des billets de la Banque d'Italie" n'avait point été abrogée, pas plus que les décrets du 26 février 1928 obligeant la Banque d'Italie à délivrer contre billets des lingots d'un poids minimum de 5 kilogrammes et à maintenir le cours de la lire entre les limités de 18,90 et 19,10 lires par rapport au dollar-or, défendant ainsi une dépréciation de plus de 0,5%.

A côté de la dépréciation du cours officiel, nous notons de mai 1934 à octobre 1936, d'autres symptômes nombreux de l'affaiblissement de la lire. Ainsi, sur le marché des changes à l'étranger, la lire-billet fut traitée avec un escompte élevé. Ensuite, le décret-loi du 14 novembre 1935 fit reprendre la cotation officielle du prix de l'or et l'Istcambi offrait alors 15,50 liras par gramme, ce qui représente un contenu de 0,0645 grammes par lire et par conséquent une dépréciation virtuelle de 18,5% de la lire de 1927 qui contenait 0,0792 grammes d'or. Le cours officiel était alors déprécié de 8,4% seulement; le décret-loi du 20 mars 1936 autorisa l'Istcambi à émettre des titres de crédit touristiques (lettres de crédit et ordres de paiement) et l'escompte de la lire touristique par rapport à la lire officielle—elle aussi dépréciée—fut d'environ 23,5%. Enfin, pour les échanges commerciaux la dépréciation se traduisit par les primes à l'exportation sous les différentes formes que nous avons examinées: "facilitations," compensation privée, "primes" et "droit" en clearing.

De 1934 à 1936 se forme donc une multitude de lires avec des escomptes plus ou moins importants par rapport à la lire de la loi monétaire de 1927. Les facteurs de cet affaiblissement sont 1) la hausse des prix particulièrement vive en 1935 par suite de la mauvaise récolte de 1934, du contingentement des importations et de la politique de crédit libérale de l'Institut d'émission tenu de faciliter la mobilisation militaire et économique pour la guerre éthiopienne, 2) quelques fuites de capitaux (exportation de lires-billets), 3) la diminution de l'encaisse-or qui, étant donné l'expansion parallèle de la circulation, força le gouvernement à suspendre le 21 juillet 1935, la proportion-limite de 40% que selon la loi monétaire de 1927, l'institut d'émission devait maintenir entre la réserve en or et devises, et ses engagements à vue.

2) "L'alignement" de la lire en octobre 1936

Après la dévaluation, du franc français, du franc suisse et du florin, en septembre 1936, le gouvernement italien décida une opération similaire pour la lire par le décret-loi du 5 octobre 1936. On prit comme modèle la stabilisation du dollar de février 1934, en diminuant la valeur-or de la lire de 1927 de 40,94% et en laissant au gouvernement la faculté de dévaluer par décret jusqu'à 50%. Nominalement, la dévaluation était donc plus forte que la dévaluation simultanée des autres monnaies de l'ancien bloc-or, mais cette différence est réduite si on se rappelle la dépréciation de fait antérieure à la dévaluation officielle; par rapport au cours de la lire officielle en septembre 1935, la dévaluation d'octobre ressort à environ 33%. Depuis octobre 1936, la lire officielle n'a pas été touchée et s'est maintenue invariablement an cours de 19 par rapport au dollar. La dévaluation avait fait cesser la disparité entre prix italiens et prix étrangers. En conséquence, on abolit toutes les primes à l'exportation énumérées ci-dessus; la lire touristique fut maintenue mais son cours se rapprocha considérablement du cours général; l'écart ne fut plus que de 6,5%. De même, le cours officieux des billets de banque circulant à l'étranger vit diminuer son écart du cours officiel.

La loi monétaire du 5 octobre 1936 avait formellement ouvert la voie vers l'atténuation et même l'abolition progressive du contrôle par article 5 dont voici la teneur: "*Les dispositions en matière de mouvements de capitaux et d'échanges avec l'étranger*, édictées à la suite du décret-loi du 29 septembre 1931 n° 1207[10] et les dispositions contenues dans les mesures successives pourront *être suspendues en tout ou en partie* par décrets royaux sur la proposition du Chef du Gouvernement et du Ministre des Finances." Cet article démontre que le gouvernement italien n'avait pas encore définitivement choisi son chemin en matière de politique monétaire.

On constate, en effet, à la fin de 1936, une certaine tendance à l'atténuation du contrôle. Ainsi, en décembre, la permission de tenir des comptes en devises étrangères fut étendue des Compagnies d'assurance et de navigation à toutes les sociétés dont l'activité s'effectue surtout à l'étranger. Enfin, quant à la cession obligatoire de crédits et de titres étrangers, certaines exonérations ont été accordées.

3) L'évolution des prix après l'alignement et ses répercussions sur la lire

Mais ces velléités ne devaient pas aller loin; le déficit commercial important de 1937 rendit plus que jamais nécessaire le monopole des changes et l'évolution des prix italiens par rapport à celle des prix étrangers fit bientôt réapparaître une certaine disparité affaiblissant de nouveau la lire. Dans le tableau 7.8. on a indiqué l'évolution comparée des prix de gros-or on Italie, en France et en Angleterre sur la base de 1913. Malgré les précautions qu'il faut

10 Ce décret-loi avait donné au Ministre des Finances la faculté de réglementer par décret les opérations de change.

prendre avant vouloir tirer des conclusions trop formelles de ces indices souvent hétérogènes, il n'y a pas à se méprendre sur le sens général de l'évolution qui, seul, nous importe ici.

Tableau 7.8. *Indices-or des prix de gros en Italie, France et Grande-Bretagne*

	Italie (Conseil Economique De Milan)	France (S.G.F. 126 articles)	Grande-Bretagne (Board of Trade)
1930	112	112	120
1931	94	112	98
1932	85	87	73
1933	77	81	70
1934	73	76	65
1935	81	69	64
1936 août	88	81	70
septembre	89	85	71
octobre	66	67	70
novembre	60	70	70
décembre	61	74	72
1937 janvier	63	72	73
février	65	76	74
mars	66	77	76
avril	68	76	77
mai	69	75	79
juin	71	76	79
juillet	72	67	80
aout	72	69	80
septembre	73	66	79
octobre	74	64	79
novembre	75	64	79
décembre	76	66	78
1938 janvier	76	64	78
février	75	63	77
mars	75	59	75
avril	75	60	74
mai	76	56	74
juin	76	56	72
juillet	75	55	72

Tableau 7.8. *Suite*

	Italie (Conseil Economique De Milan)	France (S.G.F. 126 articles)	Grande-Bretagne (Board of Trade)
aout	75	54	71
septembre	76	53	69
octobre	76	54	68
novembre	76	54	68
décembre	76	55	66

Jusqu'en 1933, les prix italiens sont soumis à une déflation sévère qui n'arrive, toutefois, pas à compenser la dévaluation de la livre. De 1933 à 1934, la baisse se ralentit et fait place de 1934 à 1935 à une hausse de 11%, de sorte qu'à partir de 1935 jusqu'à la veille de la dévaluation, l'Italie a le niveau de prix le plus élevé des trois pays. Par la dévaluation, la situation se renverse et, vers la fin de 1936, et pendant le premier semestre du 1937, l'indice italien se trouve au-dessous des indices français et anglais avec des marges qui se rétrécissent, car les prix italiens montent plus vite que les prix anglais et l'indice français, avantagé par la chute du franc, se trouve au-dessous de l'indice italien dès juillet. Alors que les prix mondiaux descendent dans la deuxième moitié du 1937 et en 1938, les prix italiens continuent à monter pendant l'année 1937 et restent complètement stationnaires en 1938.

Enfin, la dépréciation de la lire par rapport à l'or pendant les derniers mois de 1938 donne à l'indice anglais un avantage supplémentaire sur l'indice de l'Italie dont la monnaie est en rapport fixe avec l'or. L'indice anglais tombe donc au-dessous de l'indice italien on avril 1938, et depuis lors ne fait qu'augmenter sa distance. Ainsi, tandis qu'en novembre 1936, l'indice italien était inférieur de 14% aux indices anglais et français, (égaux en ce moment) ceux-ci sont inférieurs en décembre 1938 de 13% et de 28% respectivement à l'indice italien. D'ailleurs, s'il est certain que les dévaluations successives du franc et la dépréciation récente de la livre ont accentué la nouvelle disparité entre prix italiens et prix franco-anglais, la transition d'une situation favorable en fin 1936 à la situation défavorable en fin 1938 se retrouve vis-à-vis des indices de pays dont la monnaie est également fixe par rapport à l'or, comme la Belgique et les États-Unis. Le nouveau rajustement des salaires au coût de la vie ne pourra qu'aggraver cotte situation.

C'est donc bien la forte hausse des prix italiens d'abord et la résistance à la baise mondiale, ensuite, qui ont entraîné une nouvelle "surévaluation" de la lire et qui fait, tout naturellement, apparaître des symptômes d'affaiblissement semblables à ceux que nous avons observés dans la période précédant l'alignement de 1936. Ainsi, le rabais de la lire touristique a dû être augmenté et on parle d'une nouvelle lire pour les remises des émigrants et surtout pour ceux qui veulent être rapatriés. Le cours des billets est tombé très bas (60% du cours officiel) mais moins à cause de l'évolution des prix que de certaines fuites de capitaux qui se sont produites dernièrement à cause de la situation internationale et des lois contre les Juifs.

Enfin, quoiqu'aucune norme générale n'ait été émise jusqu'ici, tout indique que les primes à l'exportation sont en train de réapparaître. On a déjà vu que les accords de devises attribuant des matières premières aux industries exportatrices correspondent à une nouvelle forme de compensation privée et comportent, comme celles-ci, des primes importantes. Dans l'exportation de la soie grège, les primes ont toujours subsisté et ont dû être relevées et de nouvelles facilités pour les exportateurs sont couramment demandées par la presse économique qui se plaint des profits sûrs et commodes—obtenus par les importateurs en regard des risques de l'exportation que personne ne veut assumer, faute de rémunération suffisante. Actuellement, la formation de Compagnies d'exportation qui seront de grands Comptoirs de vente par catégories d'articles doit donner une nouvelle force à l'exportation qui a difficilement maintenu sa position en 1938 et commence à fléchir pendant ces derniers mois. Mais ces Compagnies, une fois formés, réussiront probablement beaucoup mieux à obtenir des subventions et primes de l'État qu'à se frayer de nouveaux chemins sur le marché international.

4) Causes de l'évolution des prix

La hausse des prix intérieurs italiens et leur résistance ultérieure à la baisse est d'autant plus remarquable que, lors de la dévaluation, diverses mesures furent prises pour maintenir la hausse dans des limites étroites: on abolit la surtaxe *ad valorem* de 15% imposée sur toutes les importations après septembre 1931, et on réduisit dans de fortes proportions les droits de douane sur de nombreux articles alimentaires. Les prix des transports, de l'eau, du gaz, de l'électricité et des loyers furent "bloqués" pour deux ans et en juin 1938, le Comité Corporatif Central a décidé de ne pas admettre d'augmentation pour les années ultérieures. (Les tarifs de chemins de fer pour voyageurs ont, toutefois, été relevés de 20% à partir de 1939, et on parle de nouvelles hausses sur le prix des services publics). Quant aux *autres prix*, une surveillance étroite fut établie—dévolue d'abord au parti fasciste et à partir d'avril 1937 aux organes corporatifs—et toute hausse "non justifiée" devait être sévèrement réprimée. Si, malgré tout cela, l'évolution des prix a été telle que nous l'avons vue, cela s'explique: a) par les besoins financiers de l'Italie provoqués par sa politique africaine et européenne, b) par le politique économique de l'autarcie, et c) par la moindre disponibilité de biens de consommation résultant des deux premiers points.

a) Quant aux *Finances publiques*, elles ont connu des déficits extraordinairement élevés depuis 1935. Dans les trois exercices de 1935–1936, 1936–1937, et 1937–1938, les dépenses non couvertes par les recettes budgétaires s'élèvent à 41 milliards de lires, c'est-à-dire à environ 40% des dépenses totales. On ne connaît pas le résultat pour 1938–1939. Pour 1939–1940, le déficit du seul budget ordinaire ressort dans les prévisions à 4.775 millions de lires. Malgré ces charges lourdes et constamment renouvelées, les financiers italiens ont mis toute leur ingéniosité à éviter, autant que possible, l'inflation. On a fait appel à l'emprunt, à long, à moyen et à court terme et surtout à une série de mesures extraordinaires frappant le capital; 1935: conversion de la rente amortissable 3½% en 5% perpétuel par versements à fonds perdu de 15 lires par 100 lires de capital; 1936: emprunt forcé immobilier et taxes immobilières destinées à payer les intérêts de l'emprunt; 1937: impôt de 10% sur le capital et les réserves des sociétés par actions; 1938: impôt de 7,5% sur le capital des sociétés de personnes et des entreprises individuelles. Mais on n'a a pu écarter complètement le recours à l'Institution d'émission, soit pour des avances directes, soit au moyen de l'utilisation du bénéfice de la réévaluation du stock or, soit par la création de circuits inflationnistes pour le paiement des emprunts et des impôts ci-dessus. En outre, on a introduit de nouveau des billets d'État pour les petites coupures. Il a été calculé que l'inflation représente durant les années 1935, 1936 et 1936–1937, 25% environ des moyens de couverture des dépenses extraordinaires. Ce qui est certain, c'est que l'armement et la mise en valeur des Colonies demandent des capitaux que l'impôt et l'épargne volontaire sont incapables de fournir intégralement à eux seuls. La pression qui en résulte sur le système des prix dans le sens de la hausse est évidente.

b) Une cause plus profonde encore c'est l'évolution des prix et la *politique autarcique* qui conduit à un renchérissement, soit par l'exploitation plus intensive et, par conséquent, à coût croissant des ressources nationales, soit par la substitution de produits nationaux plus coûteux ou de qualité inférieure aux produits d'importation étrangère. En outre, la construction de nouveaux établissements industriels, la mise en œuvre de nouvelles cultures, et la mise en exploitation de nouvelles mines ou de mines abandonnées antérieurement demandent des capitaux d'investissement importants dont l'amortissement s'incorpore dans les prix de revient.

c) Il *résulte* des besoins de l'État pour ses défenses militaires et commerciales et des besoins d'investissement de la politique autarcique que la production s'oriente principalement vers les biens de production. La disponibilité réduite des biens de consommation renforcée par la tendance de forcer les exportations de denrées alimentaires et de produits textiles fait naturellement monter le coût de la vie. Cela entraîne avec un certain retard des augmentations de salaires, la première de 6 à 12% eut lieu en août 1936, la deuxième de 10% en mai 1937 et une troisième augmentation d'environ 8% vient d'être décidée. Ces augmentations agissent, à leur tour, sur tous les prix.

La hausse des prix italiens et leur résistance à suivre la baisse des prix mondiaux nous paraît ainsi suffisamment expliquée; elle n'est pas une conséquence directe du Contrôle des Changes, mais est, comme celui-ci une conséquence de la politique économique et générale du Gouvernement italien.

Si on voulait abolir aujourd'hui le Contrôle des Changes italien, il faudrait, sans doute, procéder à un nouveau rajustement de la valeur de la lire, rajustement qui pourrait, d'ailleurs, être relativement modéré; l'exercice par le gouvernement de la faculté qu'il tient du décret-loi du 5 octobre 1936, de dévaluer la lire jusqu'à 50% de sa parité de 1927, ce qui correspondrait à une dévaluation de 16% de la lire actuelle, suffirait probablement à ramener l'équilibre entre prix italiens et étrangers. Mais l'opération serait entièrement vaine si après quelques mois, devait réapparaître un nouveau déséquilibre du fait des tendances autonomes du système de prix italien; pour éviter cela, il faudrait que l'Italie ait un budget en équilibre approximatif et qu'elle ralentisse son action autarcique qui renchérit, en même temps, biens de production et biens de consommation. On n'en est pas là.

L'expérience italienne du Contrôle des Changes par rapport à l'évolution de la valeur de la monnaie enseigne que le Contrôle n'implique pas, à tout moment, un divorce entre la valeur externe et la valeur interne de la monnaie. La preuve en est la situation italienne à la fin de 1936. Le Contrôle peut continuer à subsister même quand il y a équilibre entre prix nationaux et prix étrangers, soit à cause de mouvements de capitaux qu'il doit empêcher, soit parce qu'on prévoit à brève échéance, une nouvelle disparité de prix à cause d'une tendance autonome des prix nationaux. Dans ce cas, le Contrôle des

Changes deviendrait sans objet seulement si cette tendance, c'est-à-dire, la politique économique qui la provoque venait à cesser.

VI. Économie intérieure

1) Relation entre le Contrôle des Changes et le Contrôle étatique de l'Économie et la politique autarcique

Les rapports du Contrôle des Changes avec les changements de la structure économique interne sont très enchevêtrés. On trouve des exemples pour toutes sortes de relations causales, parmi lesquelles il faut essayer de distinguer la relation directrice, c'est-à-dire celle qui nous semble le mieux correspondre à ce qui se passe le plus souvent, en réalité. Quant à l'évolution des prix, par exemple, il est certain qu'on peut trouver des exemples de la hausse des prix à l'importation par suite de tel contingentement, des exemples de hausse de prix à l'exportation par suite des intérêts pour la période d'attente en clearing qui sont incorporés dans les prix de vente; mais d'autres faits suggèrent que c'est la hausse des prix intérieurs qui rend nécessaire l'établissement d'abord et le maintien ensuite de la réglementation du commerce intérieur et c'est plutôt dans ce sens que nous avons interprété les relations entre prix intérieurs et contrôle.

On sait que l'Économie italienne est devenue de plus en plus une Économie strictement contrôlée par l'État. Cette évolution remonte aux années de la crise économique pendant lesquelles l'État a dû procéder à des sauvetages qui ont mis dans ses mains, principalement par l'entremise de l'Institut de Reconstruction Industrielle, le Contrôle financier de plusieurs industries-clés (métallurgie, électricité, marine marchande, chantiers navals), et des trois principales banques commerciales (Banca Commerciale Italiana, Credito Italiano, Banco di Roma). En 1934, ces Banques qui avaient été mixtes selon le modèle allemand, transmirent définitivement leurs participations industrielles à l'IRI et ainsi, la voie fut libre pour la réforme bancaire de 1936 qui créa avec l'"Inspection pour la Défense de l'Épargne et la Direction du Crédit" l'organe de contrôle et de direction du système bancaire.

Un autre point de départ de l'organisation de l'Économie italienne est constitué par la création de 22 corporations, par branches d'activité économique. La loi s'y référant date du 5 février 1934 et est ainsi, tout comme le début du Contrôle bancaire et industriel, antérieure aux premières mesures du Contrôle des Changes (mai 1934). La fonction principale de ces corporations consistait, suivant la loi, dans "la discipline unitaire de la production." Les années 1934–1935 étaient occupées par l'établissement des corporations, rouages nouveaux qui devaient prendre contact avec la réalité qu'ils avaient la tâche de réglementer. A partir de 1936, elles commençaient réellement à fonctionner et plusieurs fonctions nouvelles et très importantes: surveillance des prix, décisions sur les demandes d'établissement nouveau ou d'agrandissement, norme générale, en matière de salaires, leur furent confiées.

Un troisième fait qui travailla dans la même direction fut la crise agraire. La chute des prix agricoles entraîna l'aide de l'État et aboutit à la constitution facultative d'abord et bientôt obligatoire d'office ("ammassi") pour plusieurs produits parmi les plus importants de l'agriculture italienne: blé, cocons de soie, chanvre, laine. Les "ammassi" quand ils devinrent obligatoires, étaient les seuls à avoir la droit d'acheter aux producteurs et de vendre aux consommateurs les produits en question et contrôlaient ainsi entièrement le marché et les prix.

Ainsi, la crise industrielle et agricole et l'exécution du programme corporatif du gouvernement fasciste concourent de côtés divers à soumettre l'Économie italienne tout entière à un contrôle toujours plus serré de la part de l'État et de ses multiples organes appelés "para-étatiques," à cause de leur autonomie relative et de leur caractère souvent corporatif; quant aux relations économiques avec l'Étranger, le Contrôle des Changes nous paraît donc s'insérer presque tardivement, dans cette tendance fondamentale qui se manifeste à partir de 1930.[11]

Le Contrôle des Changes a entraîné, à son tour, de nouveaux contrôles et monopoles; en particulier, du côté de l'importation, il a conduit à la formation près du l'Istcambi de ces Juntes corporatives qui doivent décider de l'attribution des licences d'importation et du côté des firmes d'importation à la constitution de nombreux comptoirs d'achat.

A partir de 1935, toute l'activité économique italienne a été soumise aux nécessités résultant de la guerre abyssine et des sanctions, d'abord, de la politique autarcique, ensuite. Les corporations et les confédérations des industriels ont travaillé à l'élaboration et ont procédé à l'exécution des plans autarciques dans chaque secteur. L'État lui-même a financé, par des organes interposés, la réalisation de certains plans là ou l'initiative privée était insuffisante; l'IRI

11 Il ne faut pas oublier que la doctrine économique initiale de M. Mussolini et la pratique de ses premiers gouvernements, en particulier de 1922 à 1925, était celle du libéralisme le plus orthodoxe.

pour la sidérurgie et le caoutchouc synthétique, l'AGIP, (Agenzia Generale Italiana Petroli) pour l'hydrogénation et le raffinement des pétroles, l'AMMI (Azienda Minerali Metallici Italiani) pour les minerais, etc.

L'autarcie s'inspire, en premier lieu, de considérations militaires; elle doit assurer à l'Italie les matières premières et les aliments indispensables dans l'éventualité de guerre et de blocus. Pour autant qu'elle possède des motifs économiques, elle a la même base que le Contrôle des Changes: le déséquilibre de la balance des comptes. Tandis que l'action du Contrôle s'étend sur tous les postes passifs et actifs de la balance et est essentiellement orientée vers un équilibre à court terme, l'autarcie exerce une action sur une seule partie du passif: les matières premières et denrées alimentaires d'importation étrangère qu'elle se propose de réduire de façon durable.

Lu rôle que l'autarcie assigne au Contrôle des Changes, et en particulier, au Contrôle des importations est 1) de forcer les industriels par des restrictions d'importation de matières premières étrangères, de substituer à celles-ci, dans la plus grande proportion possible, des matières premières nationales, c'est-à-dire de hâter l'"autarcisation" par une pression directe, 2) d'enregistrer les succès et d'assurer les résultats de l'autarcie, c'est-à-dire de fermer la porte aux quantités de matières premières étrangères dont on n'a plus besoin grâce aux produits nationaux.

Ainsi, le contrôle des changes est, en partie, subordonné à la politique autarcique; d'une façon générale, il apparaît comme une pièce importante du système de la direction étatique de l'activité économique plutôt que comme la cause de ce système.

2) Le Contrôle des Changes et l'approvisionnement en matières premières et en articles de consommation

Le Ministre des Échanges et Devises, M. Guarneri, avait déclaré à la Chambre, le 22 mars 1938, que les contingentements d'importations étaient répartis dans le cadre des disponibilités en devises, en tenant compte successivement: 1) des nécessités fondamentales du peuple italien; 2) des besoins de matières premières de l'industrie, en particulier, de celle travaillant pour la défense nationale ou pour le commerce d'exportation; 3) des besoins des nouvelles industries autarciques en outillage; 4) des accords commerciaux de l'Italie avec les pays étrangers qui lui font souvent l'obligation d'acheter des produits finis en contrepartie des produits "non essentiels" qu'elle exporte.

En réalité “les nécessités fondamentales du peuple italien” ne paraissent pas avoir eu la première place dans la répartition des contingentements, soit parce que les nécessités industrielles et autarciques furent jugées plus impérieuses, soit parce qu’il était relativement plus facile d’y apporter les restrictions ou de trouver des produits nationaux de substitution. Ainsi, il résulte clairement des statistiques que la consommation a baissé fortement pendant les dernières années. Prenons l’indice des ventes au détail des matières alimentaires corrigé des mouvements de prix, et calculé à Milan:

Janvier	1934	100,0
“	1935	95,9
“	1936	78,9
“	1937	78,5
“	1938	72,0
“	1939	69,4

D’autres indices de la consommation (consommation par tête d’habitant des principaux articles alimentaires) confirment cette évolution. Ensuite, il faut tenir compte de la détérioration de la qualité. Les deux exemples les plus importants sont le pain auquel on ajoute, depuis décembre 1937, une proportion variable de farine de maïs (10% d’abord, puis 20%, puis de nouveau 10%) et les tissus textiles destinés à la consommation intérieure où les fibres “nationales” (rayonne courte, chanvre cotonnisé et lanital) représentent, en moyenne, plus de 50%. Malgré les grands progrès de la technique des fibres artificielles nouvelles, cette proportion, de l’avis même de techniciens italiens, parait préjudiciable à la qualité—de résistance surtout—des tissus et cela explique la diminution des ventes de l’habillement qu’on a pu observer récemment.

Or, il ne faut pas oublier que chèque décision du Contrôle des Importations implique la résolution d’un choix alternatif. Si on a limité l’importation de froment et de coton, et qu’on s’est vu, par conséquent, obligé de renoncer au pain en froment pur et aux vêtements en coton pur, c’est parce qu’il paraissait plus important d’importer des ferrailles, du cuivre, du pétrole et des machines.

L’approvisionnement de l’industrie en matières premières paraît avoir été assez régulier et satisfaisant, quoique à plusieurs reprises, il y ait eu des bruits incontrôlables que telle industrie a dû interrompre son travail à cause du manque de fer, en particulier. En 1938, on a pu procéder à des achats massifs (pour 700 millions de lires) de machines venant principalement d'Allemagne et destinées aux industries autarciques et aux mines nouvellement mises en exploitation.

Il serait, toutefois, faux de dire que c'est le contrôle qui a entraîné une diminution quantitative et qualitative de la consommation au profit de l'approvisionnement et de l'agencement des industries lourdes, exportatrices et autarciques. Cet avantage relatif d'une catégorie d'importations par rapport à une outre n'a pas été provoqué par quelque tendance endogène du contrôle des changes, mais le contrôle a servi comme simple instrument pour réaliser une politique qui avait été décidée en dehors et au-dessus de lui.

3) Le Contrôle des Changes et la protection de l'industrie et de l'agriculture

On a vu qu'en 1934–1935, un des buts du Contrôle des Changes était de laisser se poursuivre la reprise économique et la hausse des prix amorcées sans qu'elles se heurtent à la surévaluation de la lire; le Contrôle, principalement par la limitation des importations, devait donc arrêter l'arrivée du marchandises étrangères que, sans lui, l'écart entre prix italiens et étrangers aurait certainement fait affluer en Italie. En d'autres termes, le but du Contrôle n'était pas d'augmenter la marge bénéficiaire dus entreprises, mais de la maintenir ou d'assurer sa réapparition par la reprise; c'est dans ce sens que le Contrôle a donc exercé un rôle protectionniste un faveur de l'industrie et de l'agriculture.

A son tour, pendant les premiers mois de 1935, l'isolement du marché italien a créé des quasi-monopoles, et a favorisé la hausse des prix et la formation du bénéfices élevés, ce qui est attesté par la hausse des cours des actions et par l'augmentation de la spéculation sur valeurs à revenu variable. (Sur les affaires à terme, la part des affaires sur actions fut de 73% en 1935 contre 43% en 1934). Mais les mesures d'août 1935 limitant les dividendes à 6% et instituant un impôt de 10% sur les dividendes des titres eu porteur brisèrent ce mouvement.

Dans la suite, le contrôle quantitatif des importations a assisté, comme on a vu, la naissance des industries autarciques.

On peut faire remarquer que l'organisation monopolistique ou bien la règlementation minutieuse du marché intérieure rend inutile un contrôle *à part* des importations parce qu'elle l'implique. Ainsi, pour l'agriculture, la création d'offices d'achat et de vente pour les principaux produits enlève toute fonction économique aux droits de douane, d'abord; et quant à la quantité importée, elle est déterminée directement par l'office d'entente avec les Ministères des Échanges et Devises en tenant compte des besoins de la consommation et des disponibilités en devises. Si, à ce moment, à cause de la pénurie de devises, l'Office ne peut pas acheter tant qu'il aurait voulu, il ne s'ensuit nullement qu'il augmentera le prix du blé. De même si le contrôle était aboli et que l'Office pouvait acheter à l'Étranger tout ce qu'il voulait, il ne s'ensuivrait point un affaiblissement des marges bénéficiaires que l'Office laisse par la fixation de son prix aux cultivateurs, et qui est uniquement déterminé parce qu'il croit être la rémunération équitable aux producteurs, tout en tenant compte de l'achat du consommateur.[12]

Dans l'industrie, la réglementation et l'exécution de "plans" arrivent au même résultat que le monopole en agriculture. Nous donnerons l'exemple suivant: la limitation des importations de coton favorisait et protégeait l'industrie des fibres artificielles, que les industries du coton durent introduire en quantités croissantes dans leurs broches et métiers, mais actuellement on se propose de fixer les différents pourcentages de fibres artificielles que toute l'industrie cotonnière doit introduire dans les filets et tissus à destination du marché intérieur. Il est évident qu'avec cela, la tâche précédente du contrôle devient inutile car avec un niveau donné d'activité industrielle, la fixation des pourcentages détermine exactement la quantité de coton à importer, qu'il y ait contrôle ou non. Le contrôle peut, dans ce cas, déterminer uniquement le niveau global d'activité de l'économie textile, mais non pas favoriser telle branche aux dépens de telle autre.

VII. Évolution récente

Nous avons vu que la dévaluation de 1936 avait apporté au Contrôle des Changes italien, une simplification mais aussi certaines atténuations. Les prix italiens étaient en équilibre ou même avaient un léger avantage sur les prix étrangers, et il y avait là en somme, pour l'Italie, l'occasion de retrouver le contact avec les économies en monnaies librement négociables. Si le gouvernement n'a pas saisi cette occasion, c'était peut-être parce qu'il sentait que

12 Cela est, d'ailleurs, évident quand on pense que la notion même de protection par l'État implique concurrence dans la branche d'activité économique qu'on veut protéger. Un monopole est capable de se protéger par ses propres moyens et y réussit généralement assez bien.

la confiance des Italiens dans la lire ne serait pas très grande, mais surtout parce que la politique autarcique allait engager l'Italie dans une évolution économique autonome. Depuis la fin de 1936 on a, en conséquence, assisté à un maintien intégral du contrôle et à son perfectionnement au point de vue organisation et fonctionnement, sinon à son renforcement, surtout au point de vue des pénalités aux contrevenants.

Quelles seraient les conditions d'une abolition du contrôle? Quelles en sont les perspectives? Quelles en seraient les étapes? Essayons de puiser dans la situation actuelle et ses tendances des éléments pour une réponse à ces questions.

La condition unique pour l'abolition du contrôle des changes est, évidemment, la réalisation d'un équilibre automatique de la balance des comptes, sans oscillations monétaires violentes. Quant aux mouvements de capitaux, il faudrait donc que les Italiens s'abstinssent de pratiquer les opérations que leur seront de nouveau permises. Il y aura là, au début, toujours une phase critique parce que importateurs, exportateurs et banques voudront se reconstituer à l'étranger des disponibilités qu'ils avaient cédées à l'Istcambi. On peut, cependant, espérer que ces mouvements seront contrebalancés par des rapatriements et des venues de capitaux étrangers.

Quant aux échanges de biens et de services, les conditions préalables seraient: 1) une parité qui assure l'équilibre entre prix italiens et étrangers; 2) une politique financière et économique qui rende possible le maintien de cet équilibre, c'est-à-dire, qui n'implique pas un renchérissement continu des coûts.

Étant donné qu'un retour pur et simple au passé est à exclure, il faudra donc attendre que les productions autarciques aient atteint un certain palier et une stabilité relative et ait fait sentir toute leur incidence sur les prix pour pouvoir fixer à ce moment le cours du change.

Il resterait, cependant, un grand obstacle; c'est l'insuffisance du stock d'or qui rend nécessaire un équilibre de chaque instant qui ne saurait être obtenu que par un contrôle. Or, l'Italie est hostile à des emprunts étrangers, unique moyen pacifique que nous entrevoyons pour lui procurer de nouvelles réserves.

Donc, même si la réalisation partielle du programme autarcique et le renoncement à le poursuivre indéfiniment, et le rétablissement d'un équilibre approximatif des finances publiques devaient créer après un réajustement préalable de la lire, les conditions économiques essentielles pour rétablir la liberté monétaire, l'Italie ne pourra probablement pas y retourner faute d'une masse de manœuvre suffisante de son Institut d'émission.

Mais même dans le cas où toutes ces difficultés pourraient être aplanies, l'évolution du contrôle des changes ne se fera que graduellement. Les premières atténuations qu'on a déjà vu apparaître en 1936, seraient de laisser aux personnes privées et morales la possession des crédits non commerciaux et des titres étrangers qui entreraient dans leur patrimoine. Ce serait ensuite l'encouragement du tourisme et l'autorisation de réimportation des billets de banque. Un pas décisif qui équivaudrait, en fait, à une abolition de la défense d'exporter des capitaux serait ensuite le fait de ne plus obliger les exportateurs à céder leurs devises à L'Istcambi. C'est par des cessions des crédits des exportateurs à l'étranger que se sont, en effet, effectuées la plupart des exportations de capitaux dans la période avant la stabilisation de 1927.

Mais en supposant qu'il n'y ait point de causes propres à provoquer des exportations de capitaux, on pourra en venir là, supprimer le monopole des changes et autoriser de même l'achat de titres étrangers. Il restera alors une partie essentielle du contrôle: le contingentement des importations. Celui-ci sera certainement maintenu le plus longtemps possible, car l'abolition des restrictions quantitatives exigera, entre autres choses, des retouches aux tarifs douaniers qui devront être mûrement réfléchies.

Pour le contrôle des changes, en général, et celui des importations, en particulier, on peut entrevoir la possibilité d'une abolition non pas en revenant à un système plus libéral, mais en déplaçant le contrôle de la périphérie au centre de l'Économie; on a vu comment tel monopole ou telle règlementation rendait presque superflu le contrôle à l'importation. Une planification plus marquée encore de l'activité économique qui ne pourrait manquer de tenir compte de la balance commerciale rendrait le contrôle inutile lors de l'acte de l'attribution des devises parce qu'il aurait déjà ou lieu à une phase antérieure. Mais étant donné l'hostilité souvent proclamée du fascisme contre une centralisation totale, il nous paraît plus probable que le système actuel avec ses contrôles multiples et à divers échelons de la vie économique sera maintenu.

A côté du cours officiel du change, *L'Information Économique et Financière* a reporté à partir du l'automne 1935 le cours officieux des billets italiens, d'abord de façon plutôt sporadique, mais bientôt avec une grande régularité—et à partir de 1937 mémé sous forme de rubrique quotidienne.

Tableau 7.9. *Cours de la lire-billet (grosse coupure) sur le marché officieux de Paris en% du cours officiel(-graphique)*

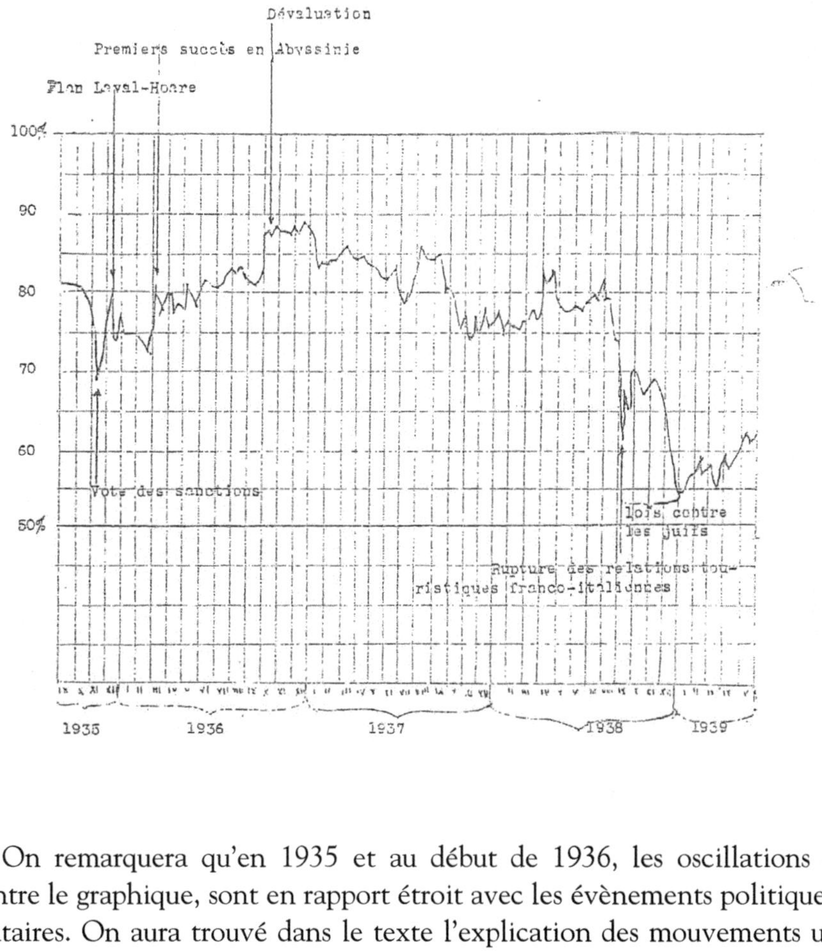

On remarquera qu'en 1935 et au début de 1936, les oscillations que montre le graphique, sont en rapport étroit avec les évènements politiques et militaires. On aura trouvé dans le texte l'explication des mouvements ultérieurs: rétrécissement de la marge séparant les deux lires lors de la dévaluation de la lire officielle, élargissement dans la suite et particulièrement accentué vers la fin de 1938. Enfin, attirons l'attention sur le facteur saisonnier qui fuit monter généralement le cours des billets au printemps et en été, époques principales du tourisme. (Ce facteur ne devant, avoir de l'influence que sur les petites coupures qu'il est seul permis d'importer en Italie en quantités limitées. Mais la contrebande effectue l'arbitrage et assure le parallélisme de l'évolution des prix de toutes les coupures de billets).

· 8 ·

ÉTUDE STATISTIQUE SUR LA TENDANCE DU COMMERCE EXTÉRIEUR VERS L'ÉQUILIBRE ET LE BILATÉRALISME*

Introduction

Quand on parle de la tendance du commerce mondial vers les échanges compensés, on confond facilement deux tendances que la présente étude se propose de distinguer: la tendance vers l'équilibre et la tendance vers le bilatéralisme. Si les déficits et les excédents des balances commerciales de divers pays se réduisaient relativement aux valeurs échangées, cela tendrait à indiquer que les mouvements de capitaux et les postes invisibles perdent de l'importance au sein de la balance des comptes dont l'équilibre devrait par conséquent être assuré par les seuls échanges de marchandises. Dans ce cas, il importe peu que l'équilibre de la balance commerciale soit réalisé isolément avec chaque pays, ou comme résultat de la compensation entre déficits et excédents des balances particulières. C'est dire que la tendance vers l'équilibre ne signifie pas abandon des échanges triangulaires.

D'autre part, le bilatéralisme n'implique pas nécessairement l'équilibre des balances commerciales. Prenons un pays assuré d'obtenir des montants

* Institut International de Coopération Intellectuelle, Société des Nations, Paris. Conférence Générale d'Études sur les Politiques Économiques de la Paix, XIIéme Session, Bergen 1939.

considérables de devises par les revenus du tourisme. Une politique d'échanges bilatéraux fixerait pour ce pays une certaine marge relative pour le déficit de sa balance commerciale et s'emploierait à reproduire cette marge dans les échanges avec tous les pays individuellement. En fait, un grand nombre d'accords de clearing et de paiement prévoient non pas l'équilibre mais le déséquilibre des échanges.

Nous allons étudier sur la base des statistiques si et dans quelle mesure, au cours des dernières années, ces tendances soit vers l'équilibre, soit vers le bilatéralisme des échanges se sont manifestées. Nous allons rechercher d'abord une méthode pour mesurer la tendance vers l'équilibre à l'échelle mondiale et nous analyserons ensuite la tendance vers le bilatéralisme dans quelques grands pays.

I. La tendance vers l'équilibre à l'échelle mondiale

La façon la plus simple de comparer le degré d'équilibre réalisé par les différentes balances commerciales est de prendre la différence absolue entre les importations et exportations et de la diviser par le total du commerce extérieur du pays en question.

Soient i_p et e_p les importations et les exportations d'un pays p, l'indice de l'équilibre de sa balance commerciale sera: $n = \frac{|i_p - e_p|}{i_p + e_p} \cdot 100$ Cet indice évolue entre 0 (cas d'équilibre parfait: $i_p = e_p$) et 100 (cas de déséquilibre parfait: $i_p = 0$ et $e_p = 100$)[1].

1 On emploie souvent les rapports $n_1' = \frac{i - e}{i} \cdot 100$ et $n_2' = \frac{e - i}{e} \cdot 100$ selon qu'il s'agit de balance déficitaire ou excédentaire, car les valeurs indiquées par ces indices ont une signification concrète puisqu'elles indiquent soit la part des importations non couverte par les exportations, soit la part des exportations non compensées par les importations. Cependant, notre indice est plus commode quand il s'agit de mesurer le déséquilibre sans tenir compte de la nature de ce déséquilibre: excèdent ou déficit. Il est d'ailleurs facile de se convaincre qu'entre les indices n' et notre indice n, il existe la relation simple: $n' = \frac{2n}{100 + n} \cdot 100$.

L'indice général N de l'équilibre des balances commerciales nous est ensuite donné par la moyenne pondérée de tous les indices nationaux:

$$N = \frac{\sum \left| i_p - e_p \right|}{\sum \left| i_p + e_p \right|} \cdot 100 = \frac{\sum \left| i_p - e_p \right|}{I + E} \cdot 100$$

en désignant par I et E les importations et les exportations mondiales. Le numérateur $\sum \left| i_p - e_p \right|$ n'est autre que la somme de tous les déficits et des excédents de toutes les balances commerciales.

Voici les resultats numeriques pour le commerce mondial de 1925 a 1938:

Tableau 8.1. Voici les résultats numériques pour le commerce mondial de 1925 à 1938:

Années	$\sum \left\| i_p - e_p \right\|$ (1)	$I + E$ (2)	$N = \frac{(1)}{(2)} \cdot 100$
En millions de dollars-or			
1925	8.698	62.872	13,9
1926	6.605	61.888	10,7
1927	7.605	65.048	11,7
1928	7.625	67.582	11,3
1929	6.390	68.606	9,3
1930	6.879	55.558	12,4
1931	6.549	39.704	16,5
1932	4.471	26.868	16,7
1933	3.762	24.224	15,6
1934	3.506	23.314	15,1
1935	3.259	23.802	13,7
1936	3.660	25.722	14,3
1937	4.643	31.592	14,7
1938	3.860	27.736	13,9

En 10 cas sur 13, les variations d'année en année de $\sum \left| i_p - e_p \right|$ et de I +-E sont dans le même sens, et dans 7 cas, la variation de $\sum \left| i_p - e_p \right|$ tout en étant dans le même sens est plus forte que celle de I + E, de sorte que notre indice varie alors parallèlement aux deux séries de base. Par contre, dans six cas, l'indice varia dans un sens opposé à celui du commerce mondial, soit que les mouvements du commerce mondial et de $\sum\left|i_p - e_p\right|$ soient divergents (1928–1929, 1929–1930, 1934–1935) soit que, tout en étant dans le même sens, la variation du commerce mondial soit plus accentuée que celle de $\sum\left|i_p - e_p\right|$ (1927–1928, 1931–1932, 1932–1933).

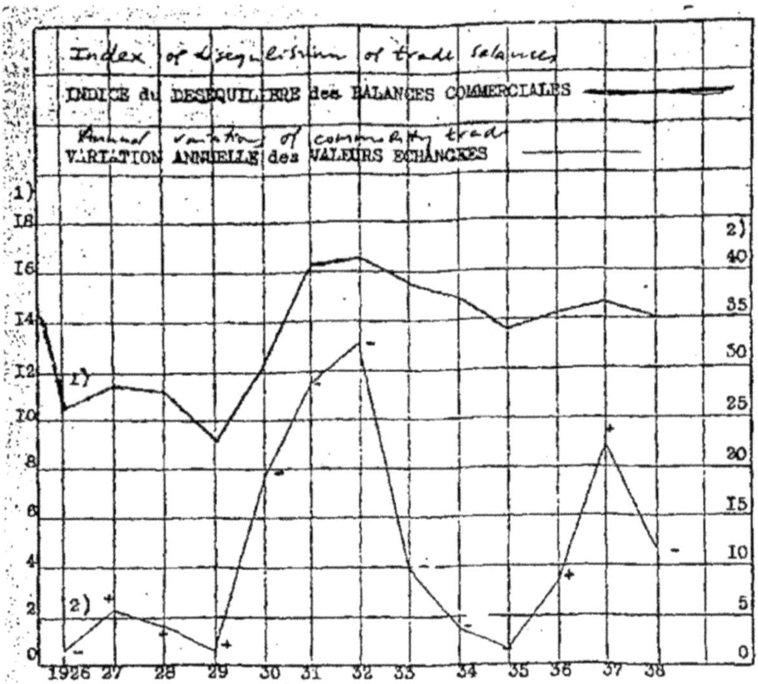

Graphique 8.1. Les signes + ou - dont chaque point de la courbe fine est affecté indiquent s'il s'agit d'une expansion ou d'une contraction du commerce mondial (en valeur) par rapport à l'année précédente.

Il s'ensuit que l'indice du déséquilibre des échanges commerciaux ne présente point une allure régulière au cours du cycle économique. Tantôt il suit la conjoncture: il baisse en 1925–1926 et se relève en 1936–1937, il hausse de 1935 à 1937 et baisse de 1937 à 1938—tantôt il montre la corrélation inverse: ainsi, il baisse de 1937 à 1929 pour monter très fortement de 1929 à 1932.

Ces observations nous ont suggéré l'idée que *l'allure de l'indice n'était pas conditionnée par les fluctuations en hausse ou en baisse de la conjoncture, mais par* ***l'intensité*** *de ces fluctuations*. Nous avons donc calculé les pourcentages de variation annuelle du commerce mondial (I + E) et nous avons relié par une courbe les valeurs ainsi obtenues, sans égard aux signes qui indiquent le sens de la variation par rapport à l'année précédente. Le résultat représenté par le Graphique 8.1 est frappant: sans la moindre exception, l'indice du déséquilibre et la courbe des variations annuelles du commerce mondial varient dans le même sens do 1925–1926 jusqu'en 1938. La traduction en paroles du graphique conduit à l'énoncé suivant: une variation du commerce mondial de l'année x + 1 par rapport à l'année x, qui soit plus forte (dans le sens de la hausse ou de la baisse) que celle de l'année x par rapport à l'année x - 1, s'accompagne d'une hausse de l'indice du déséquilibre des échanges de l'année x, à l'année x + 1, et inversement.

Ainsi, de fortes contractions et expansions du commerce mondial—qui se concentrent toujours sur un nombre limité d'années et per conséquent font hausser la courbe des variations annuelles (courbe 2)—ne vont pas sans renforcer le déséquilibre des balances commerciales des différents pays. Par contre, dès que le mouvement s'amortit, se ralentit et que le commerce international se stabilise ainsi sur un niveau donné—soit bas, soit élevé—le déséquilibre diminue.

Les observations précédentes peuvent être mises en parallèle avec un phénomène souvent constaté dans les sciences économiques, sociales, et même en physiologie: à savoir qu'une forte croissance (ou décroissance) s'accompagne de disproportionnalités qu'un arrêt de croissance tend ensuite à faire diminuer.

En examinant dans le détail les variations annuelles de notre indice, l'épisode le plus intéressant est sa montée en flèche de 1929 à 1931. En se reportant au Tableau 8.1, on remarque qu'entre ces deux dates, le commerce mondial a diminué de 42,1% tandis que la somme des déficits et excédents *augmentait* de 2,5%. On peut expliquer cette anomalie par le fait que les paiements internationaux d'intérêt et d'amortissement ne diminuaient pas avec la même rapidité que le commerce mondial, de sorte que les déséquilibres des échanges commerciaux nécessaires pour le transfert de ces paiements devaient être maintenus coûte que coûte. En effet, ce sont les *excédents* qui de 1929 à 1931 augmentent de 1.913 millions de dollars-or à 21.331 millions de dollars-or et ceci malgré la chute des prix des matières premières exportées surtout par les payer à balance excédentaire; tandis que la somme des déficits baisse de 4.477 à 4.218 millions de dollars-or.[2]

D'autre part, non seulement les autres parties de la balance des comptes ne se contractaient pas au même rythme que les échanges commerciaux, mais encore il s'y ajoutait des mouvements de capitaux qui forcèrent alors des mouvements de marchandises à sens unique. Rappelons comme exemple le cas de l'Allemagne avec ses excédents anormaux de 1930 et 1931.

Jusqu'ici on n'a fait attention qu'aux mouvements annuels et cycliques de notre indice. Quant au *trend*, nos chiffres ne nous permettent qu'une conclusion négative: dans la période observée, il n'y a certainement pas eu une tendance nette vers l'équilibre des balances commerciales. On dirait plutôt que le déséquilibre a augmenté, mais il reste à voir si l'élévation du niveau de l'indice due à la hausse rapide des années 1930–1931 est stable ou passagère. Il est assez significatif que l'indice ait retrouvé en 1938 sa valeur exacte de 1925, début de la période sous observation.

L'absence d'une tendance prononcée vers l'équilibre à l'échelle mondiale s'explique par le fait: 1) que les efforts désespérés des pays à balance déficitaire pour équilibrer leur balance commerciale, s'ils n'ont pas été frustrés par d'autres éléments de la politique économique de ces mêmes pays, ont été contrecarrés par les efforts non moins énergiques de tous les pays à balance excédentaire de conserver et d'augmenter leurs excédents; 2) que même s'il y a diminution du déséquilibre de la part d'un pays ou d'un groupe de pays, cela peut entraîner une désorganisation des échanges d'un autre groupe de pays et avec cela une augmentation des déséquilibres de leurs balances commerciales.

II. Tendance vers le bilatéralisme

Pour étudier la tendance vers l'équilibre à l'échelle mondiale, nous avons considéré les indices nationaux du déséquilibre des balances commerciales comme les termes d'une série statistique élémentaire dont l'indice général du déséquilibre était une des caractéristiques. A l'opposé de cette étude qu'on pourrait appeler macrocosmique, nous allons considérer maintenant l'indice

2 Si les importations mondiales étaient égales aux exportations mondiales, la somme des déficits devrait être égale à la somme des excédents. En fait, les exportations sont toujours inférieures aux importations, principalement parce que les prix à l'importation comprennent les frais de transport. Il est pourtant extrêmement rare que la somme des déficits et la somme des excédents n'évoluent pas dans le même sens.

national du déséquilibre comme la moyenne d'une série élémentaire dont les termes seront les déficits et excédents relatifs des balances particulières du pays considéré dans son commerce avec chaque pays étranger pris isolément. Et nous adopterons une autre caractéristique de cette série, à savoir la plus ou moins grande concentration des termes autour de leur moyenne comme l'indice du bilatéralisme.

Pour rendre plausible notre procédé, considérons d'abord le cas simple d'un pays dont la balance commerciale générale soit en équilibre: cet équilibre peut provenir soit de l'équilibre des balances particulières, soit d'une compensation entre les soldes passifs et actifs de ces balances. Il est évident que selon le premier ou le deuxième cas, le système des échanges du pays en question sera bilatéral ou plurilatéral. Pour le cas plus général d'un pays à balance déficitaire (excédentaire), on dira qu'il y a bilatéralisme si les balances particulières sont toutes déficitaires (excédentaires) dans à peu près la même mesure, tandis qu'on sera en présence d'un système d'échanges triangulaires si on rencontre dans les balances particulières tantôt des déficits (excédents) très importants, tantôt des déficits (excédents) très faibles, ou même des excédents (déficits). *La dispersion de la série des déficits et excédents particuliers-* mesurés en termes relatifs—*par rapport à leur moyenne—qui est le déficit ou l'excédent relatif général—est donc plus qu'une simple caractéristique statistique: elle a la signification économique d'indice du bilatéralisme des échanges.*

Soient I et E, les importations et exportations totales du pays observé, et $D = \frac{I - E}{I + E}$, le déficit relatif général, soient $i_1, i_2, \ldots i_n$ et $e_1, e_2, \ldots e_n$ les importations et exportations en provenance ou à destination des différents pays étrangers, et $d_k = \frac{i_k - e_k}{i_k + e_k}$ la valeur relative du déficit avec l'un quelconque ces pays, valeur qui sera négative s'il s'agit d'un excédent. En mesurant la dispersion de la série par l'"écart moyen" et en pondérant chaque écart suivant l'importance du commerce dont il provient, nous obtenons comme indice du bilatéralisme:

$$e = \frac{\sum |d_k - D| \cdot (i_k + e_k)}{I + E} \cdot 100$$

Cet indice évolue entre 0 et 100. En cas de bilatéralisme parfait, nous avons $d_1 = d_2 = \ldots . d_n = D$, et par conséquent $e = 0$. Il y aurait par contre absence complète de bilatéralisme si la balance générale étant en équilibre, les importations venaient exclusivement d'un pays et les exportations d'un autre. Dans ce cas, l'indice devient 100.

Cependant, soit pour la commodité du calcul, soit pour faire ressortir un certain nombre de qualités de l'indice, nous allons le transformer de la façon suivante:

$$e = \frac{\sum \left| \frac{i_k - e_k}{i_k + e_k} - \frac{I - E}{I + E} \right| (i_k + e_k)}{I + E} \cdot 100$$

$$= \frac{\sum \left| (i_k - e_k)(I + E) - (i_k + e_k)(I - E) \right|}{(I + E)^2} \cdot 100$$

$$= \frac{\sum \left| 2E \cdot i_k - 2I \cdot e_k \right|}{(I + E)^2} \cdot 100$$

$$= \frac{\sum \left| E \cdot i_k - I \cdot e_k \right|}{I \cdot E} \cdot \frac{2I \cdot E}{(I + E)^2} \cdot 100$$

$$= \frac{1}{2} \frac{\sum \left| E \cdot i_k - I \cdot e_k \right|}{I \cdot E} \cdot \frac{4I \cdot E}{(I + E)^2} \cdot 100$$

$$= \frac{1}{2} \sum \left| \frac{i_k}{I} - \frac{e_k}{E} \right| \cdot \frac{(I + E)^2 - (I - E)^2}{(I + E)^2} \cdot 100$$

$$= \frac{1}{2} \sum \left| \frac{i_k}{I} \cdot 100 - \frac{e_k}{E} \cdot 100 \right| \cdot \left(1 - D^2\right)(1a)$$

L'indice ainsi transformé nous permet de faire les constatations suivantes:

1°) Il est beaucoup plus commode pour le calcul. En effet $\frac{i_k}{I} \cdot 100$ et $\frac{e_k}{E} \cdot 100$ sont les pourcentages dans les importations et les exportations totales des importations et exportations en provenance et à destination de différents pays. Ces pourcentages sont d'un calcul facile; ils sont d'ailleurs donnés dans un certain nombre de publications statistiques nationales et sont calculés chaque année pour tous les pays par le Service économique de la S.D.N. qui les publie dans les volumes annuels sur le commerce international. La formule $(1a)$ a de plus l'avantage de rester inchangée en cas de balance excédentaire; en effet D^2 est toujours positif.

2°) En cas c'équilibre parfait I = E et D = 0, et l'indice devient pour les deux formules:

$$1' = \frac{\sum |i_k - e_k|}{2I} \cdot 100 = \frac{\sum |i_k - e_k|}{2E} \cdot 100$$

Dans ce cas, par conséquent, l'indice du bilatéralisme est au commerce d'un pays ce qu'était l'indice du déséquilibre des balances commerciales au commerce mondial.

3°) Le coefficient $\left(1 - D^2\right)$ diffère généralement très peu de 1. Supposons un pays à balance très déficitaire de sorte qu'il importe le double de ce qu'il exporte: en ce cas, $D = \frac{2-1}{2+1} = \frac{1}{3}$ et $1 - D^2 = \frac{8}{9}$. On se rend compte ainsi que pour des déficits et excédents d'une ampleur normale, le facteur $1 - D^2$ n'apporte qu'une correction très légère aux chiffres trouvés par le calcul de l'expression $\frac{1}{2} \sum \left| \frac{i_k}{I} \cdot 100 - \frac{e_k}{E} \cdot 100 \right|$.

On peut même dire que notre indice a sa valeur d'indicateur du bilatéralisme seulement à condition que $\left(1-D^2\right)$ ne s'écarte pas trop de 1. En effet, les notions même de triangularité et de bilatéralisme des échanges impliquent qu'il y ait importations et exportations en quantités *d'un même ordre de grandeur*. Si nous avons dit au début que nous nous proposons ici de distinguer nettement l'équilibre et le bilatéralisme, nous n'entendons pas pour cela dissocier entièrement les deux conceptions.

4°) Le terme central de la formule (1a) est donc

$\frac{1}{2}\sum\left|\frac{i_k}{I}\cdot 100-\frac{e_k}{E}\cdot 100\right|$. Moins grand sera l'écart entre les deux pourcentages occupés par chaque pays dans les importations et les exportations totales du pays considéré, moins grande sera cette expression, plus le commerce du pays sera bilatéral.

La politique commerciale actuelle de beaucoup de pays tend ou aboutit effectivement à obtenir une plus forte concentration des déficits ou excédents relatifs des balances particulières autour du déficit (ou de l'excédent) relatif général. Nous citerons le cas de la Turquie qui veut obtenir qu'avec tous les pays, ses exportations se trouvent par rapport aux importations dans la relation de 5 à 4, Dans la mesure où cette relation est respectée, les importations en provenance du pays étranger sont entièrement libres. Dans le cas contraire, elles sont frappées par des contingentements et restrictions divers.[3] Mais même sans vouloir réaliser d'une façon aussi consciente la notion de bilatéralisme telle qu'elle est donnée par notre indice, les négociateurs des traités de commerce y travaillant chaque fois qu'ils mettent en avant dans la discussion plutôt que les chiffres absolus du commerce, les pourcentages dans les importations et les exportations totales. Égaliser ces pourcentages ne veut pas dire équilibrer le commerce entre les deux pays; cela veut dire précisément faire concorder le déficit (ou l'excédent) relatif de la balance particulière avec le déficit (ou l'excédent) relatif général.

Avant cette étude, le Service économique de la S.D.N. a entrepris dans son « Aperçu général du commerce mondial » de donner une mesure du bilatéralisme (voir *Aperçu général du commerce mondial*, 1933 p. 61 et suivantes, 1935, p. 65 et suivantes, 1934, p. 70 et suivantes.)

3 Voir le mémoire présenté à la Conférence des Hautes Études Internationales: *Exchange Control in Turkey* p. 41.

A cet effet, l'Aperçu distingua dans le commerce d'un pays—par exemple la Grande-Bretagne—trois parties:

1°) le déficit général,
2°) la somme des déficits et excédents des balances particulières diminuée de 1°), ce que l'Aperçu général appelle le commerce triangulaire de marchandises,
3°) ce qui reste, ce sont les exportations vers les pays avec lesquels le commerce de l'Angleterre est déficitaire plus les importations des pays avec lesquels le commerce de l'Angleterre est excédentaire, c'est-à-dire le commerce compensé bilatéralement.

Cette troisième quantité rapportée au commerce total est l'indice du bilatéralisme de l'Aperçu. Il correspond exactement au nôtre s'il y a équilibre parfait de la balance commerciale générale (sauf qu'il varie de 0 à 100, là où notre indice varie de 100 à 0) mais la différence peut devenir assez sensible dès que cela n'est plus le cas. L'indice de l'Aperçu en effet ne tient aucun compte du groupement des déficits (excédents) particuliers autour du déficit (excédent) général. Pour donner une idée de l'insuffisance de l'indice dans des circonstances déterminées, nous formulerons l'exemple suivant du commerce d'un pays dans deux années différentes, le pays ayant par hypothèse des échanges commerciaux avec deux autres pays seulement:

	Année *a*		Année *b*	
	Imp.	Exp.	Imp.	Exp.
Pays I	125	125	150	100
Pays II	175	75	150	100
Total	300	200	300	200

L'indice du bilatéralisme de l'Aperçu resterait inchangé de l'année *a* à l'année *b*, étant dans l'année *a* de: $\frac{2 \cdot 125 + 2 \cdot 75}{500}$ et dans l'année *b* $\frac{2 \cdot 100 + 2 \cdot 100}{500}$ tandis que notre indice indiquerait bilatéralisme parfait (I = 0) dans l'année *b* contre bilatéralisme incomplet (I = 20) pour l'année *a*. Or, il est évident qu'en effet, le bilatéralisme a augmenté considérablement pour notre pays de l'année *a* à l'année *b* et c'est donc l'indice proposé ici qui "a raison."

III. Résultats

Nous avons calculé l'indice du bilatéralisme des échanges pour la Grande-Bretagne, l'Allemagne, la Belgique, les Pays-Bas et la Suède et pour tous ces pays de 1929 à 1937. Voici les résultats:

Tableau 8.2. *Indices du bilatéralisme*

	Angleterre	Allemagne	Pays-Bas	Belgique	Suède
1929	25,8	25,2	23,7	22,3	25,6
1930	25,0	26,1	27,3	22,3	26,9
1931	24,9	29,0	31,0	25,3	31,6
1932	24,3	28,5	28,3	24,8	29,1
1933	24,3	28,9	24,9	23,2	26,7
1934	22,8	28,8	24,1	20,8	22,6
1935	21,2	22,8	22,6	22,5	18,0
1936	19,2	17,8	23,0	22,8	19,2
1937	17,5	21,5	21,2	20,8	18,2

Le Graphique 8.2 reproduit ces séries; rappelons qu'une diminution de l'indice (courbe descendante) indique un renforcement du bilatéralisme.

Nous avons choisi les pays qui par leur structure économique sont en quelque sorte préposée au commerce international. Non seulement ces pays avaient un important commerce triangulaire, mais encore ce commerce est reparti sur un grand nombre de pays, ce qui permet la compensation des oscillations accidentelles. Il est ainsi permis de voir dans les variations de l'indice auprès de ces pays, le reflet de la tendance générale du commerce international. Ceci vaut particulièrement pour l'Angleterre dont le commerce extérieur ne connaît qu'un seul pourcentage qui soit supérieur à 10%: il s'agit des importations des Etats-Unis qui occupent généralement 11% des importations anglais totales.

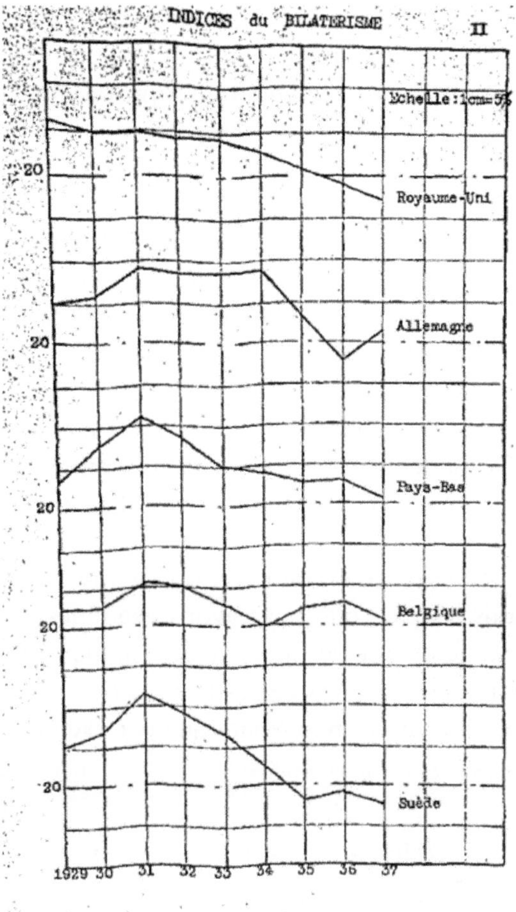

Graphique 8.2.

Or, c'est précisément l'indice anglais qui, par sa diminution continue d'année on année, fuit rassortir le renforcement le plus notable du bilatéralisme, par contre, le déficit de la balance commerciale anglaise ne s'est point atténué: après des mouvements dans les deux sens, il a été en 1937 plus élevé—par rapport au commerce total—qu'en 1929. Soit politique voulue, soit évolution naturelle, soit tendance imposée du dehors, le déficit du commerce extérieur anglais a donc tendance à se répartir de façon de plus en plus uniforme sur toutes les balances particulières. Ajoutons que, poux l'année 1913, l'indice anglais est de 29,5 c'est à dire le beaucoup supérieur au niveau d'après-guerre, quoiqu'il y oût en 1913 moins de pays indépendants et par conséquent, moins de possibilités de commerce triangulaire qu'aujourd'hui.

La tendance générale vers le bilatéralisme apparaît nettement dans le graphique. En particulier, si l'on compare les deux années de prospérité 1929 et 1937, on trouve que pour tous les pays examinés, l'indice est inférieur en 1937 à sa valeur de 1929.

Rappelons que, par contre, l'indice mondial du déséquilibre avait nettement augmente de 1929 à 1937; cela prouve encore une fois que dans certaines limites, la tendance vers le bilatéralisme est indépendante de la tendance vers l'équilibre. *Dans certaines limites*: car des mouvements violents de la tendance vers l'équilibre ont de grandes chances d'entraîner la tendance vers le bilatéralisme. Ainsi nous observons qu'en 1931 presque tous nos indices atteignant leur maximum et font ainsi ressortir un minimum de bilatéralisme, tout comme en 1931-1932 le déséquilibre des balances commerciales s'était fortement accentué.

Finalement, il est intéressant de noter que le niveau des indices est très semblable pour tous les pays que nous avons examinés. L'Allemagne qui a fait du bilatéralisme le dogme de sa politique commerciale n'est pas arrivée à abaisser son indice plus que les autres pays et même le cours de l'indice est d'une interprétation moins immédiate que par exemple celui des indices anglais et suédois.

Explications statistique—Sources

1) *Tendance vers l'équilibre*. Pour calculer $\sum |i - e|$, on s'est servi du tableau donnant pour tous les pays la valeur du commerce extérieur calculée en dollars-or. Ce tableau a été publié pour la première fois à partir de l'année 1928 dans l'*Annuaire statistique* de la S.D.N. de 1933–1934 (p. 194); ensuite, il a été régulièrement publié en annexe à l'*Aperçu général du Commerce mondial.* Pour les années 1925 à 1927, le Service économique de la S.D.N. a bien voulu mettre à notre disposition des données sur le commerce d'un certain nombre de pays, données qui avaient été rassemblées dans la rubrique "Autres pays" dans les publications précédentes de la S.D.N.: *Mémorandum sur le Commerce International* 1912 à 1926 et 1926 à 1928.

2) *Tendance vers le bilatéralisme.* Nous avons déjà indiqué que pour le calcul des indices du bilatéralisme, nous nous sommes servis de la formule (1a) qui demande la connaissance des importations et exportations en provenance et à destination des différents pays dans les importations et exportations totales du pays considéré. Pour l'Allemagne, ces pourcentages sont publiés par le *Statistiches Jahrbuch* pour une liste complète de pays. Quant aux autres pays, nous nous sommes servis des *Statistiques du Commerce international* de la S.D.N. qui donnent elles aussi les pourcentages à côté des chiffres absolus du commerce de chaque pays avec les pays étrangers. Ces statistiques cependant avaient l'inconvénient de laisser une rubrique "Autre pays" assez importante; pour l'Angleterre, les Pays-Bas et la Belgique, elle dépassait parfois 15%, soit pour les importations, soit pour les exportations. Or, c'est souvent avec les petits

pays que les déséquilibres les plus importants se produisent. C'est pourquoi nous avons tenu à spécifier—en nous servant des statistiques nationales du commerce extérieur—les pourcentages des importations et des exportations en provenance et à destination d'un certain nombre du pays non énumérés par les statistiques de la S.D.N. Nous avons ainsi ramené le pourcentage des "Autre pays" aux environs de 5%.

INDEX OF NAMES

INDEX OF CONTENT

www.ingramcontent.com/pod-product-compliance
Ingram Content Group UK Ltd.
Pitfield, Milton Keynes, MK11 3LW, UK
UKHW020217290926
15470UKWH00001B/243

9 781636 675398